MARY BERRY'S
COOKERY COURSE

About the author

Mary Berry is one of Britain's most popular cookery writers and has written over twenty books. She is a regular contributor to BBC Woman's Hour and often takes part in BBC and local radio phone-in programmes. She was for several years cookery editor of *Ideal Home* and now writes regularly for *Family Circle*.

Her most popular books include *Fast Cakes*, *Buffets* and *Mary Berry's Food Processor Cookbook*, all published by Piatkus.

MARY BERRY'S
COOKERY COURSE

PIATKUS

© 1991 by Mary Berry

First published in Great Britain in 1991 by
Judy Piatkus (Publishers) Limited,
5 Windmill Street, London W1P 1HF

First paperback edition published 1993

The moral right of the author has been asserted

A catalogue record for this book is available from the British Library

ISBN 0 7499 1078 X
ISBN 0 7499 1279 0 **Pbk**

Designed by Paul Saunders
Photographs opposite pages 192 and 193 by John Lee
(for other photographic credits see page 6)
Illustrations by Dick Vine and Paul Saunders

Front cover photograph is by Tim Imrie and shows
Victoria Sandwich Cake, Wild Bramble Mousses,
Monkfish Kebabs, Brioche, white and wholemeal bread
rolls, Gooseberry and Elderflower Jam, Red Tomato
Chutney, Eastern Stir-Fry, Steak, Kidney and
Mushroom Pie, Really Good Shortbread, Brandy Snaps
and Whisky Marmalade

Back cover photograph shows Sunday Tea Chocolate
Cake

Typeset in Lintron Sabon by
Phoenix Photosetting, Chatham
Printed and bound in Great Britain by The Bath Press, Avon

Contents

Foreword

This cookery course is the largest and most comprehensive book that I have written over the years. I have been so lucky to have Joanna Drew working with me sharing this monumental task. I have to confess that we have enjoyed the challenge and somehow have managed not to increase our waist measurements with all the tasting. I appreciate Joanna's lively contribution and keen creative ability.

Now our young are living in London during the week they often take back some of the spoils of the kitchen with them on Sunday night. It is always interesting to have their comments to add to the recipes, also to include some of their ideas. My son Thomas's latest invention, last Pancake Day, was to make savoury pancakes and to toss finely sliced peppers, onions and garlic straight into the batter. Such a good idea uses few pans – less washing up too!

Acknowledgements

The publishers would like to thank the following organisations for supplying photographs for use in this book:

British Egg Information Service
British Chicken Information Service
Potato Marketing Board
Alaska Canned Salmon Information Service

Introduction

Learning to cook should be fun, not a chore. The best way is to learn as you go along, so that you see results right from the very beginning and don't become bored before you have really achieved anything.

My cookery course is designed to guide and tempt the beginner or inexperienced cook with easy-to-make recipes that produce impressive and delicious results. The recipes have been arranged so they are progressive within each chapter. In other words those towards the end of a chapter involve different techniques or are slightly more advanced than those at the beginning. Try a few recipes from the beginning of each chapter before you attempt those further on in the same chapter – you will then find them easier to make and you will be learning and gaining confidence with each new recipe accomplished. Doing it this way you won't have the offputting feeling that you are following a rigid structured course.

These days we are eating less red meat and more poultry, fish, and vegetable dishes. We also cook vegetables faster to give a crisper, more healthy result. Fresh herbs (or frozen or dried when out of season) are being used more and more, as are the many interesting new ingredients that are becoming widely available. Ethnic foods too have become increasing popular. All these things influence our style of cooking today, so that alongside many traditional recipes I have included others with a more international flavour, or a more modern lighter touch. You will find, for example, easy-to-make recipes for classic French dishes, Mediterranean specialities, spicy curries and Eastern stir fries.

I have also included the traditional roasts, which we are all called on to make at one time or another, and which for the inexperienced cook can be daunting. Follow my simple instructions, however, and you will be able to produce a Sunday roast, plus gravy and all the trimmings, with the minimum of effort.

Many recipes in this book are real family favourites that you will receive requests for time and time again. Others make smarter dishes for entertaining. I do hope you will enjoy trying out all the recipes.

Mary Berry

Your Kitchen

If you have the luxury of planning your kitchen from scratch you can decide exactly what style you really want – don't go for the starkly clinical kitchen with a white floor if your life consists of a rowdy family tearing through the kitchen in their wellies followed by a muddy dog. Also, is your kitchen going to be purely a room for preparing meals or will you eat in it as well – and, if so, do you want to be able to seat six or eight people or just have a breakfast bar? Whatever the answer, it is likely that you are going to spend a lot of time in your kitchen so allow yourself plenty of time to plan it.

The work triangle, as the experts call it, is very important. It consists of the storage, preparation and cooking areas and, as these three areas are in constant use, they need to be easily accessible to one another. The refrigerator and larder, if you are lucky enough to have both, should be near the preparation area of sink and work surface, which in turn should be in a direct line to the cooker – not a long walk across the kitchen.

The shape of the room will determine to some extent how you plan the kitchen; a long thin kitchen need not be looked upon as a disadvantage as in many ways it is ideal to have everything along one wall.

Kitchen units, choose the best you can afford. If you want open shelves and a farmhouse type kitchen with old unsealed pine this will mean more cleaning. Handles and knobs must be robust; check hinges on the cheaper ranges of units as these can cause trouble. Remember you can often change the handles on wooden doors. Allow enough storage space for your 'batterie de cuisine' (kitchen utensils).

Work surfaces should be easy to clean and should also be heatproof. Probably the most popular is laminate, with tiles and wood next on the list. Include a built-in marble slab for pastry making if you have the space, this need not be expensive – the top of an old wash-stand can be cut down. If you are using tiles, continue them up the wall for two or three courses to act as a splashback. Coloured grouting is now available in most colours to match the tiles. Try to avoid using white grouting as this very quickly discolours.

Electric plug sockets are essential if you are gadget minded. If you are, be sure to give yourself plenty of double sockets above your work surface, as well as storage space for the machines. Also, consider whether your kitchen is going to include the utility area, as this will mean yet more sockets.

Flooring must be practical – a pristine white kitchen floor may be wonderful in a flat with no children or animals, but it will become a nightmare when you start a family. Again, your budget will have a strong bearing on your decision. The first consideration will be ease of cleaning, which automatically cuts out ordinary carpet or rush matting, for instance. Vinyl is infinitely variable and, in its sheet form, is easy to lay and easy to clean. Vinyl tiles are less wasteful for a small area and can be used to create a pattern. Cork tiles, providing they are *really* well sealed, look and feel wonderfully warm and are comparatively inexpensive; the more expensive type with a vinyl skin are tougher and stand up to more wear and tear. Quarry tiles and ceramic tiles, once laid, are there for life which can balance up the initial expense if you are not planning to move. Do not rule out wooden floor boards. With several coats of polyurethane they can be just as practical and when this eventually wears off you can always sand them down and start again. There are special tough kitchen carpets, a good idea for the eating area.

Lighting is very important. Small fluorescent lights can be fixed under wall units or shelves and are probably the best way to light work surfaces. Overhead lighting will depend on the ceiling heights, but make sure that when standing at the sink and your main working area, you are not standing in your own shadow. It is sensible to have a master switch by the door to turn them all off at once.

Heating is often not considered. If you are lucky enough to have an Aga, Rayburn or woodburning stove this will not be a problem but cooking by gas or electricity can be quite chilly, unless you are a very keen baker! Even more important to me are dry tea towels, so think about running your kitchen radiator off the hot water, then you can turn it on even when the central heating is off, or have an electric radiator instead.

Ventilation is vital. Condensation and cooking smells can both be got rid of with an extractor fan or cooker hood.

Rubbish bins should be bigger than you think you will need. A pedal bin may be sufficient for a newly married couple but will not cope with the cans and waste paper of an average family. If you have room to keep a separate bin for dry waste, it does simplify life, and have a generous cupboard to hide the swing bin. Keen gardeners will want a separate bin for kitchen waste for compost.

Altering an existing kitchen

Make a scale plan and cut out dummies, list the things that you need in order of priority, then see if you can make better use of the available space by moving the various pieces of equipment. It might be worth the cost of moving one or two electric sockets in order to reorganise certain items.

If you are re-using existing units, bear in mind that wood cupboards, such as pine or oak can be painted or stained; units that cannot be altered might possibly have new handles fitted to them to give a different look or colour scheme.

Most machines like dishwashers and washing machines are a standard width and height but check this carefully before buying a new one.

Lighting can radically alter your kitchen so take a long hard look at your work area and think how you can light it best.

EQUIPMENT

It is very difficult to decide exactly what you will need when you are equipping a kitchen – there are gadgets, equipment and machines for just about every task! The following list is a guide to the equipment I find most useful in my kitchen.

Pepper grinder
Kettle
A set of saucepans, the best quality you can afford
A very large pan which can double up as a preserving pan
Milk pan, non-stick
Egg poacher
Frying pan, non-stick
Colander
Wire strainers, large and small
Kitchen scales
Chopping board
Cake tins
Cooling racks
Measuring jug, pyrex or metal
Mixing bowls
Salad spinner
One or two baking trays
Cooks' knives
Measuring spoons

Wooden spoons
Tablespoons and forks
Kitchen teaspoons for tasting
Fish slice
Spatula
Slotted draining spoon
Scissors
Potato peeler
Lemon zester
Balloon whisk
Tin opener
Stainless steel grater
Potato masher
Lemon squeezer
Rolling pin
Carving knive and fork
Food processor or blender
Coffee maker
Fish kettle – if you are likely to want to cook whole large fish
Whereas in time past you might have included a pressure cooker or slow cooker, today the microwave oven has really taken their place.

THE STORE CUPBOARD

The following are all useful things to have in your kitchen store cupboard.

Flavourings and seasonings
Dried herbs, choose a few of your favourites and renew them each year
Spices, a few of the ones you use most
Stock cubes, beef, chicken and fish
Salt, kitchen and table
Black peppercorns
Mustard powder
French mustard
Tomato purée, in cans or tubes
Olives
Gravy browning
Worcestershire sauce
Soy sauce

Baking ingredients
Sugar, granulated, caster, brown and icing
Flour, plain, self-raising and wholewheat

Dried fruits, apricots, currants, dates, prunes, raisins, sultanas
Cornflour
Baking powder
Custard powder
Essences, vanilla and almond
Shelled nuts, such as almonds and walnuts, ideally kept frozen
Glacé cherries, candied peel, angelica
Longlife milk
Gelatine

Staple foods
Rice, brown, short grain and long grain
Pasta, a selection of your favourites
Dried vegetables, lentils, haricot beans, kidney beans and split peas
Dried soup mix

Canned foods
Fish, tuna, salmon, sardines, anchovies and prawns
Meat, chopped ham, corned beef and pâté
Soup, consommé, tomato and a good 'meal' soup
Vegetables, tomatoes – chopped and whole, new potatoes, sweetcorn, pimentos and mushrooms
Fruit, blackcurrants, cherries, pineapple, raspberries and peaches, which are all now available in natural juice

Miscellaneous
Coffee, tea, chocolate and cocoa
Jams and preserves
Oil, salad and cooking
Vinegar, distilled malt and wine
Good quality mayonnaise
Wine for cooking
Cider for cooking

FREEZERS

There are different types of freezers to choose from and it is mainly a matter of personal choice, taking in to account the space you have available, how much you want to store, and the running costs.

A **chest freezer** is the cheapest to buy and run. There is little loss of cold air when the lid is opened. It is difficult to get food from the bottom of the freezer and it is not easy to clean out. It takes up more space and is not easy for short people to reach to the bottom – and if you have a back problem, beware!

An **upright freezer** is more expensive to buy and run. There is greater temperature variation when the door is opened. It is easy to organise because of drawers and shelves, and it takes up less space than a chest freezer.

A **fridge freezer** which incorporates the refrigerator and freezer in one unit with separate doors is ideal where space is short, though very limited on size. There is temperature loss when the door opens and it only freezes small amounts.

Points to consider

Before buying a freezer consider how much space is available and where? Is the kitchen hot? Freezers run more economically in a cool place. Buy a larger model than you think you need, if in doubt – it's better to have too much space than not enough. Shop around for a good price.

Freezing can save time and money. You can cook dishes two at once and freeze one. You can buy and freeze food when it is cheap and plentiful, or you have a glut of garden produce. You can freeze carcasses for soups, left-overs and single portions, and foods that won't keep for a long time in a cupboard or fridge.

A freezer is invaluable for cooking ahead for dinner parties or special occasions like Christmas.

Freezing food

Freeze only food that is in peak condition. A freezer will not improve poor quality food. Any food that is past its best before freezing will deteriorate very quickly when thawed. Freezing does not alter the nutritional value of food. Apart from salad ingredients, most vegetables freeze well. Soft fruits generally freeze well though some, like strawberries, go soft when thawed. Dark coloured stone fruits freeze well though light coloured ones can discolour. Apples freeze well as blanched slices or purée.

MICROWAVE OVENS

Before buying a microwave, decide exactly what you want from it. Consider how many are likely to be at home and the family lifestyle. If you want it mainly for bought recipe dishes and reheating foods, there is no point in spending a mint of money on anything too sophisticated.

A **small basic microwave** has low power and is the cheapest in the range. It will probably have dial controls, two or three power levels and is ideal for one or two people, cooking baked potatoes and other vegetables, warming soups and sauces, thawing food and heating recipe dishes.

A **family-sized microwave** has more features, such as a turntable or stirrer, and some have automatic defrosting and cooking by weight which is calculated by the machine. The various types have a higher power output than the basic model, several variable power settings, a larger capacity oven and electronic touch or dial controls. All can cope successfully with family-sized meals, joints, chickens, and up to several portions of food at a time.

Combination ovens are the newest addition to the range, incorporating a microwave and conventional oven in one unit. They cost more than microwave-only cookers, but do perform a much more varied job. The advantage of cooking in a combination oven is that it browns, and crisps foods such as bread, cakes and pastries. They save space too. The drawbacks are that only one dish can be cooked at a time, splashes inside the oven get baked on – though most ovens are easy to clean, and that they are the most expensive type of microwave oven.

Getting the best from the microwave

Before you cook for the first time, read the manufacturer's instruction book carefully. Refer to it constantly, initially making notes to help next time.

Choose suitable containers to use in the microwave, such as heatproof glass, china and pottery. Many of the dishes you already have will be suitable, so check them before rushing out to buy expensive new ones. Dishes that are not suitable are metal ones or ones with metallic trims, as sparking (arcing) could occur. Fine bone china should only be used for reheating foods for short periods or it might crack. Unglazed pottery can be used but as it is porous it slows down the cooking time. Some plastic buckles or melts.

Food cooks more evenly in a shallow, round dish with straight sides, as it allows even penetration by the microwaves.

Preparing food to cook in the microwave

Large whole vegetables and fruit with skins on should be pierced before cooking, as should egg yolks. Never cook eggs in their shells in the microwave as they explode.

For most things it is best to cover food, as it speeds up the cooking. Specially designed clingfilm, microwave safe lids or plates are useful; absorbent kitchen paper will mop up splashes when laid over a dish.

Food with uniform thickness, such as potatoes or fish portions, cook evenly if arranged around the edge of a round container whereas chicken pieces or chops cook better if the thick end is towards the outside of the dish.

Bones that protrude and fish fins need protecting from the microwaves with a small piece of baking foil wrapped closely over the food to prevent burning.

Thick liquids need stirring during cooking.

Tips for success with microwave cooking

1. If you are a first time user, try a few simple recipes from the manufacturer's handbook before attempting a complete meal.

2. Cook for the minimum recommended time, test, then add on further cooking time in 30 second bursts if necessary.

3. Stand food for the recommended time after cooking; it will continue to cook for 5–10 minutes after the cooker has been switched off.

4. Thaw food according to packet instructions. Don't attempt to rush it, the outside may cook before the centre has thawed.

5. Food straight from the microwave can be very hot and burn the mouth, especially hot drinks and foods with jam or sugar. So take care. If heating mince pies in the microwave remember the mincemeat centre becomes excessively hot very quickly.

6. Use suitable containers. Very thick glazed pottery or thick oven glass bowls slow down the cooking process. A very good buy is a deep toughened plastic bowl with fitting lid, as it prevents splashes and conducts heat equally.

7. Reheat casseroles until the liquid is bubbling throughout, stirring from time to time.

8. To double a recipe, add an extra third or half to the cooking time. When halving a recipe, decrease the microwave time by a third to a half.

Stocks and Soups

STOCKS

A good basic home-made stock gives flavour and body to soups or casseroles and gives soup a velvety texture. It has the advantage over cubes or stock powders in that it contains no additives, colourings or preservatives, and you can tailor make it to suit your family's taste.

Making stock takes several hours of gentle simmering in a large covered pan on top of the cooker or 1–1½ hours in a pressure cooker according to manufacturers' instructions. Stock ingredients are cheap to buy and a good way to use up bones from meat and carcasses from birds, though it is best not to mix raw butcher bones and cooked meat bones. A strong jellied stock can be made from pig's trotters or veal bones. Fish stock takes about 30 minutes simmering.

In general, stock ingredients should harmonise with the end product for which it is intended. This is particularly important for soups.

Stock cubes or powder are sometimes a useful addition as a seasoning rather than a base for stock. They tend to be strong and salty so use less than the manufacturers recommend. Add some wine or sherry with the water when using cubes.

Tinned clear consommé makes an excellent substitute for stock in an emergency.

Basic stocks

Brown stock Use beef marrow bones sawn into pieces if possible, and browned in the oven to give colour. Place in a saucepan, cover with water and add salt, a few peppercorns, a bay leaf, a carrot, an onion in its skin, a leek and a stick of celery, together with any root vegetables or vegetable trimmings as liked for flavour. Bring to the boil, cover and simmer for about 8 hours. Strain and leave to cool. When cold remove any fat from the surface.

White stock As for brown stock, but without browning the bones in the oven.

Poultry and game stock Use the carcass from a cooked chicken, turkey, pheasant (the best for flavour) and other game birds. Giblets can be added if liked. Cover with water and add salt, a few peppercorns, a bay leaf and an onion for extra flavour. Bring to the boil, cover and simmer for about 4 hours. Continue as for brown stock.

Fish stock Use bones, trimmings and skin from white fish such a cod, plaice, haddock etc. Fish heads which are often thrown away in fish shops, are good for making stock. Don't use oily fish such as mackerel or herring as the flavour is too strong. Place in a saucepan and cover with water. Add carrot and parsley stalks and season with salt and white pepper. Bring to the boil, cover and simmer for 20 minutes. Strain and use immediately or cool and freeze.

Vegetable stock Use washed outside leaves and trimmings from cabbage, lettuce and Brussels sprouts, cauliflower leaves and stalks, and the scrubbed peelings of carrots and celeriac. A small quantity of turnips and parsnips are good too. Add salt, a bay leaf and mild herbs in season – chervil and lovage are delicious. Avoid potatoes as they make stock cloudy. Place in a saucepan, cover with water, bring to the boil and simmer for about

30 minutes. Strain and use or allow to cool and freeze.

Storing stocks

It is more economical to make stock in large quantities, then if it is not all needed the remainder can be kept in the refrigerator or frozen. Meat and bone stock will keep in the refrigerator for up to 1 week. Store it in a covered container and boil up every other day to prevent off flavours. Fish and vegetable stocks do not keep so well and are best used the same day. To save on space and storage cost, reduce the amount of finished meat stock by rapidly boiling. Skim any fat or scum from the top, pour into conveniently sized containers, cool, then refrigerate until quite cold. Seal and label the stock, then freeze. To use, thaw and make up to the required amount with cold water. Bring to the boil and use as needed. Fish and vegetable stocks are best not reduced.

SOUPS

As with stock, a home-made soup is totally free from artifical flavouring and colourings. Soup can be a good source of vegetables for people, especially children, who are reluctant to eat them whole with the main meal.

Soups can be smooth or chunky, clear or creamy, thick and hearty, a meal in itself, or a sophisticated prelude to a delectable meal. Food processors and blenders cut out the laborious work of sieving. I refer to using a processor or blender in the recipes where a soup of smooth consistency is required. But if you don't own either, simply push the mixture through a sieve with the back of a spoon. Make sure you cook the soup until all the pieces are soft or they won't go through the sieve.

Most fresh vegetables make delicious soups either on their own or in combinations. By adding ingredients just before serving, such as fresh cream, a little brandy or port to meat soups, a little dry white wine to fish soups, or chopped fresh leafy herbs, the variations are endless. Some good winter soups can be improved by adding a couple of tablespoons of dried pulse soup mix, which contains, lentils, peas, beans, and pearl barley, but remember to soak them them first.

Hot soups should be served piping hot, and cold soups chilled but not so cold that the flavour is impaired.

Storing soup

Soup is nicer if eaten freshly made, but it will keep for up to 3 days in the refrigerator. Remember to bring to the boil before serving. If you have made a large quantity of soup, it is best frozen in several small servings rather than in a huge amount. If the soup has added milk or cream, omit these if you are going to freeze it and add them after thawing and reheating.

Good things to go with soup

Apart from traditional additions, such as French bread topped with grated cheese in French Onion Soup, there are other things you can add to a plain soup just before serving to make it look more attractive.

- Croûtons (see page 237) of toasted or fried bread.
- Cream or yoghurt, swirled in a pattern.
- Fresh vegetables, cut in wafer thin slices or matchsticks, add a crunch to a cold soup.
- Fresh herbs, such as parsley, dill, mint, either tiny whole leaves or chopped, look attractive on soups.
- Rice or pasta, cooked and added to the soup, can not only be decorative but make the soup more substantial.

Crusty French bread or fresh rolls are the best accompaniments to soup. Herb or Garlic Bread are also good with many soups (see page 236), while Bouillabaise has it's own traditional accompaniments of Garlic Croûtons, Sauce Rouille and freshly grated Parmesan cheese.

CHICKEN AND VEGETABLE SOUP

SERVES 6

A main meal using perhaps the leftover carcass from the weekend chicken. With enough added vegetables, this is a meal in itself. The onion and vegetables are softened in butter before adding the stock to obtain the best flavour.

INGREDIENTS

1 cooked chicken carcass
3 pints (1.8 litres) water
salt and freshly ground black pepper
1 large onion
2 large carrots
3 or 4 sticks celery
1 leek
generous knob butter
1 heaped teaspoon flour

HOW TO MAKE

Break the carcass into pieces, so the water will cover the bones, and put into a large pan with a well fitting lid. Add the water with some seasoning. Bring to the boil, then cover and simmer for at least 3 hours, or longer if time permits.

Next prepare the vegetables. Chop the onion, cut the carrots into neat matchstick-sized pieces, cut the celery thinly on a slant and the leek into rings.

Strain the stock from the chicken bones and set aside. When the bones are cool enough to handle, pick off any remaining meat and reserve. Rinse out the stock pan, melt the butter in the pan, add the vegetables and allow to soften without colouring. Sprinkle on the flour and stir. Blend in the stock, bring to the boil, stirring, then simmer gently, until the vegetables are cooked but not soggy. Chop any large pieces of chicken removed from the bones and add to the soup. Taste for seasoning.

Serve piping hot, with garlic bread or fresh crusty rolls.

FAST TOMATO SOUP

SERVES 2 TO 3

I've made this easy soup for many years from ingredients likely to be on hand. It takes 15 minutes from start to finish. If the soup needs stretching, I add a can of chopped tomatoes too.

INGREDIENTS

1 oz (25 g) butter
1 small onion, finely chopped
1 oz (25 g) flour
½ pint (300 ml) water
2½ oz (62 g) can tomato purée
½ pint (300 ml) milk
1 teaspoon caster sugar
salt and freshly ground black pepper
grated Parmesan cheese
chopped parsley

HOW TO MAKE

Melt the butter in a saucepan, add the onion and fry gently for about 5 minutes, or until soft but not coloured. Stir in the flour and cook for 1 minute, without colouring.

Remove the pan from the heat and gradually add the water and tomato purée. Stir until smooth, then return to the heat and bring to the boil, stirring until thickened. Add the milk, sugar and seasoning, stir until well blended, then simmer gently for 7 minutes.

Taste and check the seasoning. Pour the soup into bowls, sprinkle with cheese and parsley, and serve at once.

LENTIL SOUP

SERVES 4–6

Like most pulses, lentils are very high in food value. They do not need soaking before cooking. The better the stock, the more delicious the soup will be. To dice potatoes or any other ingredient simply cut into small even-sized cubes.

INGREDIENTS

8 oz (225 g) red lentils
1 large onion, chopped
3 sticks celery, chopped
2 medium potatoes, diced
2 pints (1.2 litres) chicken stock (see page 14)
salt and freshly ground black pepper

HOW TO MAKE

Rinse the lentils well under cold running water. Put all the ingredients in a large saucepan, bring to the boil and cover with a lid. Reduce the heat and simmer for about an hour, until the lentils are tender.

Allow the soup to cool slightly, then reduce to a purée in a blender or food processor. Reheat the soup in a clean saucepan, check the seasoning and serve very hot.

GAZPACHO

SERVES 4–6

A classic cold Spanish soup that is not cooked. Best served on a warm summer's day. Serve very chilled.

INGREDIENTS

2 lb (900 g) ripe red tomatoes, skinned and sliced (see page 125)
1 large Spanish onion, sliced
1 small can red peppers, drained well
2 fat cloves garlic, crushed
4 tablespoons red wine vinegar
5 tablespoons olive oil
1/2 pint (300 ml) chicken stock (see page 14)
juice of 1/2 lemon
salt and freshly ground black pepper
diced cucumber, diced green pepper and small fried bread
*   croûtons, for garnish*

HOW TO MAKE

Put the tomatoes, onion, red peppers, garlic, vinegar, oil and stock in a blender or food processor and process for a few seconds until the mixture is well blended.

Turn the mixture into a bowl, then stir in the lemon juice and seasoning. Chill for at least 6 hours.

Serve garnished with diced green pepper, diced cucumber and fried bread croûtons.

LEEK AND POTATO SOUP

SERVES 4–6

This traditional soup can be served piping hot in winter, or chilled in summer. Served cold it is known as Vichysoisse. You may need to thin the cold soup down with a little extra stock or some milk, and you will find that soups need more seasoning when served cold.

INGREDIENTS

2 oz (50 g) butter
3 medium leeks, trimmed and sliced
1 small onion, finely chopped
12 oz (350 g) potatoes, sliced
2 pints (1.2 litres) chicken stock (see page 14)
salt and freshly ground black pepper
a little freshly grated nutmeg
1/4 pint (150 ml) single cream (optional)
2 tablespoons snipped chives or chopped parsley

HOW TO MAKE

Melt the butter in a saucepan, add the leeks and onion and cook gently, without boiling, for about 10 minutes. Add the potatoes, stock, seasoning and nutmeg. Bring to the boil, cover and simmer gently until the vegetables are tender.

Allow to cool slightly, then purée in a blender or food processor until smooth. Reheat thoroughly and check the seasoning. Stir in the cream, if using, and sprinkle with chives or parsley.

KINGS SPICED PARSNIP SOUP

SERVES 4–6

An excellent soup, well worth making when parsnips are at their best and cheapest. If they are at the end of the season, cut out the woody centre of the parsnip.

INGREDIENTS

3 oz (75 g) butter
8 oz (225 g) onions, chopped
1 lb (450 g) parsnips, cubed
1 fat clove garlic, crushed
1 oz (25 g) flour
1 rounded teaspoon curry powder
2 pints (1.2 litres) beef stock (see page 14)
salt and freshly ground black pepper
1/4 pint (150 ml) single cream
snipped chives

HOW TO MAKE

Melt the butter in a large pan, add the onions, parsnips and garlic and fry gently for about 5 minutes. Stir in the flour and curry powder and cook for a minute, then blend in the stock and seasoning. Bring to the boil, stirring, then cover and simmer gently for about 20 minutes, until the parsnip is tender.

Purée the soup in a blender or food processor until smooth. Reheat until piping hot, then taste and check the seasoning. Stir in the cream just before serving, and sprinkle chives on top.

COOK'S TIP
Generally speaking, soups will need *more* seasoning if they are to be served chilled.

FARMHOUSE PEA SOUP

SERVES 4–6

This fresh tasting summer soup uses fresh peas, but out of season you can make it with frozen peas.

INGREDIENTS

2 oz (50 g) butter
1 large onion, chopped
2 streaky bacon rashers, chopped
1 tablespoon flour
1½ lb (675 g) fresh peas (shelled weight)
2 pints (1.2 litres) chicken stock (see page 14)
½ teaspoon sugar
2 large sprigs fresh mint
salt and freshly ground black pepper
mint leaves, for garnish

HOW TO MAKE

Melt the butter in a large saucepan, add the onion and bacon and cook gently until the onion is soft. Sprinkle on the flour and cook for 1 minute, stirring. Add the peas, stock, sugar and mint sprigs. Bring to the boil, cover and simmer for about 20 minutes. Remove the mint sprigs and allow the soup to cool a little, then purée in a blender or food processor. Return to the pan and add seasoning to taste. Heat thoroughly, check the seasoning again, then garnish with tiny mint leaves.

CURRIED APPLE SOUP

SERVES 6

This unusual soup is equally delicious served hot or cold.

INGREDIENTS

1 oz (25 g) butter
1 onion, roughly chopped
1 tablespoon curry powder
1½ oz (40 g) flour
1½ pints (900 ml) chicken stock (see page 14)
1½ lb (675 g) cooking apples, peeled and roughly chopped
2 tablespoons mango chutney
Juice of ½ lemon
salt and freshly ground pepper
¼ pint (150 ml) natural yoghurt

HOW TO MAKE

Melt the butter in a large saucepan, add the onion, cover the pan and fry slowly for 5 minutes or until soft. Stir in the curry powder and cook for 1 minute, then add the flour and cook for a further minute. Add the stock and apples.

Bring to the boil, stirring, and simmer for 15 minutes. Allow to cool a little, then add the mango chutney and lemon juice. Purée in a blender or food processor in two or three batches, until smooth.

Rinse out the saucepan, return the soup to it and bring to the boil. Taste and check the seasoning and consistency. Add a spoonful of yoghurt to each bowl of soup to serve. Thin down with a little more stock or water to serve cold.

WATERCRESS SOUP

SERVES 4–6

This is a refreshing soup when served cold in summer and actually tastes quite different when served hot.

INGREDIENTS

2 bunches of watercress
2 oz (50 g) butter
1 onion, chopped
2 oz (50 g) flour
1 pint (600 ml) milk
¾ pint (450 ml) chicken stock (see page 14)
salt and freshly ground black pepper
¼ pint (150 ml) single cream

HOW TO MAKE

Wash the watercress well. Reserve a few nice sprigs for garnish and chop the remainder. Melt the butter in a large saucepan, add the watercress and onion and cook gently until soft. Sprinkle in the flour, stir and cook for 1 minute. Gradually blend in the milk and chicken stock and bring to the boil slowly, stirring continuously. Cover and simmer for about 20 minutes, stirring from time to time. Cool slightly, then purée in a blender or food processor. Return to the pan and reheat gently. Taste for seasoning, then stir in the cream. Garnish with watercress to serve.

To serve cold, after puréeing chill in refrigerator for at least 4 hours before swirling in cream and garnishing with watercress.

> **COOK'S TIP**
> Cream stirred into soup at the last minute will make the soup rich, smooth and luxurious. Natural yoghurt or soured cream can also be used to give a more piquant flavour, but avoid reboiling in each case.

MUSHROOM SOUP

SERVES 4

Closed cup mushrooms will make the lightest creamy-coloured soup, but they lack the flavour of open mushrooms which will produce a darker coloured end result. Field mushrooms have the best flavour and the darkest colour.

INGREDIENTS

1 lb (450 g) mushrooms, cut into quarters if large
2½ oz (65 g) butter
¾ pint (450 ml) chicken stock (see page 14)
1½ oz (40 g) flour
1 pint (600 ml) milk
salt and freshly ground black pepper
¼ pint (150 ml) single cream

HOW TO MAKE

Put 1 oz (25 g) butter into a pan, add the mushrooms, cover with a lid and gently soften for 1–2 minutes, depending on the size.

Pour on the stock, bring to the boil, cover and simmer for about 5 minutes.

Measure the remaining butter into another pan, sprinkle on the flour and cook for 1 minute. Gradually blend in the milk and bring to the boil, stirring until thickened. Add salt and pepper to taste. Set aside.

Purée the mushrooms in a blender or food processor, add to the white sauce, taste for seasoning and mix well together. Reheat gently until boiling, then stir in the cream.

CARROT AND ORANGE SOUP

SERVES 6–8

Large old carrots are fine for this soup. Use orange juice from a carton, the kind you have for breakfast and keep in the refrigerator. Omit the cream if you like it less rich.

INGREDIENTS

2 oz (50 g) butter
1 lb (450 g) onions, roughly chopped
2 lb (900 g) carrots, roughly sliced
1 pint (600 ml) unsweetened orange juice
salt and freshly ground black pepper
2 pints (1.2 litres) chicken stock (see page 14)
¼ pint (150 ml) double cream
2 tablespoons snipped chives or chopped parsley

HOW TO MAKE
Melt the butter in a pan, add the onions and fry until soft but not brown, then tip into a blender or food processor. Cook carrots in boiling salted water for about 15 minutes, until just tender, then drain and add to onion. Process to a purée, then add the orange juice and seasoning through the lid or funnel of the blender or food processor. Blend in the stock. Either serve very cold or piping hot. Stir in the cream and chives just before serving.

COOK'S TIP
For really smooth soups, when using a processor strain off the liquid and process only the chunky pieces. Mix the purée into the liquid. When using a blender/liquidiser however, blend the solids with the liquids.

FRENCH ONION SOUP

SERVES 8
A wonderful main meal soup. Served with slices of French bread and grated melted cheese floating on each bowl, it makes a substantial soup or light lunch.

INGREDIENTS
4 tablespoons oil
1½ oz (40 g) butter
2 lb (900 g) Spanish onions, thinly sliced
1 tablespoon sugar
2 oz (50 g) flour
3 pints (1.8 litres) beef stock (see page 14)
salt and freshly ground black pepper
8 slices French bread ½ inch (1.25 cm) thick
4 oz (100 g) Gruyère cheese, grated

HOW TO MAKE
Melt the oil and butter in a large pan, add the onions and fry gently to soften. When the onions are soft, add the sugar and continue cooking for about 20 minutes until they are a good brown colour, then sprinkle in the flour and cook for 1–2 minutes.

Gradually add the stock and bring to the boil, stirring all the time. Add the seasoning, cover with a lid and simmer for about 30–40 minutes.

Toast one side of the French bread slices under the grill. Sprinkle the grated cheese on to the untoasted side of the bread and brown and melt the cheese under a hot grill when ready to serve.

Taste the soup for seasoning, then float one slice of toasted cheese on each bowl of soup and serve immediately.

BOUILLABAISE

SERVES 4 AS A
MAIN COURSE
OR 6 FOR A
FIRST COURSE

Traditionally Bouillabaise was made with sole, turbot or John Dory which are more expensive than the fish used here, but do give a firmer result. Do not add any oily fish. Saffron is very expensive, turmeric can be used instead, if preferred.

INGREDIENTS

2 lb (900 g) mixed fish, such as monkfish, red mullet, cod or
*   haddock, skinned*
2 pinches saffron
¼ pint (150 ml) boiling water
¼ pint (150 ml) olive oil
2 large onions, chopped
1 celery stick, sliced
14 oz (400 g) can chopped tomatoes
2 fat cloves garlic, crushed
1 bay leaf
2 sprigs lemon thyme
few sprigs of parsley
finely grated zest of 1 lemon
salt and freshly ground black pepper
2 oz (50 g) shelled prawns

TO SERVE
Garlic Croûtons (see page 237)
Sauce Rouille (see page 226)
freshly grated Parmesan cheese

HOW TO MAKE

Cut the fish into fairly large thick pieces. Place the saffron in a small bowl, cover with the boiling water and leave to soak for 30 minutes.

Measure the oil into a large pan, add the onions and celery and cook gently to soften. Stir in the tomatoes, garlic, bay leaf, thyme, parsley, lemon zest and seasoning.

Arrange the fish in a layer over the vegetables, pour on the saffron liquid and just enough water to barely cover the fish. Bring to the boil and simmer, uncovered, for 7–10 minutes. Add the prawns and cook for about 5 minutes, until the fish is cooked but still whole. Taste the soup for seasoning. Stir gently so as not to break up the fish.

Serve with Garlic Croûtons, Sauce Rouille and freshly grated Parmesan cheese.

First Courses

The first course is a vital part of the meal, not least because first impressions count. Always remember that its purpose is to whet the appetite, so don't serve huge filling portions or you will spoil the effect of what follows.

When entertaining it's a sensible idea to choose a cold first course that you can prepare ahead and keep in the fridge. Before guests arrive arrange the food on individual plates and put round the table so that you are not darting backwards and forwards to the kitchen at the beginning of the meal.

The first course should always contrast with, as well as complement, the rest of the meal. If there's cream in the main course or dessert, choose a lighter, fresh tasting first course. If the main course is meat-based, then a fish, vegetable or fruit starter would be best. Consider texture too; if the dessert is a mousse or smooth ice cream then something nice and crunchy to begin with would fit the bill, such as Palm Hearts with a Cheesy Top (page 28) or a crisp salad sprinkled with fried bacon pieces and croûtons. If you are serving a rich or substantial main dish, fruit is the perfect first course. It is light, refreshing and appetising and particularly welcome on warmer days. Try tossing together orange and grapefruit segments with slices of avocado and a little French dressing. Or cut a really ripe and juicy melon into chunks, add a little sliced stem ginger and some ginger syrup and chill well for 20 minutes.

Soups and salads also make excellent first courses and you'll find lots of ideas in those chapters. And any of the recipes in this chapter can be served in larger quantities for lunch or supper dishes.

MELON AND PARMA HAM

SERVES 4

Choose a good ripe melon in season. Press the top and smell it. If ripe it will be slightly soft and most important of all, smell ripe.

INGREDIENTS

1 medium melon, chilled
8 thin slices Parma ham
juice of 1 lemon
freshly ground black pepper
curly and red lettuce, for garnish

HOW TO MAKE

Cut the melon in half lengthwise and scoop out the seeds. Cut each half into four wedges. With a sharp knife cut away the skin. Slice each wedge into three slices and arrange spaced out in a fan shape on four plates.

Roll each slice of ham loosely and place two on each plate between the melon slices. Squeeze a little lemon juice over the melon and some black pepper on the ham. Garnish with a little lettuce.

SCOTS HERRINGS

SERVES 8

One of the most delicious and simple first courses. It's quite an unusual combination, the bananas taking away the sharpness of the rollmop herrings. Serve with brown bread and butter.

INGREDIENTS

6 firm bananas
juice of 1 lemon
½ pint (300 ml) mayonnaise (see page 126)
4 rollmop herrings
enough mixed green salad to cover eight plates
parsley, dill or fennel, for garnish

HOW TO MAKE

Peel the bananas, cut them in half lengthwise, then slice them diagonally into a bowl. Pour the lemon juice over the bananas and mix together, then stir in the mayonnaise. Cut the rollmops into small, manageable pieces and stir into the mayonnaise.

Arrange the green salad over eight individual plates and divide the herring mixture between them. Garnish with parsley, dill or fennel.

FRENCH DRESSED YOUNG LEEKS

SERVES 4

Young leeks are best for this dish, being the most tender and looking pretty on the plate. If you like nuts try using walnut oil in the dressing and scattering a few coarsely chopped walnuts over the leeks instead of parsley.

INGREDIENTS

4 small leeks
8 tablespoons French dressing (see page 127)
4 large ripe tomatoes, thinly sliced
1–2 tablespoons chopped parsley

HOW TO MAKE

Cut off any torn leaves from the leeks, trim off the green ragged ends. Cut the leeks into 2 inch (5 cm) lengths, then into thin strips. Wash well. Blanch the strips in boiling salted water for 2 minutes, then drain on a colander and refresh under cold running water. Drain well. Turn into a bowl, pour over half the French dressing and leave to marinate for 4 hours.

Arrange slices of tomato round the edge of four flat plates or salad plates; season. Pile the leeks in the centre. Spoon the remainder of the dressing over the tomato slices. Scatter the parsley over the leeks. Serve with brown bread and butter.

Variation

French Dressed Artichokes   Drain two 7 oz (200 g) cans of artichoke hearts, quarter each artichoke. Marinate as for leeks and proceed as above.

GARLIC MUSHROOMS WITH CREAM

SERVES 4

Use only really small, fresh, white button mushrooms for this dish, otherwise the creamy sauce will be grey.

INGREDIENTS

12 oz (350 g) small button mushrooms
1½ oz (40 g) butter
1 fat clove garlic, crushed
salt and freshly ground black pepper
¼ pint (150 ml) double cream

HOW TO MAKE

Clean the mushrooms and trim the ends off the stalks. Melt the butter in a large frying pan or saucepan, add the garlic and mushrooms and fry gently for 5 minutes.

Season well, stir in the cream and simmer gently for a further 5 minutes, or until the mushrooms are tender but still crisp. Divide between four ramekins or small dishes and serve hot.

COOK'S TIP
Never peel cultivated mushrooms as much of the flavour and goodness lie in or just under the skin. The best way to clean them is by wiping with a damp cloth.

PALM HEARTS WITH A CHEESY TOP

SERVES 6

Buy canned palm hearts in a good delicatessen, they are delicious and crunchy. Creamy white in colour, they look rather like the base of a leek.

INGREDIENTS

14 oz (400 g) can palm hearts
1½ oz (40 g) butter
1½ oz (40 g) flour
¾ pint (450 ml) milk
4 oz (100 g) Emmenthal or Gruyère cheese, grated
1 good teaspoon Dijon mustard
Generous pinch of freshly grated nutmeg
salt and freshly ground black pepper

HOW TO MAKE

Heat the oven to 425°F/220°C/gas mark 7. Drain the palm hearts and throw away the liquid. Slice the palm hearts in half lengthways and then into three or four pieces.

Next, make a white sauce. Heat the butter in a pan, add the flour and cook for 1 minute, then gradually blend in the milk, stirring until smooth and thickened. Add two-thirds of the cheese, the mustard, nutmeg and salt and pepper, then stir the palm hearts into the sauce. Taste and check the seasoning.

Divide the mixture between six large ramekin or individual shallow oval dishes and sprinkle over the remaining cheese. Cook in the oven for 20 minutes, until crispy brown on top.

SARDINE PÂTÉ

SERVES 4

This makes a small amount, but it is plenty for four people as a starter because it is very rich. Serve with crusty French bread or hot toast.

INGREDIENTS

2 oz (50 g) butter, softened
2 oz (50 g) cream cheese
4½ oz (125 g) sardines in oil or brine
juice of about ½ lemon
freshly ground black pepper
salt (optional)
bay leaves or other herbs, for garnish

HOW TO MAKE

Measure butter and cheese into a blender or food processor. Drain the sardines, remove the backbones and add the fish to the blender or processor. Add the lemon juice, black pepper, a little salt, if liked, and process briefly until mixed but not altogether smooth. Scrape down sides, taste, add a little more lemon juice, if needed.

Pack the mixture into small ramekins or a terrine. Decorate with bay leaves or other herbs. Chill for 1 hour before serving.

Variation

Sardine-stuffed Lemons   For an elegant way of serving this pâté, cut a thin slice from the bases of 4 lemons so they stand steadily. Cut and reserve a larger slice from the top of each lemon. Scoop out the flesh from the 4 lemons using a serrated or grapefruit knife. Fill the lemons with the pâté and sit the lids on top.

SMOKED TROUT PÂTÉ

SERVES 6

Melted butter poured over the pâté keeps it beautifully moist.

INGREDIENTS

2 smoked trout
10 oz (275 g) butter, melted but not hot
4 oz (100 g) cream cheese
juice of ½ lemon
small sprigs of parsley, for garnish

HOW TO MAKE

Remove the skin from the trout, separate the fillets and discard the backbone. Put the fillets with 8 oz (225 g) of the butter, the cream cheese and the lemon juice in a blender or food processor and blend until smooth.

Divide the pâté between six individual serving dishes and smooth the tops, or put in a small loaf-shaped terrine or dish, about 1 pint (600 ml) size. Spoon on a little of the remaining butter, remelted so that it pours on top of each dish, and leave in a cool place until set.

Garnish with small sprigs of parsley and serve with hot toast and butter.

TARAMASALATA

SERVES 4

Fresh smoked cod's roe is sometimes difficult to get, but I find it is usually available in jars from the fishmongers. Taramasalata is delicious served, as in Greece, with hot pitta bread.

INGREDIENTS

8 oz (225 g) smoked cod's roe
2 small slices white bread, crust removed
2 tablespoons milk
1 clove garlic, crushed
4 fl oz (125 ml) olive oil
2 tablespoons lemon juice
salt and freshly ground black pepper

HOW TO MAKE

Remove the skin from the cod's roe, place the roe in a blender or food processor and purée until smooth.

Soak the bread in the milk, then squeeze out as much milk as possible and add the bread to the blender or processor with the garlic. Add the oil a little at a time, processing between each addition, until it has all been absorbed, then add the lemon juice and seasoning to taste. Turn the pâté into a small serving dish and chill well before serving.

HUMMUS

SERVES 10 AS A DIP

A great favourite with vegetarians, hummus is good in pitta bread with salad, but is more usually served as a dip with raw vegetable sticks. If in a hurry, buy canned or frozen chick peas which will cut down the time taken, but naturally you would need twice as many as they don't need soaking. Tahini is a paste made from sesame seeds. It is best kept in the refrigerator once opened.

INGREDIENTS

8 oz (225 g) dried chick peas
3 fat cloves garlic, crushed
3 tablespoons lemon juice
3 tablespoons oil
2 tablespoons tahini
plenty of salt and freshly ground black pepper

HOW TO MAKE

Measure chick peas into a bowl, cover with cold water and leave to soak overnight.

Next day, drain the chick peas, put in a pan and cover with cold water. Bring to the boil and simmer for 1–1½ hours, until tender. Do not add salt at this stage as it tends to toughen the skin on the peas. Leave the chick peas to cool in the cooking liquid, then drain, reserving the liquid.

Put the garlic, lemon juice, oil, tahini and chick peas into a blender or food processor and process until smooth. Add a tablespoon or two of the reserved cooking liquid to thin it down a little if needed. Scrape down the bowl sides and process until you have the consistency you like. Add plenty of seasoning, again process briefly and taste. Transfer to a pretty bowl and serve surrounded by fresh vegetable sticks or pitta bread.

SPECIAL CHICKEN LIVER PÂTÉ

SERVES 8–10

A useful pâté as it is quick to make and perfect for picnics and light lunches. It will keep in the refrigerator for about a week or in the freezer for up to a month – it's one of the few meat pâtés that will freeze well.

INGREDIENTS

6 oz (175 g) butter
1 onion, chopped
2 cloves garlic, crushed
1 lb (450 g) chicken livers
1 teaspoon chopped lemon thyme
salt and freshly ground black pepper
2 tablespoons brandy
2 oz butter, melted

HOW TO MAKE

Melt 1 oz (25 g) butter in a large frying pan, add the onion and garlic and fry for about 5 minutes on a low heat until softened. Add the chicken livers and thyme, increase the heat and cook for about 5 minutes, stirring well. Season to taste.

Turn the mixture into a blender or food processor. Pour the brandy into the pan and scrape up any remaining bits in the pan and pour over the livers. Melt the remaining 5 oz (150 g) butter and add to the other ingredients, then process briefly until the pâté is smooth. Check the seasoning and turn into ramekin dishes or a suitable dish. Leave to cool for about 30 minutes, then pour melted butter over the pâté to seal it.

COOK'S TIP
Each time you buy a chicken with giblets, remove the livers and freeze until you have sufficient to make a quantity of pâté.

COARSE FRENCH PÂTÉ WITH GARLIC

SERVES 8

A coarse pâté that is very quick to make if you own a food processor, but if not, it can easily be done with a mincer.

INGREDIENTS

4 oz (100 g) chicken livers
8 oz (225 g) pig's liver
4 oz (100 g) braising steak, finely cubed
12 oz (350 g) belly of pork, finely cubed
2 cloves garlic, crushed
1 tablespoon chopped fresh mixed herbs or
    1 teaspoon dried herbs
salt and freshly ground black pepper
1/4 teaspoon ground mace
1 small egg, beaten
1 tablespoon sherry
6 oz (175 g) thin rashers streaky bacon, rinded

HOW TO MAKE

Heat the oven to 325°F/160°C/gas mark 3. Well grease a 2 lb (900 g) loaf tin.

Put the livers, steak and pork into a food processor and process until a chunky purée. Alternatively put the meat through a mincer. Turn the meat into a large bowl and mix with the garlic, herbs, seasoning, mace, egg and sherry. Line the loaf tin with the bacon and fill with the mixture. Cover with foil and stand in a small roasting tin half-filled with boiling water.

Cook in the oven for about 2 hours, until when pierced with a skewer the juices that flow are clear. Leave to cool in the tin and chill well before turning out.

Serve with French bread and unsalted butter.

COOK'S TIP
Meat pâtés do not freeze well for any length of time; they crumble on thawing and have a disappointing flavour.

Right: *Salmon and Broccoli Roulade (page 36)*

SALMON MOUSSE

SERVES 6

This quick and easy-to-make mousse can also be made with canned crab. For special occasions, top with a dollop of soured cream and a teaspoon of black lumpfish roe.

INGREDIENTS

½ oz (15 g) packet powdered gelatine
3 tablespoons cold water
7½ oz (210 g) can pink salmon
about 1 tablespoon lemon juice
10 fl oz (300 ml) mayonnaise (see page 126)
¼ pint (150 ml) double cream
salt and freshly ground black pepper
sprigs of parsley, for garnish

HOW TO MAKE

Sprinkle the gelatine over the water in a small bowl and leave for 3 minutes to become spongy. Stand the bowl in a pan of simmering water and stir until the gelatine has dissolved, then leave to cool.

Drain the salmon, flake the flesh and remove any pieces of black skin and bone. Place the salmon in a bowl with 1 tablespoon lemon juice and the mayonnaise and mix thoroughly. Stir in the gelatine.

Whisk the cream until it is thick and just forms soft peaks, then fold it into the salmon mixture with seasoning to taste, adding a little more lemon juice, if liked.

Divide the mixture between six ramekin dishes, smooth the tops and leave in a cool place to set. Garnish each dish with a small sprig of parsley.

Left: *Soused Herrings (page 63)*

Avocado Mousse

SERVES 8

Serve with salad and crusty brown rolls. For more special occasions, fill the centre of the mousse with a prawn mixture (see below).

INGREDIENTS

¾ oz (20 g) gelatine
4 tablespoons cold water
¼ pint (150 ml) chicken stock (see page 14)
3 ripe avocado pears
salt and freshly ground black pepper
2 fat cloves garlic, crushed
juice of ½ lemon
½ pint (300 ml) mayonnaise (see page 126)
¼ pint (150 ml) double cream, lightly whipped
a bunch of watercress sprigs, for garnish

HOW TO MAKE

Sprinkle the gelatine over the water in a small bowl and leave for about 3 minutes to become spongy. Stand the bowl in a pan of simmering water and stir until the gelatine has dissolved. Allow to cool, then stir the gelatine into the stock.

Peel and quarter the avocados, removing the stone from each. Place the flesh in a blender or food processor with the stock, salt, pepper, garlic and lemon juice. Reduce to smooth purée, then gently fold in the mayonnaise and cream.

Lightly oil a 2½ pint (1.5 litre) ring mould and turn the avocado mixture into the mould. Leave to set in the refrigerator. Turn the mousse out into a damp, flat plate, and fill the centre with watercress.

Variation

Avocado Mousse with Prawns   Fill the centre of the mousse with the following mixture. Blend ½ pint (300 ml) mayonnaise with 3 teaspoons tomato purée, the juice of ½ lemon, a little Worcestershire sauce and lots of black pepper. Mix in 12 oz (350 g) well-drained, shelled prawns.

Samosas (Curry Puffs)

MAKES 30

I use frozen pitta filo pastry, the slightly thicker variety, for these samosas. Each packet contains two polythene packs containing three sheets of filo in each. If you use the thinner filo, use two layers, brushing with butter between the layers. Samosas are best served hot. They can be made in advance then reheated in a hot oven for about 5 minutes.

INGREDIENTS

6 sheets filo pastry, thawed
melted butter

FILLING
1 tablespoon oil
1 lb (450 g) minced raw beef
1 onion, finely chopped
1 teaspoon ground cumin
½ teaspoon chilli powder
1 rounded teaspoon garam masala
2 potatoes, cooked and mashed
2 tablespoons mango chutney, chopped

HOW TO MAKE

Make the filling. Heat the oil in a non-stick pan, add the meat and fry until golden. Stir in the onion then the spices and fry for 3 minutes. Season, then cover with a lid and simmer gently for 30 minutes. Add the mashed potato and chutney, mix well, then transfer to a shallow dish to chill until thoroughly cold. Divide the mixture into 30 portions.

Heat the oven to 425°F/220°C/gas mark 7. Unwrap the thawed pastry and carefully unfold one sheet. Cover the rest with a damp cloth to prevent it drying out. Brush the pastry sheet with melted butter and cut into 2½ inch (6 cm) strips.

Put a portion of the mixture on to the corner of the pastry strip and fold over to form a triangle, then keep folding the triangle over until you reach the end of the strip. If there's a spare piece of pastry at the end, cut it off. Repeat with remaining pastry and filling.

Arrange the triangles on a backing sheet, brush again with melted butter, then bake in the oven for about 10 minutes, until crisp and golden brown. Serve hot.

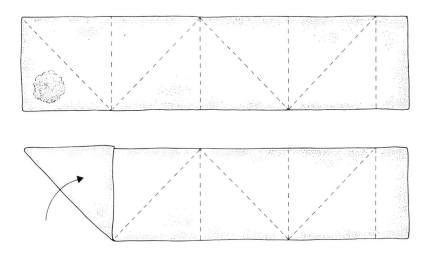

SALMON AND BROCCOLI ROULADE

SERVES 6

An impressive looking starter that's also ideal to take on picnics. Extra thyme and grated lemon rind can be added to the sauce, if liked.

INGREDIENTS

7 oz (175 g) can Alaska pink or red salmon
1 inch (2.5 cm) piece fresh root ginger, peeled and chopped
1 clove garlic, peeled and chopped
8 oz (225 g) broccoli florettes, cooked until soft
3 eggs, separated
salt and freshly ground black pepper
1 oz (25 g) freshly grated Parmesan cheese
½ oz (15 g) butter
½ oz (15 g) plain flour
¼ pint (150 ml) soured cream
½ teaspoon finely grated lemon rind
¼ teaspoon chopped fresh thyme
4 tablespoons natural yoghurt
juice of ½ lemon

HOW TO MAKE

Heat the oven to 400°F/200°C/gas mark 6. Grease and line a 13 × 9 inch (33 × 23 cm) Swiss roll tin with greased greaseproof paper or silicone paper.

Crush the ginger and garlic together to make a paste and put into a blender or food processor along with the broccoli and egg yolks. Process until smooth.

Whisk the egg whites until stiff and fold into the broccoli mixture. Season with salt and pepper. Pour into the prepared tin and sprinkle the Parmesan evenly over the surface. Bake for 10 minutes or until well risen and firm to the touch.

Meanwhile, drain the salmon, reserving the juice and making it up to 3 fl oz (80 ml) with water, if necessary.

Melt the butter in a saucepan and stir in the flour. Cook for a minute, then gradually blend in the salmon stock and bring to the boil, stirring until thickened. Stir in 3 fl oz (80 ml) of the cream, the lemon rind and the chopped thyme. Flake the fish and mix in. Set aside.

Blend together the remaining cream with the yoghurt and lemon juice. Set aside.

Turn the cooked roulade out on to a clean tea towel and peel away the lining paper. Spread evenly with salmon filling and quickly roll it up from a short edge. Serve warm or cold in slices accompanied by the yoghurt sauce.

Eggs

Size

I am often asked what size eggs to use, and I, like most cookery writers, buy size 3. The recipes in this book have all been tested with eggs this size. The smallest eggs are size 6 and the largest are size 1.

Storing

Eggs should always be stored with the pointed end downwards. It's best to keep them in the refrigerator, but remember to bring them out and allow them to come to room temperature before using for baking or boiling.

Eggs can absorb strong flavours or smells, so don't store them next to strong smelling foods like onions or garlic.

If in doubt whether an egg is really fresh, lower it into a bowl of cold water. If it floats it is old and should be discarded. If it sinks to the bottom or stays just above the bottom, then it is all right to use.

For storing leftover egg whites or yolks, see the Cook's Tips on pages 182 and 184.

Cooking eggs

The traditional methods of cooking eggs are boiled, poached, fried or scrambled.

Boiled   When simply hard-boiling eggs, remember that it is best to use an egg that is at least a week old, otherwise the white will stick to the shell, making it difficult to peel. Take care not to overboil hard-boiled eggs. A size 3 egg takes about 10 minutes, and if cooked longer will have a black rim round the outside of the yolk.

Soft-boiled eggs   These take only a few minutes, depending on how runny you like them, and whether they are placed in already boiling water, or cold water which is then brought to the boil.

Poached   The classic way to poach an egg is to break it into a shallow pan of just under-boiling salted water, and to cook over gentle heat until the white is firm and the yolk still runny. The poached egg is carefully lifted out with a fish slice. Nowadays people tend to buy so-called egg poachers. The egg is broken into one of the buttered compartments then steamed over boiling water with the lid on. Technically these are buttered eggs.

Fried   For flavour, eggs are best fried in bacon fat. Cook them in the frying pan after you have fried the bacon. To get a white top to the yolk spoon over a little bacon fat or put a lid on the pan. The American 'sunny side up' is simply an egg flipped over once the first side is set.

Scrambled   Beaten eggs are mixed with a little milk or cream, seasoned and cooked in melted butter in a saucepan. Keep stirring the mixture until it thickens and turns creamy. Scrambled eggs should not be cooked until they are dry and powdery. See page 39 for a luxurious variation of scrambled eggs.

Quails' eggs

These pale blue speckled eggs are delicious hard-boiled – they only take a minute. To serve, either peel and serve with celery salt to accompany drinks, or serve with a herb-flavoured mayonnaise and a little salad for a simple first course.

CURRIED EGG MAYONNAISE

SERVES 4

For plain egg mayonnaise, omit the curry powder and chutney.

INGREDIENTS

4 hard-boiled eggs
4 tablespoons mayonnaise (see page 126)
2 teaspoons lemon juice
1½ tablespoons mango chutney juice
½–1 teaspoon curry powder
salt and freshly ground black pepper
cress or parsley sprigs, for garnish

HOW TO MAKE

Cut the hard-boiled eggs in half lengthwise and arrange on a serving dish. Measure the mayonnaise, lemon juice, chutney juice and curry powder into a bowl and blend together. Season to taste, spoon over eggs and garnish with cress or parsley.

> **COOK'S TIP**
> Hard-boiled eggs will be easier to handle if you put them straight into cold water when cooked, and leave for a few minutes. This will also stop a black ring forming round the yolk. Very fresh eggs are difficult to peel when hard-boiled.

BAKED EGGS

SERVES 4

Also known as *Oeufs en cocotte*, baked eggs make a delicious late snack, special breakfast or hot first course.

INGREDIENTS

1 oz (25 g) butter
4 thin rashers lean bacon, chopped
2 oz (50 g) button mushrooms, chopped
salt and freshly ground black pepper
4 eggs
4 tablespoons double cream

HOW TO MAKE   Heat the oven to 350°F/180°C/gas mark 4. Melt the butter in a non-stick frying pan and fry the bacon until beginning to brown. Add the mushrooms and cook for 2 minutes, then season well with salt and pepper.

Divide the mixture between four buttered ramekins. Break an egg into each one, then spoon 1 tablespoon cream over each one. Place the dishes on a baking tray and bake in the oven for about 8–10 minutes, until the egg whites are just set. Serve straight away.

Variation

Instead of bacon and mushrooms, divide 4 oz (100 g) smoked salmon pieces, cooked smoked haddock, diced ham or prawns between the dishes. Cook as above.

SCRAMBLED EGGS WITH SMOKED SALMON

SERVES 4   This delicious version of scrambled eggs makes a luxurious light lunch or special breakfast. Use smoked salmon pieces which are much cheaper than buying slices.

INGREDIENTS

4 thick slices bread
3 oz (75 g) butter
7 eggs
2 tablespoons double cream
3 oz (75 g) smoked salmon pieces, chopped
salt and freshly ground black pepper
sprigs of parsley, for garnish

HOW TO MAKE   Cut 4 rounds from the bread using a 3 inch (7.5 cm) pastry cutter. Melt 2 oz (50 g) butter and dip both sides of the bread circles in butter. Grill both sides of bread under a hot grill until golden brown and crispy. Keep warm on a serving dish.

Beat the eggs lightly in a bowl and stir in the cream and smoked salmon. Season to taste. Melt 1 oz (25 g) butter in a non-stick pan over a low heat. Pour in the egg mixture and stir until the mixture is creamy and beginning to thicken. Remove from the heat, stir gently, then spoon on to the hot toast circles. Garnish with parsley and serve immediately.

PIPERADE

SERVES 4–6

This is a wonderful Spanish version of scrambled eggs. It's essential to use olive oil and fresh basil for the true flavour.

INGREDIENTS

2 tablespoons olive oil
2 large onions, thinly sliced
1 clove garlic, crushed
1 red pepper, sliced
1 green pepper, sliced
1 lb (450 g) tomatoes, skinned and chopped
6 eggs
1 teaspoon basil or parsley, chopped
salt and freshly ground black pepper
fried bread triangles, for garnish

HOW TO MAKE

Heat the oil in a deep frying pan, add the onions and garlic and fry gently until golden. Add the peppers and cook until soft, then stir in the tomatoes. Increase the heat and cook until the mixture is thick and pulpy.

Beat the eggs in a bowl and add the herbs and plenty of seasoning. Pour into the pan and stir gently until beginning to set. Remove from the heat while still creamy, and serve straight on to warmed plates. Garnish with triangles of fried bread.

EGGS FLORENTINE

SERVES 4

Poached eggs served on a bed of spinach, and covered with cheese sauce can be served as a light lunch or supper dish with brown French bread.

INGREDIENTS

2 lb (900 g) fresh spinach
1½ oz (40 g) butter
1 oz (25 g) flour
½ pint (300 ml) milk
3 oz (75 g) mature Cheddar cheese
salt and freshly ground black pepper
4 eggs

HOW TO MAKE

Wash the spinach in several changes of water. Put in a pan with just the water that clings to the leaves. Cover and cook for 5–10 minutes, until tender. Drain well. Chop roughly and reheat with ½ oz (15 g) butter. Spread out in a shallow ovenproof dish.

Melt the remaining butter in a pan, stir in the flour and cook for 1 minute, stirring. Gradually blend in the milk, and bring to the boil slowly, stirring until thickened. Add 2 oz (50 g) cheese and the seasoning.

Poach the eggs and gently transfer on to the bed of spinach. Pour on cheese sauce. Sprinkle with the remaining cheese and brown under the grill.

CLASSIC FRENCH OMELETTE

SERVES 1

An omelette is one of the quickest things to make, and you usually have all the ingredients to hand in a fridge or store cupboard. Make more of a meal of an omelette by serving with a mixed green or tomato salad and warm bread – garlic or otherwise.

I have given some favourite filling suggestions below, but for a more substantial omelette combine any freshly cooked leftover vegetables, chicken or ham with ½ pint (300 ml) cheese sauce (page 228) and divide between 3 or 4 omelettes for the family.

INGREDIENTS

3 eggs
1 tablespoon water
salt and freshly ground black pepper
a good knob of butter

HOW TO MAKE

Blend the eggs in a bowl. Add the water and seasoning. Heat a 7 inch (18 cm) pan – preferably non-stick or heavy iron with a good surface – until very, very hot. Drop the butter into the pan and run it around quickly by tilting the pan. Pour the egg in and stir lightly two or three times only. Leave until just set. The inside should still be soft and creamy.

Unless making a plain omelette, add any heated filling (see below) on the half of the omelette at the far end from the pan handle. Flip the uncovered half over the filling using a fish slice. Turn the omelette out on to a heated plate and serve at once.

Variations

Mixed Herbs   Add a tablespoon of mixed chopped leafy herbs to the omelette mix before cooking. Try parsley, chervil, basil, tarragon and marjoram.

Mushroom   Fill the just cooked omelette with 2 oz (50 g) mushrooms that have been sautéed in butter.

Cheese and Ham   Fill the just cooked omelette with 1½ oz (50 g) well-flavoured grated cheese and a slice of chopped ham.

SPANISH OMELETTE

SERVES 4

A variety of lightly cooked vegetables can be added to the basic omelette such as chopped red pepper, mushrooms, sweetcorn, tomatoes, peas and beans to add colour and make a more substantial meal. Add them to the pan after cooking the potatoes and onions.

INGREDIENTS

3 tablespoons olive oil
2 large potatoes, cubed
2 large onions, chopped
salt and freshly ground black pepper
6 eggs, lightly beaten

HOW TO MAKE

Heat the oil in a medium-sized frying pan, add the potatoes and onions and fry gently for about 15 minutes, stirring to coat in oil, until softened and golden brown. Season well with salt and pepper. Drain off the excess oil.

Stir in the beaten eggs, mixing them with the vegetables. Cook for about 5 minutes until almost set, then brown the top under the grill, if liked. Slide on to a serving dish and cut into four wedges to serve.

OMELETTE ARNOLD BENNETT

SERVES 2

This version of Omelette Arnold Bennett is a soufflé omelette – the egg whites are separated from the yolks, whisked until dry then folded into the omelette mixture. The result is a lovely fluffy omelette. The same method can be used to make a sweet omelette. Omit the seasonings and fish and fill the cooked omelette with warmed strawberry jam. Slide on to a plate and sprinkle with icing sugar.

INGREDIENTS

4 oz (100 g) smoked haddock fillet
2 oz (50 g) butter
¼ pint (150 ml) double cream
3 eggs, separated
salt and freshly ground black pepper
2 oz (50 g) mature Cheddar cheese, grated

HOW TO MAKE

Place the fish in a saucepan, just cover with water, then bring to the boil and simmer gently for about 10 minutes. Drain and flake the fish, discarding the skin and any bones.

Melt half the butter in the rinsed-out pan over a high heat, add fish and 2 tablespoons of cream and remove from the heat. Beat the egg yolks and 1 tablespoon cream in a bowl. Season well and add to fish mixture.

Whisk the egg white until dry, then fold into the seasoned fish and yolks. Heat the remaining butter in a non-stick frying pan and pour in the egg mixture. Cook for 1–2 minutes to set the bottom of the omelette. Mix the cheese with the remaining cream, pour on to the omelette and brown under the grill. Slide on to a warm serving dish and serve immediately.

BACON AND LEEK QUICHE

SERVES 4–6

If you want to save on effort, you can use 7½ oz (215 g) frozen shortcrust pastry, thawed, for the base of this quiche. To get a brown base to the quiche, preheat a thick metal baking sheet in the oven and bake the quiche on it. Serve hot with French bread or a simple salad.

INGREDIENTS

PASTRY CASE
4 oz (100 g) plain flour
2 oz (50 g) butter or block margarine, cut into pieces
About 1 tablespoon cold water

FILLING
1 leek
1 oz (25 g) butter
6 oz (175 g) lean cooked forehock of ham or bacon
2 eggs
¼ pint (150 ml) plain yoghurt or single cream
salt and freshly ground black pepper

HOW TO MAKE

Put the flour in a bowl and rub in the butter or margarine until the mixture resembles fine breadcrumbs. Add the water and mix until the pastry forms a ball. Roll out on a lightly floured surface and use to line an 8 inch (20 cm) flan case.

The pastry can be baked straight away, but it is better if allowed to rest for about 20 minutes in the refrigerator.

Heat the oven to 425°F/220°C/gas mark 7. Bake the pastry blind by lining it with a circle of greaseproof paper or foil and filling with baking beans (available from kitchen ware shops). Bake for 15–20 minutes, removing the paper and beans for the final 10 minutes.

While the flan case is cooking, wash and cut up the leek into fine rounds and cook for 1–2 minutes in the butter, stirring all the time. Cut the ham into small pieces and place in a bowl. Mix in the eggs, yoghurt or cream, seasoning and cooked leek. Pour the mixture into the cooked flan case and cook for about 25–30 minutes, until puffy and golden brown.

QUICHE LORRAINE

SERVES 8

A really large quiche for a crowd, delicious served warm with salad. If you prefer, halve the ingredients and bake it in a 7–8 inch (18–20 cm) flan tin. (A smaller quiche will need a slightly shorter cooking time.)

INGREDIENTS

1 oz (25 g) butter
1 tablespoon sunflower oil
1 large onion, chopped
12 oz (350 g) streaky bacon, snipped into small pieces
8 oz (225 g) well-flavoured Cheddar cheese, grated
4 eggs, beaten
1½ pint (300 ml) milk
¼ pint (150 ml) single cream
salt and freshly ground black pepper
1–2 tablespoons chopped parsley

PASTRY
8 oz (225 g) flour
4 oz (100 g) butter or block margarine, cut into pieces
about 3 tablespoons water

HOW TO MAKE

Make the pastry, put the flour in a bowl and rub in the butter or margarine, until the mixtures resembles fine breadcrumbs. Add the water and bind together to form a firm ball. Knead the dough until smooth, then roll out on a lightly floured surface and use to line a deep 11 inch (27.5 cm) loose-bottomed flan tin. Chill in the refrigerator for about 20 minutes. Meanwhile, heat the oven to 425°F/220°C/gas mark 7.

Place a thick baking sheet in the oven (standing the quiche on a hot baking sheet to cook will ensure that the bottom browns nicely). Line the flan case with greaseproof paper and baking beans, or a piece of foil, and bake in the oven for about 20 minutes, removing the paper and beans or foil for the final 10 minutes.

Meanwhile, heat the butter and oil in a pan and fry the onion and bacon for about 10 minutes, until the onion is golden brown and the bacon crisp. Spoon over the base of the flan case and sprinkle the cheese on top. In a large jug, mix the eggs, milk, cream, seasoning and parsley until thoroughly blended, then pour into the flan case.

Reduce the oven temperature to 350°F/180°C/gas mark 4. Bake the quiche in the oven for about 35 minutes, until the filling has set.

WATERCRESS AND EGG MOUSSE

SERVES 8

A great standby that makes a most attractive and delicious first course. If I can get quails' eggs I use them, hard-boiled, to decorate the mousse (see page 37).

INGREDIENTS

½ oz (15 g) packet powdered gelatine
2 tablespoons cold water
10½ oz (298 g) can condensed consommé
1 bunch of watercress
¼ pint (150 ml) double cream
6 hard-boiled eggs, chopped
¼ pint (150 ml) mayonnaise (see page 126)
salt

HOW TO MAKE

Sprinkle the gelatine over the water in a small bowl or cup and leave to stand for about 3 minutes until the gelatine is spongy. Place the bowl in a pan of gently simmering water and stir until the gelatine has dissolved.

Put the consommé in a measuring jug and stir in the gelatine. Keep a few sprigs of watercress for decoration and chop the rest. Whisk the cream until it forms soft peaks. Mix together the chopped watercress, cream, eggs and mayonnaise. Stir in three-quarters of the consommé. Taste and check the seasoning.

Divide the mixture between eight individual ramekins and leave to set. Spoon over the remaining consommé, reheating it gently if it has already set. Decorate with reserved sprigs of watercress.

Variation

Mild Curry Mousse   Add 2 tablespoons chopped mango chutney and 2 teaspoons curry powder with the mayonnaise.

Salmon and Egg Mousse   Add a small can of salmon, well drained and with bones removed, before adding the eggs. Taste the mixture and add the juice of half a lemon if you think the mousse needs to be sharper.

COOK'S TIP
To dissolve gelatine successfully always sprinkle the gelatine over the cold water, never add the water to the gelatine as it could go lumpy.

CHEESE SOUFFLÉ

SERVES 4

There's nothing complicated about making a soufflé. It's simple a white sauce with added egg yolks and whisked egg whites to make it rise. The most important thing to remember is that a soufflé waits for no one. If you want to make it ahead, prepare it to the stage before adding the egg white. Any strong-flavoured cheese can be used to flavour a cheese soufflé. Try Sage Derby as an alternative to cheddar.

INGREDIENTS

1½ oz (40 g) butter
1½ oz (40 g) flour
½ pint (300 ml) hot milk
salt and freshly ground black pepper
1 level teaspoon Dijon mustard
4 oz (100 g) well-flavoured Cheddar cheese, grated
4 large eggs
1 tablespoon dried fine breadcrumbs, optional

HOW TO MAKE

Heat the oven to 375°F/190°C/gas mark 5 and place a baking tray in the oven. Butter a 2 pint (1.2 litre) soufflé dish.

Melt the butter in a pan, stir in flour and cook for 1 minute. Gradually blend in the milk and bring to the boil slowly, stirring until thickened. Add the seasoning and mustard and leave to cool. Stir in the cheese.

Separate the eggs and beat the yolks one at a time into the cheese sauce. Whisk the egg whites in a large bowl until stiff but not dry. Stir one heaped tablespoon of egg white into the cheese sauce, then carefully fold the cheese sauce into the remaining egg whites.

Pour into the soufflé dish and sprinkle over breadcrumbs if using. Bake on a hot baking tray in the centre of the oven for about 40 minutes, until well risen and golden brown.

Variations

Instead of cheese, add one of the following flavourings to the sauce before the egg yolks.

Ham   Add 4–6 oz (100–175 g) ham or cooked bacon, chopped.

Fish   Add 4–6 oz (100–175 g) cooked smoked haddock, flaked.

Shellfish   Add 4 oz (100 g) peeled prawns or shrimps.

Mushroom   Add 8 oz (225 g) mushrooms, finely chopped and cooked in 1 oz (25 g) butter.

Soufflés can also be made and served in individual ramekins. The amount given in the recipe will make 6–8 individual soufflés depending on the size of the ramekins. Cooking time will be about 20 minutes.

Fish and Shellfish

Fish is an excellent source of protein in the diet and white fish is very low in fat, making it relatively low in calories. Oily fish has a higher fat content, but the fat that fish does contain is largely polyunsaturated which is better for us than saturated animal fat. Oily fish and fish liver contain a good supply of vitamins A and D.

White fish has a delicate flavour, while oily fish has stronger flavoured flesh.

Buying fresh fish

Fish is a highly perishable food so there are certain points to look out for when buying fresh fish.

Whole fresh:
- The fish should be shiny and firm.
- Have clear bright eyes.
- The smell should be mild and fresh.

Fillets, steaks and cutlets:
- No sign of dryness or discoloration.
- Mild, clean smell.

Shellfish:
- Cooked shellfish should smell fresh.
- Live lobsters are varying shades of black and brown.
- Live mussels, scallops or oysters should have tightly closed shells when tapped. Discard any with shells that are broken.
- Prawns and shrimps should have their tails curled well under them.

Cleaning fish

A good fishmonger will always clean, skin and bone fish as required – try to choose a non-busy time to shop. However, if given a present of fish, it is good to know how to tackle the job.

To remove scales   Hold fish by the tail and scrape the back of a knife from tail to head, in the opposite direction to which the scales lie. Rinse under cold running water. To help grip the fish wrap a piece of kitchen paper round the tail first.

To gut round fish   Make a slit with a sharp knife from the gill below the head to the vent just above the tail. Insert fingers and pull insides out gently. Wash away any blood, rinse and dry with kitchen paper.

To gut flat fish   Make a slit on the upper body under the gills towards the backbone and clean out the entrails.

To finish   Cut off the fins and gills if serving the fish whole. Otherwise remove head. Wash well under cold running water and drain, then dry.

Skinning fish

Whole flat fish   Wash the fish and cut off the fins. Make a shallow cut across the tail, insert your thumb between the skin and the flesh and loosen enough skin to get a good grip. Hold the tail with one hand and the skin with the other hand, then pull the skin down towards the head. Do the same on the other side, or, if preferred, leave the white skin on. Use a cloth to hold the tail end if it's too slippery to get a good grip, or put some salt on your fingers.

Fillets of flat fish   Lay the fillet on a chopping board, skin side down. Make a cut as near the tail end as possible through the flesh to the skin but not through the skin. Hold the skin and, with the knife blade at a slight angle away from you, move the knife in a sawing action, taking care not to cut through the skin. As you cut, the flesh will fold over away from the knife leaving a clean whole skin.

Filleting fish

Flat fish Place the fish on a chopping board to avoid slipping. With the point of a sharp knife, cut straight down the backbone. To remove the first fillet, insert the knife between the backbone and the flesh and, cutting carefully, work the knife with smooth strokes from the head end to the tail on the left hand side. To remove the second fillet, turn the fish and cut in the same way but from tail end to head. The remaining two fillets come from the underside in the exactly the same way. With practice there should be no flesh left on the bones.

Round fish Lay the fish on a board and, using the point of the knife, cut all the way down the backbone but not too deeply. Gently insert the knife and pressing down slightly on the bones, make smooth cuts following the contour of the bones, working from head to tail. As you cut, it becomes easier to lift the flesh from the bones. Remove the second fillet from head to tail from the other side in the same way.

Filleting herring and mackerel To keep both fillets joined together, it is useful to know how to remove most of the bones from the fish. Cut off the head, tail and fins. Make an incision on the underside to remove insides, then rinse out the cavity. Lay fish on a board, cut side down, and press lightly with the fingers down the middle of the back to loosen the bone. Turn the fish over and ease the backbone up, removing with it as many of the smaller bones as possible to leave a whole boned fish.

Methods of cooking fish

Baking Fish such as salmon or trout retain their flavour cooked this way. Seasoned then wrapped in buttered foil and baked in the oven they cook perfectly, keep moist and do not loose their delicate flavour. This method is suitable for whole fish, fillets or steaks.

Frying Shallow frying in a little butter is more popular today than deep frying. Fillets of white fish cook quickly retaining most of their natural juices. Can be dipped in egg and breadcrumbs or just a light coating of seasoned flour. If you enjoy fish and chips, an electric deep fat fryer is an excellent idea as it controls the temperature of the fat and gives good results.

Grilling A very healthy way of cooking. It is necessary to lightly brush the fish with melted butter or oil first. Grill as near to a preheated hot grill as possible, and turn over once the fish is golden on top. Most types take only about 10 minutes as they cook so quickly under a hot grill.

Poaching The usual way of cooking fish if it is to be served with a sauce. I simply put mine in a lightly buttered dish, season and cover with a little milk or fish stock, or half milk and water. Cook in the oven for about 10 minutes until the fish flakes easily or just comes away from the bone. The liquid can be used to make a sauce.

Pickling or curing Another method of preparing fish is to pickle or cure it. This is done with vinegar or salt. Gravadlax (see page 64) is a traditional Scandinavian recipe for fresh salmon. The raw fish is spread with a salt paste then wrapped and weighted down. It is left to pickle for up to three days in the refrigerator. Soused herrings (see page 63) are baked in a pickling liquid then left to go cold.

BAKED SALMON WITH FENNEL AND LEMON

SERVES 6

This is easy to prepare and quick to cook. For entertaining, assemble all the ingredients and prepare the dish as far as the actual cooking, then keep in a cool place. All you have to do then is put the dish in the oven 15 minutes before you are ready to eat. Set your timer and do not be tempted to cook for any longer.

INGREDIENTS

1 oz (25 g) butter
1 head fennel thinly sliced
chopped fresh dill
6 salmon steaks
juice of ½ lemon
salt and freshly ground black pepper
fresh Herb Cream Sauce (page 230) to serve

HOW TO MAKE

Heat the oven to 425°F/220°C/gas mark 7. Lightly grease a shallow ovenproof dish.

Melt the butter in a saucepan, add the sliced fennel and cook for about 10 minutes, stirring occasionally until tender. Remove the fennel from the heat, add the chopped dill and spoon into the fish cavities. Any fennel left over can be arranged on top of the fish.

Place the salmon steaks in the prepared dish. Pour the lemon juice over the fish and season with salt and pepper. Cover the dish with foil, wrapping it well over the sides, and bake for 15 minutes until the fish has changed colour and is cooked through.

Serve immediately with fresh Herb Cream Sauce.

Variation

Baked Trout with Fennel and Lemon Ask the fishmonger to remove the bones from 6 fresh pink trout. Ask him to leave the skin on. Open the fish out flat and put the cooked fennel and chopped dill in the middle. Fold the fish back over and bake as for salmon. Sprinkle with chopped fennel fronds or dill before serving.

FISH CAKES

MAKES 16–20

These are very quick and easy to make using leftover cooked fish. Alternatively use canned salmon or tuna. Serve with Parsley or Tomato Sauce (see pages 228 and 232).

INGREDIENTS

6 oz (175 g) fresh bread
good bunch of parsley
2 lb (900 g) potatoes, boiled
2 oz (50 g) butter
2 lb (900 g) white fish, cooked and flaked
salt and freshly ground black pepper
1 egg, beaten
a little oil for frying

HOW TO MAKE

Put the bread in a blender or food processor and process to crumbs, then spread out on a plate. Process the parsley and put in a large mixing bowl. Mash the potatoes with the butter and turn into the bowl with the parsley. Add the flaked fish and seasoning and mix well together.

Using your hands, shape the mixture into 16–20 flat cakes. Coat in beaten egg, then in the breadcrumbs. The fish cakes can be made in advance up to this stage and then kept in the refrigerator until needed.

Heat some oil in a heavy frying pan and fry the fish cakes a few at a time for about 5 minutes on each side, until golden brown.

SKATE WITH BLACK BUTTER

SERVES 4

Skate is a flat fish with white meaty flesh. It is sometimes referred to as ray. The traditional way of serving it is with black butter, which is not really black but dark brown. The flavour is sharp and rich.

INGREDIENTS

piece of skate wing about 2 lb (900 g)
salt
2 oz (50 g) butter
1 tablespoon white wine vinegar
1 tablespoon capers
1 tablespoon chopped parsley

HOW TO MAKE

Cut the fish into four wedges, place in a shallow pan and cover with cold, salted water. Poach for 10 minutes, until tender, then drain and place on a warm serving dish. Cover and keep warm.

Melt the butter in a saucepan and cook until it turns golden brown, add the vinegar and capers and cook for about 2–3 minutes.

Pour the butter over the fish, sprinkle with parsley and serve.

MONKFISH KEBABS

SERVES 4

Fish kebabs are excellent done on the barbecue as a change from steaks. You need a firm meaty fish like monkfish or it will drop off the skewer when cooking. Save washing up by using to stuff pittas instead of eating from plates.

INGREDIENTS

1 lb (450 g) monkfish
8 small scallops
8 baby tomatoes
4 courgettes, cut into thick slices
2 oz (50 g) button mushrooms
1 green or red pepper, seeded and cut into 8 pieces
oil for brushing
4 pitta breads, split in half

HOW TO MAKE

Cut the fish into neat squares. Thread all the ingredients on to large skewers, alternating fish with vegetables. Season and brush with oil.

Cook on the barbecue or under the grill for about 7 minutes, turning once or twice. Remove the fish and vegetables from the skewers and fill the pittas.

COOK'S TIP

If you use wooden kebab skewers on a barbecue they will need soaking in water for 30 minutes before use to prevent them catching light.

MORAYSHIRE SMOKED HADDOCK

SERVES 4

The haddock will be easier to skin and bone when it is cooked. It's easy to tell when it's cooked because the flesh will start to flake. Buttery tagliatelle makes a good accompaniment.

INGREDIENTS

1 lb (450 g) smoked haddock fillet
³/₄ pint (450 ml) milk
1½ oz (40 g) butter
1½ oz (40 g) flour
6 oz (175 g) button mushrooms, sliced
salt and freshly ground black pepper
juice of ½ lemon
2 oz (50 g) well-flavoured Cheddar cheese, grated

HOW TO MAKE

Heat the oven to 350°F/180°C/gas mark 4. Put the haddock and milk into a large pan and simmer for about 10 minutes until the haddock flakes. Drain the fish and leave to cool. Reserve the cooking liquid.

When cool enough to handle, remove skin and any bones from the fish and roughly flake. Melt the butter in a saucepan, stir in the flour and cook for about a minute. Gradually add the reserved cooking liquid stirring until blended in. Bring to the boil slowly, stirring until the sauce thickens.

Add the sliced mushrooms to the sauce and cook for about 2 minutes. Season to taste.

Mix the fish, lemon juice and sauce together, turn into a shallow ovenproof dish and sprinkle the cheese over the top. Cook in the oven for about 20 minutes, until the cheese is golden and bubbling.

HERRINGS WITH MUSTARD SAUCE

SERVES 4

Herrings are an oily fish with a delicate flavour. When smoked they become kippers. It is essential for the herrings to be really fresh for this dish.

INGREDIENTS

4 large herrings
oil
1 oz (25 g) butter

SAUCE
1½ oz (40 g) butter
1 oz (25 g) flour
½ pint (300 ml) milk
1 tablespoon Dijon mustard
salt and freshly ground black pepper
parsley and lemon wedges, for garnish

HOW TO MAKE

Heat the oven to 400°F/200°C/gas mark 6 and butter a deep ovenproof dish. Remove the heads from the fish, clean, gut and bone them. Rinse and pat dry.

Slash the skins diagonally with a sharp knife two or three times on each side. Brush with a little oil. Put the herrings in the dish, cover and bake in the oven for about 20 minutes, until the flesh is no longer pinky.

Meanwhile, make the sauce. Melt the butter in a saucepan, stir in the flour and cook for a minute. Gradually blend in the milk, stirring. Add the mustard and bring to the boil slowly, stirring until thickened. Season to taste.

Serve the herrings garnished with sprigs of parsley and lemon wedges. Serve the sauce separately.

COOK'S TIP
When adding flour to melted butter to make the thickening base of a sauce, always cook for 1 minute before blending in the milk or other liquid. This prevents the sauce having a floury taste and the sauce will thicken more readily.

DOUBLE FISH PIE

SERVES 6

This recipe has been used for my family gatherings for years! Mixing smoked and unsmoked fish adds interest to the pie. Do use a shallow dish so that everyone gets plenty of the crispy brown topping.

INGREDIENTS

12 oz (350 g) smoked haddock
12 oz (350 g) unsmoked haddock
1 pint (600 ml) milk
2 oz (50 g) butter
2 oz (50 g) flour
3 hard-boiled eggs, roughly chopped
½ teaspoon grated nutmeg
juice of ½ lemon
salt and freshly ground black pepper

POTATO TOPPING
1½ lb (675 g) potatoes
milk and butter for mashing
4 oz (100 g) mature Cheddar cheese, grated
salt and freshly ground black pepper

HOW TO MAKE

Heat the oven to 425°F/220°C/gas mark 7. Grease a shallow 3 pint (1.75 litre) ovenproof dish.

Boil the potatoes for the topping until they are tender. Meanwhile, put the fish in a pan with the milk and simmer gently for 10 minutes, or until the fish can be flaked with a fork. Strain and reserve the milk. Skin and flake the fish, removing any bones.

Rinse out the pan. Melt the butter, add the flour and cook for a minute, then gradually blend in the reserved milk and bring to the boil slowly, stirring until thickened. Add the chopped egg, nutmeg, lemon juice and flaked fish. Mix well, then taste and check the seasoning. Turn into the ovenproof dish. Cool until the mixture is firm enough to pipe the mashed potato over.

Drain the potatoes and mash with plenty of milk and butter, then stir in three-quarters of the cheese and the seasoning. (The mixture should be fairly soft, like whipped cream.) Transfer the potato to a piping bag fitted with a large nozzle, and pip zig-zags over the fish from side to side of the dish, or spread the potato over, if preferred. Sprinkle the remaining cheese over the potato.

Cook for 30–40 minutes, until the topping is golden brown. Serve at once.

SOLE FLORENTINE

SERVES 4

Sole is expensive – use cod fillet instead, if preferred. There is no need to cook the fish before the dish is assembled. If you have fresh spinach, cook it first then drain well.

INGREDIENTS

4 large sole fillets, skinned
salt and freshly ground black pepper
juice of ½ small lemon
1½ oz (40 g) butter
1½ oz (40 g) flour
¾ pint (450 ml) milk
1 lb (450 g) frozen cut-leaf spinach, thawed and drained
3 oz (75 g) well-flavoured Cheddar cheese, grated
1 oz (25 g) fresh white breadcrumbs

HOW TO MAKE

Heat the oven to 400°F/200°C/gas mark 6. Season the fillets well with salt, pepper and lemon juice, roll them up and set aside.

Melt the butter in a pan, add the flour and cook for a minute. Gradually blend in the milk and bring to the boil slowly, stirring until thickened. Simmer for 2 minutes, then season to taste.

Blend half of the sauce with the spinach and spread in a shallow 3 pint (1.75 litre) ovenproof dish. Arrange the fish on top and pour over the remaining sauce.

Mix the cheese and breadcrumbs together and sprinkle on top of the sauce. Bake in the oven for 30–40 minutes, until the topping is pale brown and the fish perfectly white all through.

COOK'S TIP
Heels of cheese, or small pieces that have dried out, can be grated and stored in the refrigerator ready for sprinkling on dishes before baking or grilling, or to flavour sauces.

SPICED FISH IN YOGHURT AND MAYONNAISE SAUCE

SERVES 4

This light summer dish is delicious with a simple wild rice salad. Simply mix a little cooked wild rice with some cooked brown rice and stir in a tablespoon or two of French dressing.

INGREDIENTS

12 oz (350 g) haddock fillet, cooked
6 oz (175 g) peeled prawns
1 yellow pepper, seeded
1 avocado pear
2 bananas
juice of 1 lemon
5 tablespoons natural yoghurt
4 tablespoons mayonnaise (see page 126)
2 teaspoons curry powder
1 clove garlic, crushed
salt and freshly ground black pepper
fresh herbs, for garnish

HOW TO MAKE

Flake the fish coarsely in a large bowl and add the prawns. Cut the pepper in fine strips and add to the bowl. Halve the avocado, remove the stone and peel, then slice thinly into a separate bowl.

Peel the bananas, slice diagonally and add to the avocado, then turn both in the lemon juice to prevent discoloration. Add to the fish mixture, spoon into a serving dish, cover and chill.

Put the yoghurt, mayonnaise, curry powder, garlic and seasoning into a bowl, mix thoroughly and spoon over the fish. Decorate with fresh herbs.

PRAWNS IN MILD CURRY SAUCE

SERVES 4

Best served with boiled rice and a green salad.

INGREDIENTS

2 tablespoons olive oil
1 onion, chopped
1 rounded teaspoon curry powder
2 tablespoons flour
1/2 pint (300 ml) fish or chicken stock (see page 14)
1 rounded teaspoon tomato purée
2 tablespoons mango chutney juice
juice of 1/2 lemon
8 oz (225 g) peeled prawns
2 1/2 fl oz (65 ml) double cream
chopped parsley, for garnish

HOW TO MAKE   Heat the oil in a saucepan, add the onion, cover and cook gently, without colouring, until soft.

Stir in the curry powder and cook for a minute. Add the flour and cook for 1–2 minutes. Gradually blend in the stock and bring to the boil slowly, stirring until thickened. Add the tomato purée, mango chutney juice and lemon juice and simmer for a few minutes.

Dry the prawns well, add to the curry sauce and bring to the boil. Add the cream and remove from the heat.

Serve with plain boiled rice and a sprinkling of chopped parsley.

SCALLOPS IN BRANDY AND CREAM SAUCE

SERVES 4   Queen scallops are smaller and have a more delicate flavour than larger king scallops. Large scallops are best sliced through 2 or 3 times so they cook more quickly. Look for scallops with the orange coral attached, which is considered a great delicacy. These days scallops are usually sold out of the shell. Ask the fishmonger for some scallop shells if you want to serve this dish in the traditional way. Anchor the shells to the serving plates with a blob of mashed potato, and pipe swirls of mashed potato around the edge.

INGREDIENTS
1 small onion
1 oz (25 g) butter
glass white wine
¾ lb (350 g) queen scallops
salt and freshly ground black pepper
sherry glass of brandy
¼ pint (150 ml) double cream

HOW TO MAKE   Finely chop the onion. Melt the butter in a heavy pan, add the onion and cook slowly, without colouring, until soft.

Pour on the wine and turn up the heat. Bring to the boil and reduce by about half. Add the scallops and season.

Add the brandy, then the cream. Bring to the boil and boil for 2 minutes.

Serve at once with creamy mashed potatoes or white boiled rice.

COD AND MUSHROOM PANCAKES

SERVES 4

As anchovies are very salty, there is no need to add salt to this dish. Serve these crispy pancakes with a mixed dressed salad.

INGREDIENTS

1 lb (450 g) fresh cod, skinned and cut into 2 or 3 pieces
½ pint (300 ml) milk
6 oz (175 g) mushrooms, sliced
1½ oz (40 g) butter
1½ oz (40 g) flour
small can anchovies, drain and chopped
8 × 8 inch (20 cm) pancakes (see page 162)
freshly ground black pepper
little melted butter

HOW TO MAKE

Put the cod and ¼ pint (150 ml) of the milk into a saucepan and simmer for about 5 minutes until the fish flakes. Drain and reserve the liquid.

Simmer the mushrooms in the same liquid for about 3 minutes. Drain and reserve the liquid again. Rinse the pan, add the butter and melt. Add the flour and cook for a minute or two, stirring continuously. Gradually add the reserved liquid and remaining ¼ pint (150 ml) milk and bring to the boil, stirring until the sauce thickens. Add the chopped anchovies and black pepper and mix well. Allow to cool. Flake fish into a medium-sized bowl, removing any bones. Add the mushrooms, then the sauce.

Meanwhile, heat the oven to 425°F/220°C/gas mark 7. When the fish mixture is cool, lay out pancakes and divide the mixture equally between them and season lightly. Roll up pancakes and place in an ovenproof dish.

To serve, brush with a little melted butter and heat through in the oven for about 20–30 minutes until crispy.

Variation

Cod, Egg and Prawn Pancakes Omit the mushrooms and add 4 oz (100 g) shelled prawns and 3 chopped hard-boiled eggs with the anchovies.

COOK'S TIP
Pancakes freeze well. Make double quantity when baking a batch and store extras in the freezer. Layer with greaseproof paper and wrap well.

MOULES MARINIÈRE

SERVES 4

Mussels are best bought in winter and early spring. Make sure that every mussel is tightly closed before they are cooked. This means that they are all alive and there are no bad ones. Discard any that are open at this stage. The tightly closed shells should be left in a bucket of lightly salted water for an hour, then scrubbed before proceeding with the recipe.

INGREDIENTS

4 pints (2.3 litres) fresh mussels
2 oz (50 g) butter
1 onion, finely chopped
2 sticks celery, finely chopped
4 stalks parsley
2 sprigs fresh thyme
1 bay leaf
salt and freshly ground black pepper
½ pint (300 ml) white wine
1 tablespoon flour
chopped parsley, for garnish

HOW TO MAKE

Scrape and clean each mussel with a strong knife to remove all seaweed, mud and beard. Wash thoroughly in several changes of water, then drain.

Melt 1 oz (25 g) of the butter in a large saucepan over a low heat, add the onion and celery and fry until soft but not coloured. Add the herbs, salt and pepper, wine and mussels. Cover the saucepan with a tightly fitting lid and cook quickly, shaking the pan constantly, until the mussels open (about 5 to 6 minutes). Lift the mussels out and break off and discard the empty half shells. Keep the mussels warm in a covered dish. Any mussels that remain closed after cooking must not be forced open as they are probably bad. Instead remove and discard.

Cream the remaining butter with the flour. Remove the herbs from the cooking liquor, then drop the creamed butter and flour into the stock a teaspoonful at a time and whisk until the sauce has thickened. Taste and check the seasoning. Pour the sauce over the mussels, sprinkle with chopped parsley and serve.

COOK'S TIP

Eat the mussels in Moules Marinière by holding the half shell with your fingers and removing the mussel with a fork. Provide diners with a separate plate for the empty shells, finger bowls and napkins. Even more important, give everyone a soup spoon so they can enjoy the liquid in the bottom of their bowl.

KOULIBIAC

SERVES 6

This is a smart salmon kedgeree in a crisp puff pastry crust. It makes an impressive centrepiece for a buffet.

INGREDIENTS

2½ oz (65 g) long grain rice
3 oz (75 g) butter
1 large onion, chopped
14 oz (400 g) can chopped tomatoes
1 lb (450 g) salmon, cooked and flaked
2 tablespoons parsley, chopped
juice of 1 lemon
salt and freshly ground black pepper
14 oz (400 g) packet frozen puff pastry, thawed
1 egg beaten

TO SERVE
2 oz (50 g) butter, melted
juice of ½ lemon
¼ pint (150 ml) soured cream
finely chopped leafy herbs (optional)

HOW TO MAKE

Heat the oven to 425°F/220°C/gas mark 7 and grease a baking sheet.

Cook the rice in boiling salted water for about 12 minutes or until tender, then drain. Melt the butter in a pan, add the onion and cook gently until soft, without colouring. Drain the tomatoes, add to the onion and cook gently. Mix together the rice, onion and tomato mixture, flaked salmon, parsley, lemon juice and plenty of seasoning.

Roll the pastry into a rectangle about 11 × 16 inches (27.5 × 40 cm). Brush with beaten egg and pile the mixture down the centre, leaving a pastry border all round. Brush the border with beaten egg, fold long sides over to make a fat sausage shape and tuck the ends under.

Carefully lift on to the baking sheet, make several deep cuts diagonally across the sausage shape and brush with beaten egg. Bake for about 30–45 minutes, until well risen and golden brown.

Pour the melted butter and lemon juice down the cuts and serve with the soured cream. If liked, add some finely chopped green leafy herbs to the soured cream.

SALMON AND SCALLOP PARCELS

SERVES 8

A really exciting way of serving salmon, perhaps when you have a small tail end piece or odd cut left in the freezer. These are individual parcels folded up to look like dolly or money bags with a filling of salmon and scallop, a little cream sauce and a little fresh dill added if you have some. If scallops are unavailable, use prawns instead. I have made these and the sauce the day before, then cooked the parcels just when they are needed and reheated the sauce gently.

INGREDIENTS

SAUCE
1/4 pint (150 ml) vermouth or dry white wine
3/4 pint (450 ml) double cream
salt and freshly ground black pepper
1 teaspoon freshly snipped dill

PARCELS
1 1/2 lb (675 g) salmon, boned and skinned
10 oz (275 g) scallops
a little lemon juice
6 sheets filo pastry
melted butter, to brush

HOW TO MAKE

First make the sauce. Measure the vermouth or wine into a pan and boil rapidly until reduced to about 3 tablespoons. Add the cream, mix together and simmer until the sauce coats the back of a wooden spoon.

Remove from the heat, season to taste and add the dill. Transfer one-third of the sauce to a small bowl and allow to cool. Keep the remainder to reheat later.

Heat the oven to 425°F/220°C/gas mark 7 and grease a baking sheet.

Divide the salmon and scallops into 8 portions. Season and sprinkle with a little lemon juice. Lay out 6 sheets of pastry and cover with a damp tea towel. Take one sheet of pastry and lay it flat on a work surface. Brush with melted butter, then put a second sheet on top and brush again, divide into 4 squares. Put one portion of the salmon and scallop mixture in the centre and top with one-eighth of the sauce in the bowl. Bundle into a parcel shape. Do this with remaining portions of fish and 2 more sheets of pastry.

Brush the two remaining sheets of pastry with melted butter, and divide each one into four. Put one of the bundles into the centre of each and draw up the sides of pastry to form a dolly bag, leaving the pastry edges pointing upwards, squeezing the pastry at the necks.

Lift the eight dolly bags on to the baking sheet. Brush each with more melted butter. (At this stage the parcels can be kept uncovered in the refrigerator until required.) Bake for about 15 minutes until pale golden brown and crisp all over. Serve as soon as possible with the remaining cream sauce reheated but not boiled.

QUENELLES WITH CRABMEAT SAUCE

SERVES 4

To prepare the quenelles ahead, poach as suggested in the recipe, arrange in an ovenproof dish, cover with foil and keep in the refrigerator until required. Reheat in the oven for about 40 minutes, adding the sauce just before serving.

INGREDIENTS

QUENELLES
1 lb (450 g) cod fillet
2 egg whites
salt and freshly ground black pepper
¼ teaspoon ground mace
¼ pint (150 ml) double cream
chopped parsley, for garnish

SAUCE
¼ pint (150 ml) white wine
½ pint (300 ml) double cream
2 oz (50 g) crabmeat
juice of ½ lemon

HOW TO MAKE

Roughly chop the fish and place in a blender or food processor with the egg whites, salt, pepper and mace. Process for a few seconds until absolutely smooth then, with the blender or processor running, add the cream in a steady stream until thoroughly blended. Take care not to over-process, otherwise the cream may turn to butter.

Turn the mixture into a bowl, cover with clingfilm and chill in the refrigerator for several hours before cooking.

Meanwhile, make the crab sauce. Pour the wine into a saucepan and boil rapidly until reduced to a thin syrup. Remove from the heat. Pour the double cream into another pan, bring to the boil and cook until it coats the back of a metal spoon. Stir in the wine and crabmeat, season and add lemon juice to taste.

To cook the quenelles, bring a pan of salted water to the boil, dip two dessertspoons into the water, take a spoonful of fish mixture and with the other spoon shape it into an oval and gently ease the fish off the spoon into the water to poach for about 5–8 minutes. Do several at a time. Lift out with a slotted spoon when cooked and arrange on a warm serving dish. Keep warm until all the quenelles are cooked.

Reheat the sauce, pour it over the quenelles. Serve sprinkled with chopped parsley.

SOUSED HERRINGS

SERVES 6

Good with salad and dill mayonnaise, and in Scots Herrings (see page 26). Boiling the vinegar and spices first gives the best flavour, but if time is short this stage can be omitted.

INGREDIENTS

¾ pint (450 ml) white wine vinegar
1 bay leaf
8 peppercorns
6 large herrings
2 large onions, peeled

HOW TO MAKE

Measure vinegar and ¾ pint (450 ml) cold water into a saucepan and add the bay leaf and peppercorns. Bring to the boil and simmer for 10 minutes. Leave to cool.

Gut and clean fish (see page 47), remove heads and backbones but not tails. Wash and pat dry on kitchen paper.

Heat the oven to 350°F/180°C/gas mark 4. Cut the onions into thin slices, separate into rings. Place some of the small onion rings on the fish, roll up towards tail and secure with a wooden cocktail stick.

Arrange fish in an ovenproof dish, sprinkle with remaining onion, add cooled vinegar, cover with a lid or foil and bake for about 15 minutes. Leave to become completely cold in the vinegar, then refrigerate.

Serve, well drained from cooking liquor.

COOK'S TIP
Many people dislike herrings because of their many small bones. In soused herrings, the vinegar not only counteracts the oily richness of the fish, but also softens and dissolves the small bones.

GRAVADLAX

SERVES AT LEAST 10

This classic Scandinavian recipe for pickled fresh salmon is a top favourite in restaurants as an alternative to smoked salmon for a first course. I find it far easier to slice if I freeze it for about 4 hours beforehand. Scottish farmed salmon is ideal for this recipe and the price is reasonable. If pickling a whole fish increase the pickling ingredients accordingly.

INGREDIENTS

2½ lb (1.1 kg) cut from a fresh Scottish salmon

PICKLING INGREDIENTS
4 tablespoons granulated sugar
3 tablespoons coarse sea salt
masses of freshly ground black pepper
3 tablespoons chopped fresh dill or
 1 good tablespoon dried dill weed

MUSTARD DILL SAUCE
3 tablespoons Dijon mustard
2 tablespoons caster sugar
1 tablespoon white wine vinegar
1 egg yolk
¼ pint (150 ml) sunflower oil
2 tablespoons chopped fresh dill or 1 tablespoon dried dill weed

HOW TO MAKE

First bone the fish. Cut the fins off the fish. Lie the piece on the board and make a long cut down the back of the salmon slightly above the bone. Slip your fingers over the bone and take off the top fillet, then gently slip the knife under the backbone and pull it out. Pull out any tiny bones that you can see.

Mix the pickling ingredients together in a bowl. Put the two fillets skin side down on the board, spread them with the mixture, then sandwich the fillets together skin side out. Wrap the fish in double foil, lie it in a dish and place weights on top – a couple of heavy cans will do. Put the dish in the refrigerator for a minimum of 24 hours, or up to 3 days for a whole fish, turning every day. Expect a lot of sticky salty liquid to drain from the fish when it has been pickled. Remove the fish and dry well.

To make the sauce, whisk the mustard, sugar, vinegar and egg yolk together in a bowl (a balloon whisk is ideal for this), then whisk in the oil. The result will be the consistency of mayonnaise. Season the sauce with salt and pepper and stir in the dill.

To serve the gravadlax, cut each fillet into slices a little thicker than you would for smoked salmon. Cut the slices obliquely to the skin, each slice should then have an edging of dill. Serve with the mustard dill sauce.

GLAZED BONED SALMON WITH PRAWNS

SERVES 10

If you don't possess a fish kettle, the fish can be baked. Remove the head, season well and wrap in buttered foil. Lift into a large meat tin, pour in boiling water to come halfway up the fish. Cook in the oven at 400°F/200°C/gas mark 6 for 6–10 minutes per 1 lb (450 g). Turn the fish in the foil halfway through cooking. Leave in the foil until lukewarm.

INGREDIENTS

5½ lb (2.5 kg) salmon, head removed and cleaned
2 heaped tablespoons salt
3 bay leaves
1 onion, sliced
12 peppercorns
4 tablespoons white wine vinegar
1 packet Swiss or Scandinavian aspic jelly powder,
   [to make 1 pint (600 ml)]
½ cucumber
8 oz (225 g) shelled prawns
chopped parsley or dill, for garnish

HOW TO MAKE

Lift the salmon into a fish kettle, add the salt, bay leaves, onion, peppercorns and vinegar. Add just enough water to cover the fish. Cover and bring slowly to the boil, then simmer for 3 minutes. Remove from the heat and leave until the fish is warm but not hot, for about 2 hours.

Lift fish out carefully on to a board, slide a knife just above the backbone along the length of the fish and lift the fillet on to a tray and peel off the skin. Remove the bones and skin from the second fillet. Cover both fillets with clingfilm and put in the freezer for about 1 hour.

Make up the aspic following the instructions on the packet. I tend to use a little less water than the instructions say, then I make up the quantity with ice cubes to speed up the proceedings.

Slice the cucumber very thinly. Take the fish from the freezer and lift on to a tray placing the fillets side by side. Spoon over a thin layer of cold and thick, but not set, aspic. Arrange two parallel lines of cucumber the length of both fillets, leaving a space in between for the prawns.

Add the prawns and a little chopped parsley to the remainder of the aspic and spoon down the centre of each fillet. Keep cold until ready to serve. Garnish with fresh parsley or dill.

Facing page 64: *Salad Niçoise (page 134)*

Left: *Sage Derby Cheese Soufflé (page 46)*

Poultry and game

CHICKEN

There is a wide variety of both fresh and frozen birds available. Frozen chickens are often cheaper if they have been frozen and water-cooled, as they have taken up an allowed percentage of water which is included in the weight. Air-cooled birds are more expensive and better. Free range corn-fed and specially produced chickens are all there for us to choose from – the emphasis being on flavour and tenderness.

Poussins

These are young chickens, 6–8 weeks old, weighing 1–2 lb (450–900 g). Poussins can be split in half and grilled or fried or roasted for about 20 minutes in a hot oven. Serves 1–2 people depending on the size.

Roasting chicken

If using a frozen chicken, it must be completely thawed before roasting. If you are using stuffing, weigh the bird after you have stuffed it, and use this weight to calculate the roasting time. Truss with small skewers or string and lightly spread the breast with butter or bacon fat. Season with salt and freshly ground black pepper and roast, basting occasionally, according to the times given in the chart opposite. If the breast and thighs appear to be getting too brown, cover with foil.

To test that a bird is cooked

This method of testing applies to chicken, turkey, duckling and goose. Pierce the thickest part of the thigh with a fine skewer; if clear juices run out, the bird is cooked. If the juices are slightly pink-tinged, continue cooking until they are clear. After cooking, cover the bird with foil, keep warm in the oven and allow it to 'rest' for about 10 minutes before carving, as this makes carving easier.

TURKEY

Nowadays turkey can be found in the shops throughout the year. Although fresh turkeys are still most plentiful around Christmas, breeders are also producing relatively small birds with a good plump breast, which are available frozen and oven-ready all through the year. These are particularly economical if you are entertaining a number of people. In addition, frozen roasts of boned and rolled turkey meat are available. These are easy to cook, carve and serve and there is no waste. Some larger supermarkets also stock turkey portions of sliced breast or drumsticks, which are excellent in casseroles and curries.

If you are buying a fresh turkey, order it well in advance from your butcher or poulterer and ask him to draw it for you. Check that it has a plump breast of white, unblemished skin. Fresh turkey will keep for up to 3 days in the refrigerator, but remember that a frozen turkey must be completely thawed before cooking. Leave it in its wrappings and allow plenty of time for thawing at room temperature. You should allow a large bird over 12 lb (5.45 kg) in weight to thaw for 2 days; a smaller bird up to 12 lb (5.45 kg) will need 24 hours.

Roasting turkey

If using a frozen turkey, it must be completely thawed before cooking. If you are using stuffing, weigh the bird after you have stuffed it and use this weight to calculate the roasting time. Truss with small skewers or string and place on a rack in a roasting tin. Brush the

CHICKEN ROASTING TIMES

Oven-ready weight of chicken	Oven temperature	Approximate cooking time
2½ lb (1.1 kg)	400°F/200°C/gas mark 6	55 minutes
3½ lb (1.6 kg)	400°F/200°C/gas mark 6	1 hour 15 minutes
4 lb (1.8 kg)	400°F/200°C/gas mark 6	1 hour 35 minutes
5 lb (2.3 kg)	400°F/200°C/gas mark 6	2 hours
6 lb (2.7 kg)	400°F/200°C/gas mark 6	2 hours 15 minutes
Over 6 lb (2.7 kg)	375°F/190°C/gas mark 5	20 minutes per 1 lb (450 g)

TURKEY ROASTING TIMES

Oven-ready weight of turkey	Oven temperature	Approximate cooking time
5 lb (2.3 kg)	350°F/180°C/gas mark 4	2 hours 30 minutes
10 lb (4.5 kg)	350°F/180°C/gas mark 4	3 hours 15 minutes
15 lb (6.8 kg)	350°F/180°C/gas mark 4	4 hours
20 lb (9 kg)	325°F/160°C/gas mark 3	5 hours

skin with melted butter and season with salt and freshly ground black pepper. Cover loosely with foil, place in the oven on a shelf just below the middle.

Open the foil for the last 1¼ hours of cooking time for a bird over 10 lb (4.5 kg) in weight, and for the last 50 minutes for a smaller bird. Baste occasionally.

Accompaniments The traditional accompaniments to roast turkey are cranberry sauce (page 231), bread sauce (page 229), chippolata sausages (page 238), bacon rolls (page 238) and stuffing (pages 239–40).

DUCKS/DUCKLINGS

Most ducks are now labelled *duckling* in butchers and supermarkets as they are younger birds and are available throughout the year, since young tender birds are reared especially for freezing. The flesh is dark and fatty compared with that of chicken, and there is less meat on the bird, but the flavour is excellent. Duck breasts and portions can be roasted or grilled.

Roasting duckling

If using a frozen duckling, it must be completely thawed before roasting. It may be stuffed but it does tend to get rather greasy, so it is better to cook the stuffing separately in a dish. Truss the bird with small skewers or string and place on a rack in a roasting tin. Season with salt and prick the skin with a fork. As duck is fairly fatty it is not necessary to brush the skin with any fat, nor to cover it with foil unless it is browning too quickly while cooking. Roast according to the times in the chart on page 67.

To spin out a roast duckling

Try roasting a 4–5 lb (1.8–2.3 kg) duckling with a piece of pork to feed more people. Buy a 1½–2 lb (675–900 g) piece of boned belly of pork or a 1½–2 lb (675–900 g) piece of boned and rolled spare rib. Roast side by side in a roasting tin for 45 minutes at 400°F/200°C/gas mark 6. Reduce the oven temperature to 350°F/180°C/gas mark 4 and continue cooking for a further 1¼ hours. The duckling and pork will then serve eight people.

GOOSE

At its best from October to Christmas, it has a shallow breast with comparatively little flesh in proportion to its size and weight.

Roasting goose

If using a frozen goose, it must be completely thawed before roasting. A goose may be stuffed but it does tend to get rather greasy, so it is better to cook the stuffing separately in a dish. Truss the bird with small skewers or string and place on a rack in a roasting tin. Season with salt and prick the skin with a fork. As goose is very fatty, it is not necessary to brush the skin with any fat, nor to cover it with foil unless it is browning too quickly while cooking. Roast according to the times in the chart below.

Accompaniments   As goose is a relatively fatty bird, the tartness of apple sauce makes it a good accompaniment.

DUCKLING ROASTING TIMES

Oven-ready weight of duck	Oven temperature	Approximate cooking time
3 lb (1.4 kg)	350°F/180°C/gas mark 4	1 hour 40 minutes
4 lb (1.8 kg)	350°F/180°C/gas mark 4	2 hours 10 minutes
5 lb (2.3 kg)	350°F/180°C/gas mark 4	2 hours 30 minutes
6 lb (2.7 kg)	350°F/180°C/gas mark 4	3 hours

GOOSE ROASTING TIMES

Oven-ready weight of goose	Oven temperature	Approximate cooking time
8 lb (3.6 kg)	400°F/200°C/gas mark 6 for the first hour of cooking time, then reduce the oven to 350°F/180°C/gas mark 4 for the remaining cooking time	2 hours 40 minutes
10 lb (4.5 kg)		3 hours 20 minutes
12 lb (5.45 kg)		3 hours 40 minutes

GAME

Game birds are hung in feather before preparing for the oven. Supermarket-prepared game has been prepared and requires only to be cooked. If a bird is freshly killed, its flavour will not have developed and they are usually hung by the neck in a cool airy place for anything up to 10 days or when the breast feathers pull out easily. Hanging increases the flavour and tenderises the flesh. The exact hanging time depends on individual taste, the age of the bird and the weather. In a damp spell the flesh will decompose more quickly than when cold and dry.

After hanging, the birds are plucked, drawn and trussed. Traditionally the feet are left on. Young birds roast well while older birds are better casseroled. Wild duck should only hang for about 2–3 days.

Roasting game birds

Having scavenged for a large proportion of their food, most game birds have little fat and are improved if some is added in roasting by placing strips of fat bacon or pork on top. Season well inside with salt and freshly ground black pepper and a good knob of butter. Place in a roasting tin and baste frequently during cooking. Remove the bacon or pork fat 10–15 minutes before the end of the cooking time. Sprinkle a light dusting of flour on the breast for the rest of the cooking time.

Accompaniments The traditional accompaniments to roast game birds are game chips (page 238) and bread sauce (page 229).

Venison

Venison is a very lean meat with a good flavour, which is improved if marinated before roasting. Cuts include shoulder, haunch or saddle. Brown the meat in oil after marinating. Wrap in foil and roast for 35 minutes per 1 lb (450 g) at 375°F/190°C/gas mark 5.

GAME MARINADE
½ pint (300 ml) red wine
2 bay leaves
few peppercorns
2 fat cloves garlic, split in 4
2 tablespoons oil
1 sliced onion

Measure all the ingredients into a glass or china bowl. Add the meat and turn over in the marinade. Cover with a plate or clingfilm. Leave in the refrigerator for 1 or 2 days (less if the meat is cut up). To cook, lift the meat from the marinade, strain the liquid and save to use for a sauce.

Pheasants

In recent years pheasants have become more reasonable. I find that by roasting them for the length of time necessary to get the breasts cooked perfectly (about 45–50 minutes), the legs are sometimes still tough. Often I buy

---

ROASTING TIMES FOR YOUNG GAME BIRDS

Duck (wild)	425°F/220°C/gas mark 7	about 35 minutes
Grouse	425°F/220°C/gas mark 7	about 20–35 minutes
Partridge	425°F/220°C/gas mark 7	about 30–45 minutes
Pheasant	425°F/220°C/gas mark 7	about 45–55 minutes according to size
Quail	425°F/220°C/gas mark 7	about 15–20 minutes
Snipe	425°F/220°C/gas mark 7	about 15–20 minutes
Woodcock	425°F/220°C/gas mark 7	about 15–20 minutes

two brace for eight and roast and serve only the breasts. I make a casserole for eight the next day using the rest of the pheasant (see Roast Breasts of Pheasant with Port Wine Sauce and Normandy Pheasant Casserole, pages 79 and 80).

Guinea fowl

Guinea fowl is becoming more and more popular. It tastes like a slightly gamey chicken. It is best plain roasted or roasted and served with a light sauce. Roast as for chicken.

LEMONY CHICKEN

SERVES 4

This simple recipe uses boneless chicken breasts. These are quick and easy to cook and there is no waste. The dish can be prepared ahead and cooked later.

INGREDIENTS

4 oz (100 g) butter, softened
4 skinless and boneless chicken breasts
grated zest of 1/2 lemon
juice of 1 lemon
salt and freshly ground black pepper
1 tablespoon water
1/4 pint (150 ml) soured cream

HOW TO MAKE

Heat the oven to 375°F/190°C/gas mark 5. Put the butter and lemon zest into a bowl and mix together. With a sharp knife, make three deep cuts in each chicken breast and spread the butter into the cuts. Place chicken in a shallow ovenproof dish so they just touch. Sprinkle with lemon juice and seasoning.

Cook in the oven for about 20–25 minutes, until tender. Lift on to a warm serving dish. Add 1 tablespoon water to the cooking dish and stir round, scraping the bottom of the dish to dislodge any bits on the dish. Return the dish to the oven for 1–2 minutes to heat through. Stir the soured cream into the cooking dish and again heat through in the oven for a few minutes. Pour sauce over the chicken and serve.

TROPICAL CHICKEN KEBABS

SERVES 4

Succulent skewers of chicken and mango that can be cooked on the barbecue. I like to serve them with a crisp green salad and plain boiled rice with a little added wild rice (see page 118).

INGREDIENTS

3 boneless chicken breasts, skinned
2 tablespoons sherry
freshly ground black pepper
2 mangoes, peeled, stoned and cubed
bay leaves
2 tablespoons oil
1 oz (25 g) shredded almonds or shredded coconut

HOW TO MAKE

Cut the chicken into large cubes and place in a bowl with the sherry and a little pepper. Toss together.

Thread the chicken and mango cubes and bay leaves alternatively on to long skewers, then brush lightly with oil.

Preheat the grill to moderately hot and grill the skewers for 8–10 minutes, turning once, until golden on both sides. Sprinkle with shredded almonds or coconut and grill for a further 30 seconds.

DEVILLED CHICKEN

SERVES 4

So many friends make this recipe of mine because it is popular with all ages and quick to make from store cupboard and freezer ingredients.

INGREDIENTS

4 roasting joints of chicken, skinned
salt and freshly ground black pepper
1 rounded tablespoon apricot jam
1 teaspoon Dijon mustard
pinch of cayenne pepper
1 large clove garlic, crushed
1 tablespoon Worcestershire sauce
3 tablespoons tomato ketchup
1 tablespoon soy sauce

HOW TO MAKE

Heat the oven to 350°F/180°C/gas mark 4. Season the chicken joints well on both sides and arrange in a shallow ovenproof dish so that they just touch.

Measure the jam into a bowl, add the mustard, cayenne, garlic and Worcestershire sauce; blend well until smooth. Add the tomato ketchup and soy sauce, season with black pepper and a little salt. Pour the mixture over the chicken joints, coating evenly.

Bake in the oven for about 1 hour at the top of the oven. The chicken is cooked when the juices that run out when the thickest part of the thigh is prodded with a fork are clear; if pink, cook a little longer.

AMERICAN HOT CHICKEN SALAD

SERVES 4

This I would say was one of my most successful recipes. It has been served to hundreds for high days and holidays. It is very easy and quick. Best served with brown French bread and a green salad with fennel.

INGREDIENTS

12 oz (350 g) cooked chicken or turkey, diced
4 sticks celery, sliced diagonally
4 spring onions, finely sliced
1/2 pint (300 ml) mayonnaise
2 teaspoons lemon juice
4 oz (100 g) well-flavoured Cheddar cheese, grated
salt and freshly ground black pepper
a few plain potato crisps, crumbled
a little paprika

HOW TO MAKE

Heat the oven to 425°F/220°C/gas mark 7. Put the chicken, celery, spring onions, mayonnaise and lemon juice into a bowl, together with 3 oz (75 g) grated cheese. Season and mix together, then turn the mixture into a shallow ovenproof dish. Top with remaining cheese, crisps and a dusting of paprika.

Cook in the oven for about 12–15 minutes, until hot but not boiling. Don't cook any longer, otherwise the sauce will separate. Serve straight away.

PAN-FRIED CHICKEN AND ALMONDS WITH SALAD

SERVES 4

This light dish is extremely quick to prepare and perfect for a summer's day.

INGREDIENTS

small amount of oil
4 oz (100 g) thinly sliced streaky bacon, snipped into strips
3 oz (75 g) flaked almonds
3 skinless and boneless chicken breasts
salt and freshly ground black pepper
chopped parsley, for garnish

SALAD
1/2 bunch of watercress
about 8 red lettuce or radicchio leaves
1 crisp lettuce heart
4–6 tablespoons French dressing

HOW TO MAKE

First prepare the salad, trimming off the stalks of the watercress, tearing the lettuce into bite-sized pieces.

Oil the base of a non-stick pan and fry the bacon until the fat runs out. Add the almonds and cook until both the bacon and almonds are a light golden colour. Lift from the pan with a slotted spoon and keep warm.

Cut the chicken into pencil-thin strips and season. Quickly cook in the same pan, tossing all the time for about 2 minutes. Return the bacon and almonds to the pan for a moment. Toss the salad in the dressing and arrange on four plates. Top with chicken, almonds and bacon. Sprinkle with parsley.

MEXICAN CHICKEN

SERVES 4

This wonderful dish uses chicken thigh joints which are much cheaper to buy than breast portions. Rice is a good accompaniment.

INGREDIENTS

3 tablespoons olive oil
8 small chicken thigh joints
2 large onions, sliced
2 fat cloves garlic
14 oz (400 g) can chopped tomatoes
¼ pint (150 ml) chicken stock (see page 14)
½ teaspoon mixed dried herbs
salt and freshly ground black pepper
2 red peppers, sliced
1 small chilli, chopped
12 stuffed green olives, chopped

HOW TO MAKE

Heat the oil in a large pan and fry the chicken thighs quickly to brown on both sides. Lift out and set on one side on a plate. Add the onions and garlic to the pan and fry for 5 minutes. Add the tomatoes, stock, herbs and seasoning, red peppers and chilli. Return the chicken to the pan, cover and simmer for about 30 minutes until the chicken is just tender.

Lift out the chicken, place on a warm serving dish and keep warm. Purée the sauce in one or two batches in a blender or food processor. Rinse out the saucepan, return the sauce to it and reheat. Taste and check the seasoning. Stir in the olives and spoon the sauce over the chicken.

TANDOORI CHICKEN

SERVES 4

If you want to make this traditional Indian chicken dish and time is short, use a bought ready-made tandoori mix to marinate the chicken in.

INGREDIENTS

4 chicken portions
1 teaspoon salt
juice of 1 lemon
1 inch (2.5 cm) piece fresh root ginger or
  ½ teaspoon ground ginger
2 cloves garlic
a few fresh mint leaves
¼ pint (150 ml) natural yoghurt
½ teaspoon chilli powder
1 teaspoon ground black pepper
¼ teaspoon ground nutmeg
1 teaspoon garam masala
¼ teaspoon red food colouring (optional)

TO SERVE
finely shredded lettuce
finely sliced onion
lemon wedges

HOW TO MAKE

Skin the chicken and prick all over with a fork, or make small cuts with a sharp knife. Put in a dish and sprinkle with salt and lemon juice.

Peel the root ginger and garlic and crush. Chop the mint leaves and add to the ginger and garlic. Mix in all the remaining ingredients and pour over the chicken. Cover and leave to marinate overnight.

Remove the rack from the grill pan. Lay chicken in pan and cook under a hot grill for about 5 minutes on each side. Reduce the heat and cook for a further 10 minutes on each side.

Serve on a bed of finely shredded lettuce and finely sliced onion with lemon wedges to garnish.

EASTERN STIR FRY

SERVES 4

This recipe makes two chicken breasts go a long way. It helps to chill the chicken before cutting into strips.

INGREDIENTS

2 skinless chicken breasts
12 oz (350 g) white cabbage
6 spring onions
2 teaspoons cornflour
2 tablespoons sherry
2 tablespoons sunflower oil
salt and freshly ground black pepper
1 red pepper, seeded and sliced
6 oz (175 g) bean sprouts
4 oz (100 g) mange-tout, strings removed
1 clove garlic, crushed
2½ fl oz (65 ml) chicken stock (see page 14)
2 tablespoons soy sauce

HOW TO MAKE

Slice the chicken into pencil-thin strips. Shred the cabbage finely. Cut each spring onion into three. Blend the cornflour with the sherry.

Heat the oil in a wok or large frying pan until very hot. Season the chicken and cook for 2 minutes, stirring all the time. Lift out with a slotted spoon and set aside.

Reheat the pan and add the cabbage, red pepper, bean sprouts, mange-tout, spring onions and garlic. Cook for 3–4 minutes, stirring all the time. Return the chicken to the pan and stir in the stock, soy sauce and sherry mixture. Cook for another minute until the liquid has thickened slightly and the vegetables are still crisp. Taste and check the seasoning, then serve at once.

COOK'S TIP
Stir-frying is a fast and healthy way of cooking. Very little oil is used and the ingredients cook so quickly that they retain their goodness. Prepare all the ingredients and place within easy reach before you begin stir-frying.

EASY CORONATION TURKEY

SERVES 6

This traditional dish is a great standby for parties. It is usually served with rice.

INGREDIENTS

knob of butter
1 small onion, chopped
½ clove garlic, crushed
1 tablespoon tomato purée
½ teaspoon curry powder
2 tablespoons lemon juice
2 tablespoons apricot jam
½ pint (300 ml) mayonnaise
¾–1 lb (350–450 g) cooked turkey or chicken, cut into chunks
8 oz (225 g) green and black grapes, halved and stoned
1½ oz (40 g) flaked almonds, toasted
small sprigs of watercress or parsley

HOW TO MAKE

Melt the butter in a small pan, add the onion and fry until soft. Add the garlic, tomato purée, curry powder, 1 tablespoon lemon juice and the apricot jam and bring to the boil slowly, stirring all the time. Purée the mixture in a blender or food processor. Blend with the mayonnaise in a bowl and stir in the turkey or chicken. Chill overnight in the refrigerator.

Toss the grapes in the remaining lemon juice and stir into the turkey mayonnaise. Taste and check the seasoning.

Pile into a serving dish and scatter with the toasted almonds and small sprigs of watercress or parsley.

MINT AND CORIANDER SPICED TURKEY

SERVES 6

This is a good recipe for a party and can be made well in advance.

INGREDIENTS

1 lb 4 oz (550 g) cooked turkey, cut into large chunks
sprigs of mint, for garnish

SAUCE
8 oz (225 g) mayonnaise
8 oz (225 g) Greek-style yoghurt
1 teaspoon ground cumin
1 teaspoon ground coriander
2 tablespoons chopped parsley
2 tablespoons chopped mint
6 spring onions, chopped
salt and freshly ground black pepper

HOW TO MAKE

Mix all the sauce ingredients together. Add the turkey, taste and add more seasoning, if necessary. Turn into a glass bowl, cover and leave in the refrigerator overnight for the flavours to blend. Next day, serve in a shallow dish, garnished with mint sprigs. Serve with hot garlic bread and salad.

DUCK BREASTS IN GRAND MARNIER SAUCE

SERVES 4

Duck breasts are now available in most good supermarkets and make a pleasant change from chicken.

INGREDIENTS

4 duck breasts, trimmed of excess fat on the underside
1 orange
salt and freshly ground black pepper
2 tablespoons duck fat
1 shallot, chopped
1 oz (25 g) flour
about ¼ pint (150 ml) chicken stock (see page 14)
1 teaspoon apricot jam
1 liqueur glass Grand Marnier
dash of gravy browning
slices of orange and sprigs watercress to garnish

HOW TO MAKE

Heat the oven to 400°F/200°C/gas mark 6. Prick the duck skin. Cut the orange into four slices. Line a small roasting tin with foil. Arrange the breasts on the foil with a piece of orange under each one. Season.

Roast at the top of the oven for about 30 minutes, until brown. Cover with foil, turn the oven down to 350°F/180°C/gas mark 4 and move the tin to a lower position in the oven. Cook for about another 40 minutes or until the duck is tender. Strain off the liquid. Keep duck warm in oven, uncovered.

Make the sauce. Spoon off 2 tablespoons duck fat from the roasting tin into a small saucepan, add the shallot and fry until tender. Stir in the flour and cook for 1 minute. Make the skimmed juices up to ½ pint (300 ml) with stock and gradually add to the shallot and flour. Bring to the boil, stirring until thickened. Add the apricot jam, Grand Marnier, seasoning and a dash of gravy browning, if liked.

Transfer the duck breasts to a warm serving dish and garnish with slices of orange and sprigs of watercress. Serve the sauce separately.

DUCK IN PORT AND CHERRY SAUCE

SERVES 4

To carve a duck, use scissors and cut the duck's breast in half, starting from the neck end. Cut along the length of the breastbone, then through the backbone to split the bird in half. If you like, cut along the backbone, remove it and use it to make stock, so that you serve less bone on the plate. Cut each half of the bird in two, making a slanting cut between the ribs to separate the wing and the leg, so that you now have four portions.

INGREDIENTS

1 oven-ready duckling, weighing 4–5 lb (1.8–2.3 kg), with giblets
1 onion, quartered
salt

SAUCE
3 tablespoons dripping and the juices from the cooked duckling
2 tablespoons flour
½ pint (300 ml) giblet stock (see below)
1 small glass port
14 oz (400 g) can stoned black cherries, drained

HOW TO MAKE

Place the giblets in a saucepan, cover with cold water and add any seasoning and herbs to hand. Simmer for 1 hour to make stock.

Meanwhile, heat the oven to 350°F/180°C/gas mark 4. Pat the duckling dry inside and out with absorbent kitchen paper and put the quartered onion inside. Prick the skin all over with a fork and sprinkle with salt. Place the duckling on a grill rack in a shallow roasting tin, breast uppermost, and roast for 35 minutes per 1 lb (450 g), without basting.

To make the sauce, put 3 tablespoons of duckling dripping and juices into a saucepan, sprinkle in the flour and stir over a gentle heat for 1 minute. Gradually blend in ½ pint (300 ml) strained giblet stock to make a smooth sauce. Cook gently, stirring for about 2 minutes, or until thickened, then stir in the port and cherries.

Carve the duckling (see above) and spoon the sauce over.

COOK'S TIP
Ducks are fatty birds and don't need basting. You will be surprised at how much fat comes out as the bird roasts. When cooked, carefully pour off the fat from the top of the juices. Use the juices to make the gravy or sauce. The fat can be cooled and stored in the refrigerator. Use to make extra tasty roast potatoes.

ROAST BREASTS OF PHEASANT WITH PORT WINE SAUCE

SERVES 8

As the breasts tend to cook more quickly than the legs, I like to remove the breasts and make this dish, saving the rest of the pheasant to make the casserole on page 60.

INGREDIENTS

8 pheasant breasts
salt and freshly ground black pepper
8 rashers thin streaky bacon, derinded
6 oz (175 g) butter, softened
8 oz (225 g) cooked leaf spinach, well drained
a little melted butter

SAUCE
1 pint (600 ml) red wine
2 fat cloves garlic, crushed
1 bay leaf
sprig of fresh thyme
1 tablespoon redcurrant jelly
2 tablespoons red wine vinegar
4 tablespoons port
scant 1 pint (500 ml) chicken or game stock (see page 14)
a little gravy browning (optional)
a generous knob of soft butter
1 teaspoon flour

HOW TO MAKE

Heat the oven to 425°F/220°C/gas mark 7. Butter a roasting tin.

Remove skin from the pheasant breasts and make a long cut end to end on the top of each breast about ½ inch (1 cm) deep. Season in the cut. Stretch the derinded bacon on a board using the flat side of a knife blade.

Mash the butter and spinach together and season. Divide the mixture between the breasts, packing well into the slashed cut in each breast. Wrap a rasher of bacon around each breast at a diagonal. Arrange the breasts well spaced out on the roasting tin and brush with melted butter.

Roast for 15 minutes, until no longer pink in the middle but still moist.

To make the sauce, put all the sauce ingredients, except the browning, flour and butter into a pan, bring to the boil and boil to reduce to half the quantity to concentrate the flavour. Add any pan juices from the roast breasts, remove the bay leaf and thyme, taste and season.

To thicken the sauce, mash the butter and flour with a fork until creamed together. Bring the sauce back to the boil and whisk in small teaspoons of the mixed flour and butter until slightly thickened and shiny. Add a drop or two of gravy browning if you like a darker sauce.

NORMANDY PHEASANT CASSEROLE

SERVES 8

This is the second dish that can be made from a brace of pheasants after the breasts have been removed (see page 79).

INGREDIENTS

4 pheasants, breasts removed
2 onions
3 medium cooking apples, peeled, cored and sliced
salt and freshly ground black pepper
½ bottle white wine
1 oz (25 g) flour
fruit jelly, such as blackberry, crab apple or redcurrant (optional)
a little Calvados or brandy (optional)

HOW TO MAKE

Heat the oven to 425°F/220°C/gas mark 7. Flatten out the debreasted pheasants as much as you can and place them skin side uppermost in a large roasting tin. Roast in the oven for about 45–60 minutes, until the skin is nicely brown. Transfer the pheasants to a large flameproof casserole.

Skim the fat from the roasting tin and reserve it, and add the remaining liquid to the casserole. Add the onions, apples, seasoning and wine to the casserole and bring to a full rolling boil. Cover with a tight fitting lid. Lower the oven temperature to 325°F/160°C/gas mark 3 and cook the pheasants until the leg meat is tender when tested with a knife, about 1–1½ hours or longer if the birds are old. Allow the pheasants to cool.

When cool enough to handle, remove the meat from the bones in as large pieces as possible and place in a casserole dish. Reduce the juices, onions and apples to a purée in a blender or food processor, then sieve to make sure there are no small bones or shot. There should be about 1 pint (600 ml) of liquid.

Put 1 tablespoon of the roasting fat in a pan and blend in the flour. Cook for 1–2 minutes, then gradually blend in the puréed cooking liquid and bring to the boil, stirring. Taste and season, adding 1 tablespoon of fruit jelly if the apples were very sharp. Heat through until hot and bubbling. Add a little Calvados to taste, if liked.

To serve, pour the sauce over the meat and heat through in the oven. Serve with a purée of potato and celeriac (see page 143).

EIGHTEENTH CENTURY PIGEONS

SERVES 4

When I was researching for a good pigeon recipe I found no less than 18 of them in an 18th century book called *The Art of Cooking Made Plain and Easy*. In those days they were plentiful and extremely popular. Most of the recipes start off by stuffing the 'belly' with fresh sweet herbs then slow roasting or casseroling them. If you are not keen on too many bones, split the pigeons in half through the breast bone and to one side of the back bone and remove it. Alternatively this recipe can be made using just 8 pigeon breasts. Lie the herbs under the breasts in the casserole and discard at the end of the cooking time. The cooking time will be much less – if they are young birds the time could be just 45 minutes.

INGREDIENTS

4 pigeons, plucked and prepared
4 sprigs thyme
4 sprigs parsley
4 sprigs marjoram
1 tablespoon oil
large knob of butter
4 onions, sliced
4 oz (100 g) button mushrooms
1 heaped teaspoon flour
½ pint (300 ml) cider
2 stock cubes, crumbled
salt and freshly ground black pepper
a little ground mace or nutmeg
chopped parsley and thyme, for garnish

HOW TO MAKE

Heat the oven to 325°F/160°C/gas mark 3. Take each pigeon and put a bunch of the three herbs inside the carcass. Heat the oil and butter in a non-stick frying pan, add the birds and brown on all sides. Lift out and set aside.

Add the onions and toss in the fat to take up all the sediment, add the mushrooms and cook for about 1 minute, stirring. Stir in the flour, blend well, then add the cider and stock cubes. Bring to the boil and season with salt, pepper and mace or nutmeg. Pour this mixture into a casserole large enough to take the four pigeons.

Arrange the pigeons on top, season the pigeon breasts with salt and pepper. Cover and cook for 2–3 hours, until the birds are tender. (The time will depend upon the age of the birds.) Serve garnished with parsley and thyme.

JUGGED HARE

SERVES 6–8

This is an old English recipe served with forcemeat balls and redcurrant jelly. Hare benefits from marinating overnight to moisten the meat.

INGREDIENTS

MARINADE
½ pint (300 ml) red wine
2 bay leaves
freshly ground black pepper
2 cloves garlic, each split into 4
2 tablespoons sunflower oil
1 onion, sliced

JUGGED HARE
1 hare, jointed
2 oz (50 g) streaky bacon, cut into strips
1 oz (25 g) butter
2 onions, chopped
2 tablespoons redcurrant jelly
¼ pint (150 ml) inexpensive port
grated rind and juice of ½ lemon
4 sticks celery, chopped

BEURRE MANIE
2 oz (50 g) butter
2 oz (50 g) flour

FORCEMEAT BALLS
2 oz (50 g) cooked bacon rashers
2 oz (50 g) shredded suet
grated rind 1 lemon
2 tablespoons chopped parsley
4 oz (100 g) white breadcrumbs
1 egg, beaten
a little butter and oil for frying

HOW TO MAKE

Begin the day before by combining all the marinade ingredients in a glass or china bowl. Add the hare joints, cover with clear clingfilm and leave in the refrigerator overnight.

Next day, heat the oven to 325°F/160°C/gas mark 3. Remove the hare joints, strain the marinade and set aside. Fry the bacon gently for 2 minutes, add a little butter and fry the hare joints a few at a time until browned. Transfer to a casserole. Add the onion to the pan and fry until softened. Add the redcurrant jelly and stir until dissolved, then pour over the hare with the port and lemon juice. Stir in the celery and season.

Measure the reserved marinade and make up to 1 pint (600 ml) with water and add to the casserole. Bring to the boil, cover and simmer for 5 minutes. Transfer to the oven and cook for about 5 hours, until tender (the time will vary according to how old the hare is).

Make the beurre manie. Cream the butter and flour together with a fork on a plate until it becomes a smooth paste. Lift the hare joints from the casserole with a slotted spoon and add the beurre manie a little at a time to the hot liquid in the casserole. Bring to the boil and stir until thickened. Return the hare to the casserole and check the seasoning.

Meanwhile, prepare the forcemeat balls. Snip the bacon and blend all the ingredients together. Roll into about 12 balls, then fry until crisp and brown on all sides. Add to the jugged hare just before serving.

COOK'S TIP

A marinade is a highly seasoned liquid used for soaking meat, fish, poultry or game in. It not only flavours the meat, but tenderises it too, and gives moisture to dry meat like hare. Use a deep dish so that the marinade covers the meat or fish. If you don't have a dish deep enough, place the meat and marinade inside a large polythene bag, seal and place inside a second polythene bag. Seal this too.

Meat

In Britain we eat mostly beef, lamb and pork, which are now produced to a very high standard and are far leaner than they used to be. If you are not sure of what you want to buy, get to know your butcher and ask his advice.

BEEF

Although the most popular size and cut for Sunday roast is a 2 lb (900 g) piece of boned topside, it is not my favourite as I find it likely to be tough and too lean. I much prefer fore rib, either on or off the bone. Talking to butchers, I find that this cut is often a favourite with them too. Sirloin is considered to be the very best joint for a family roast, and is the most expensive other than roasting a fillet of beef. The stewing cuts of beef come from the active muscular parts of the animal, so they need longer, slower cooking to get the best flavour and tenderness.

Roasting beef

Prime cuts can be roasted uncovered in a hot oven. This gives a crisp, brown meat on the outside and you can decide how you want the meat in the centre to be done – rare and pinkish or well cooked throughout. Most people prefer the latter.

The prime joints can be roasted satisfactorily at various oven temperatures because the texture of the meat is of such good quality, but it is sensible to roast in a hot oven (fast roasting) if you are planning to serve Yorkshire pudding and roast potatoes with the meat since these must be cooked at a higher temperature. If a joint is cooked for a long time at a high temperature, there will be considerable shrinkage. Suitable cuts for fast roasting are sirloin, topside, fore rib, thick flank (the latter is likely to be less tender than the others).

Season any fat on the meat with salt and freshly ground black pepper and place the joint on a rack in a roasting tin. Roast in the oven, uncovered, according to the chart opposite. Baste occasionally.

Meat cooked on the bone requires less cooking time than a boned and rolled joint because of the heat conduction from the bone. The times given in the chart are for average roasts. If the joint is long and thin (such as the thin end of a rolled rib), cut the cooking time by about 5 minutes per 1 lb (450 g). If the joint is very thick (such as the thickest cut of rolled topside), increase the cooking time by about 5 minutes per 1 lb (450 g). If you like really rare beef, cut the cooking time of the rare times by 5 minutes per 1 lb (450 g).

Roasting fillet If roasting fillet of beef, roast at 425°F/220°C/gas mark 7 for 12 minutes per 1 lb (450 g) + 12 minutes for rare; 15 minutes per 1 lb (450 g) + 15 minutes for medium; 18 minutes per 1 lb (450 g) + 18 minutes for well done.

To test that beef is cooked

Pierce the thickest part of the joint with a fine skewer; if slightly pink-tinged juices run out, the meat is cooked and will be pink in the centre. If clear juices run out, the meat is cooked and will be well done throughout.

Slow roasting and pot roasting

It is better to cook the cheaper, coarser cuts in a cooler oven wrapped in foil or a roasting bag because the long, slow cooking tenderises the meat. The meat is first browned in hot fat on the top of the stove or in the oven, then

BEEF ROASTING TIMES (fast roasting)				
Weight of beef joint	Oven temperature	Approximate cooking time		
		Rare	Medium	Well done
2 lb (900 g)	400°F/200°C/ gas mark 6	50 minutes	1 hour 15 minutes	1 hour 40 minutes
3 lb (1.4 kg)	400°F/200°C/ gas mark 6	1 hour 5 minutes	1 hour 30 minutes	2 hours
4 lb (1.8 kg)	400°F/200°C/ gas mark 6	1 hour 30 minutes	1 hour 45 minutes	2 hours 20 minutes
Over 4 lb (1.8 kg)	400°F/200°C/ gas mark 6	10 mins per 1 lb (450 g) +15 mins	20 mins per 1 lb (450 g) + 20 mins	25 mins per 1 lb (450 g) + 25 mins

BEEF ROASTING TIMES (slow roasting)		
Weight of beef joint	Oven temperature	Approximate cooking time
2 lb (900 g)	325°F/160°C/gas mark 3	2 hours 30 minutes
3 lb (1.4 kg)	325°F/160°C/gas mark 3	3 hours
4 lb (1.8 kg)	325°F/160°C/gas mark 3	4 hours
Over 4 lb (1.8 kg)	325°F/160°C/gas mark 3	1 hour per 1 lb (450 g)

covered and cooked slowly in its own fat and steam – either in the oven or on the top of the stove, to give a moist, tender joint. Unlike the fast roasting method, it is impossible to achieve meat that is rare and pink in the centre as long slow cooking is needed to tenderise right to the centre of the joint.

Suitable cuts for slow roasting are silverside, thick flank, thick rib, thin rib, brisket.

Season any fat on the meat with salt and freshly ground black pepper. Heat a little oil in a thick-bottomed pan on the stove or in a roasting tin or casserole in a hot oven (425°F/220°C/gas mark 7). Add the meat, turning it to brown on all sides, then cover with a lid or foil and cook gently on the stove or roast according to the chart. The roasting times given are for average roasts. If the joint is long and thin, cut the cooking time by about 5 minutes per 1 lb (450 g). If the joint is very thick, increase the cooking time by about 5 minutes per 1 lb (450 g).

Cooking steaks

Steaks are best either fried in a very hot pan, or grilled under a very hot grill so that the cut sides are sealed as quickly as possible. Time will vary according to the thickness of the steak. If you are cooking a steak very rare the cooking time could be just 3 minutes each side.

LAMB

Lamb is very popular because it is good value, all the main cuts are easy to recognise and it is simple to cook. Leg, best end and shoulder are the most popular for roasting though all cuts except scrag and middle neck can be roasted. Chops and cutlets are suitable for grilling; scrag, middle neck, neck fillet and cubed shoulder for stews and casseroles.

Roasting lamb

Leg of lamb is a traditional roast, as the meat is tender and well-flavoured, but shoulder, best end of neck and loin are every bit as tasty and are even easier to carve if they are boned and rolled. Any cut of lamb, except scrag and middle neck, is suitable for roasting and no extra fat should be needed. If you like lamb to be slightly pink (as the French prefer), decrease the cooking time slightly. Long thin joints, such as best end, take less cooking time.

Season with salt and freshly ground black pepper and sprinkle with a little dried rosemary, if liked. Place the joint on a rack in a roasting tin and roast, uncovered, according to the times in the chart opposite. Baste occasionally.

To test that lamb is cooked

Pierce the thickest part of the joint with a fine skewer; if clear juices run out, the meat is cooked. If the juices are slightly pink-tinged, continue cooking until they are clear, unless you like lamb underdone. If you like it pink in the centre, reduce all cooking times.

PORK

Now that refrigeration is so reliable the old saying 'never eat pork unless there is an R in the month' can be forgotten.

Roasting pork

Roast according to the times in the chart opposite, but if the joint is long and thin, cut the cooking time by about 5 minutes per 1 lb (450 g). If the joint is very thick, increase the cooking time by about 5 minutes per 1 lb (450 g).

If you want crisp crackling on your roast pork you need to have the skin finely scored.

It is extremely difficult to score pork fat at home unless you are very skilled with a sharp knife – it is far better to get it done at the butchers or supermarket. To obtain a crisp crinkly crackling, rub the skin well with a butter paper or brush with oil and sprinkle with salt. Put the meat on a rack in the roasting tin and roast at 350°F/180°C/gas mark 4 for the time given in the chart opposite. Check the meat half an hour before the cooking time is up, and if the crackling isn't crisp, increase the oven temperature to 425°F/220°C/gas mark 7 until it is.

The best cuts for roasting are leg and loin. Spare rib, hand and spring and belly roast can also be roasted but need a lower temperature and a longer cooking time. Roast at 325°F/160°C/gas mark 3 and add 15 minutes to the cooking times given in the chart opposite. These cuts are also more fatty.

Bacon

Bacon is cured pork which has been dry salted, brined and sometimes smoked. The hind leg of the cured pig is called gammon and when cooked and sold, or served cold it is usually called ham. Uncooked joints can be boiled or roasted or a combination of the two. The trend nowadays is for milder flavours. Gammon is the most expensive cut of bacon and is usually sold in four joints – slipper, hock, middle gammon and corner gammon. Middle gammon is the most expensive. The cuts from the front end of the pig, the collar and forehock, are the cheaper ones and are good for cooking whole. Back and flank cuts are usually sold sliced into rashers for grilling and frying, streaky coming from the flank.

Soaking bacon

Ask your butcher whether he recommends you to soak the piece of bacon that you buy. Usually a large gammon should be soaked in cold water for 24 hours, whereas a smaller joint will only have to be soaked overnight or for 12 hours. Sweetcure or mildcure joints do

LAMB ROASTING TIMES

Weight of lamb	Oven temperature	Approximate cooking time
1 lb (450 g) i.e. best end neck (rack of lamb)	350°F/180°C/gas mark 4	35–40 minutes
2 lb (900 g)	350°F/180°C/gas mark 4	1 hour 10 minutes
3 lb (1.4 kg)	350°F/180°C/gas mark 4	1 hour 30 minutes
4 lb (1.8 kg)	350°F/180°C/gas mark 4	2 hours 10 minutes
Over 4 lb (1.8 kg)	350°F/180°C/gas mark 4	25 minutes per 1 lb (450 g)

PORK ROASTING TIMES

Weight of pork joint	Oven temperature	Approximate cooking time*
1 lb (450 g) i.e. loin pork	350°F/180°C/gas mark 4	1 hour 10 minutes
2 lb (900 g)	350°F/180°C/gas mark 4	1 hour 30 minutes
3 lb (1.4 kg)	350°F/180°C/gas mark 4	2 hours
4 lb (1.8 kg)	350°F/180°C/gas mark 4	2 hours 40 minutes
Over 4 lb (1.8 kg)	350°F/180°C/gas mark 4	30 minutes per 1 lb (450 g)

*Approximate cooking time depending on shape and thickness of meat. Thinner joints will require less cooking time.

not have to be soaked at all. For vacuum-packed bacon, follow the instructions on the pack for soaking.

If you think your bacon joint is salty and you cannot spare the time to soak it, use this quick method for getting rid of some of the salt. Place the joint in a pan of cold water and bring slowly to the boil, then drain off all the water. Cover the joint with fresh, cold water, bring to the boil, reduce the heat and simmer according to the recipe.

Grilling

Suitable cuts for grilling are gammon steaks, prime streaky, prime back, long back and middle cut. For gammon, use rashers 1/4–1/2 inch (0.5–1.25 cm) thick. Soak in cold water for 1 hour if they are salty. Grill for about 15–20 minutes, according to thickness, turning them frequently. For bacon, remove the rind and any pieces of bone and discard. Overlap the rashers in the grill pan and turn once during cooking.

Frying

Suitable cuts for frying are gammon steaks, prime streaky, prime back, long back, middle cut. Remove the rind and any pieces of bone and discard. Overlap the rashers in a non-stick frying pan and turn once during cooking.

Boiling

Suitable cuts for boiling are middle gammon, corner gammon, gammon hock, slipper and prime collar. Soak the joint in cold water for 24 hours. Place in a saucepan of fresh, cold water and bring to the boil. Reduce the heat and simmer very gently for about 2½ hours for a whole gammon, or for about 20 minutes per 1 lb (450 g) plus an extra 20 minutes for smaller joints. Remove from the heat and leave in the pan for 1 hour. Remove the rind, sprinkle with brown sugar, stick with cloves and brown in a hot oven for 20 minutes or until golden brown.

VEAL

Only 4 per cent of the meat sold in Britain is veal and most of that goes to the catering trade. Veal is rarely sold in any form except escalopes for frying or sometimes knuckle of veal for stewing.

OFFAL

Offal is the name given to the parts which remain after the slaughtered animal has been cut up. Liver and kidney are by far the most popular but all offal is highly nutritious.

Liver

Calf's liver The most expensive and the best liver. It is best fried or grilled. Avoid over-cooking, which produces hard, dry results.

Lamb's liver Cheaper than calf's liver and more popular. Suitable for grilling, frying, braising. Avoid over-cooking.

Pig's liver Cheaper than lamb's liver and with a slightly stronger flavour, which can be made milder by soaking it in milk for a couple of hours before cooking. Not to everyone's taste when grilled or fried, but excellent in pâtés and stews.

Ox liver The cheapest liver, coarse in texture and often varying between strong flavour and lack of flavour. Unsuitable for grilling and frying, but it can be stewed alone or with steak. It can also be braised.

Kidneys

Calf's kidney The most tender kidney, but not always easy to obtain.

Lamb's kidney Excellent for grilling and frying, they are smaller than calf's kidney. The skin, which is removed before cooking, should look slippery and the kidneys should be firm and light brown.

Pig's kidney Larger and flatter than lamb's kidney. Cut right through them for grilling or chop for risottos and stews.

Ox kidney The cheapest kidney, with a tendency to toughness. Long, slow cooking for stews, steak and kidney pies and puddings. One kidney usually weighs about 1½ lb (675 g). Since we joined the Common Market, the suet surrounding the kidney is not available. Much of it is used in meat product manufacture.

Remove the skin and core from all kidneys before cooking them.

Heart

Ox heart The largest heart, with thick strong muscle that requires long careful cooking to avoid toughness and dryness. Heart is often parboiled and then roasted. It requires robust flavourings, such as plenty of onions or well-seasoned stuffings. An economical buy, a heart usually weighs about

4 lb (1.8 kg), which will be enough for about five portions.

Calf's heart Much smaller than ox heart, usually enough for two portions. More tender than ox heart, but it still needs careful cooking.

Lamb's heart The smallest heart, enough for only one person. It is excellent stuffed and then roasted or braised.

Heads

Ox cheek Good for stews and brawn. A very economical buy.

Sheep's head Usually split in half and boiled for broth, with the meat being served as a separate dish accompanied by a sauce made from the broth.

Pig's head Fresh or boned, boiled for brawn. The cheek can be brined, boned and boiled to produce Bath Chap, which is sliced and fried or eaten cold with salad. It is essential that heads be thoroughly cleaned and blanched before cooking.

Tongue

Ox tongue Full of flavour and with a velvety texture. An ox tongue averages 4–6 lb (1.8–2.7 kg) and is usually cooked after salting.

Calf's tongue Delicate in texture and flavour, weighing 1–2 lb (450–900 g). It can be salted like ox tongue but is generally cooked unsalted.

Lamb's tongue The smallest tongue, weighing 8–12 oz (225–350 g). Excellent boiled or braised and served hot with parsley sauce.

Feet

Calf's feet The basis of the celebrated calf's foot jelly which is traditionally served to invalids. They can be cooked with other meats to make brawn or a gelatinous stock.

Pig's trotters These are ideal for making stock.

Sweetbreads

These are lamb's pancreas and thymus glands, which are tender and flavoursome. They should be bought only when fresh and cooked as soon as possible. One pound (450 g) of sweetbreads will be sufficient for 3–4 portions.

Allow one pair per portion and soak for at least 4 hours in cold water which should be changed several times. Put them in cold, salted water and bring to the boil. Remove the veins and skin, place the blanched sweetbreads between two plates to flatten them, and allow to cool. They can then be coated with egg and breadcrumbs and sautéed in butter.

Tripe

Tripe is the lining of an ox's stomach. Tripe from the first stomach is known as 'blanket' and that from the second stomach is known as 'honeycomb'. Tripe can be stewed in milk and deep fried. Tripe in a butcher's shop has already been parboiled, so consult the butcher about the length of cooking time.

Oxtail

Ideal for soups and stews. Oxtail should be lean and deep red in colour. Look out for an even ratio of meat to bone. Ask your butcher to skin and joint the oxtail. It needs long slow cooking, best done the day before. Allow the oxtail to get cold, then remove the fat on top. Reheat and if liked, top with dumplings.

Brains

Very much out of fashion and only lamb's brains are available nowadays. Like sweetbreads, brains should be bought when very fresh and used up quickly. They can be cooked with the head for stews and broth. They can also be soaked for about 2 hours in cold, lightly salted water. Simmer gently for about 20 minutes and then press them as they cool. They can then be sliced, coated in flour and fried in butter.

THIN GRAVY

Serve this with roast meat and game birds. A little sherry and redcurrent jelly can be added to a thin gravy for game birds, while red wine is nice when added for red meats and white wine for lighter meats.

To make, pour all the fat from the roasting tin, leaving only the sediment in the tin. Add ½ pint (300 ml) good stock or vegetable water. Stir well and simmer over a medium heat for 2–3 minutes to slightly reduce. Season to taste and add a little gravy browning, if liked. Serve hot in a sauceboat.

THICK GRAVY

If you prefer a thicker gravy, make as follows.

Pour off all the fat from the roasting tin, add ½ pint (300 ml) good stock or vegetable cooking water and heat over a medium heat, stirring to dislodge all the cooked-on sediment. Measure about a tablespoon of roasting fat into a small pan, stir in 1 tablespoon flour and cook for 1 minute. Blend in the stock from the tin, stirring continually until thickened. Season to taste and add a little gravy browning, if liked. Strain, if necessary, and serve hot in a sauceboat.

BRISTOL BEEF CASSEROLE

SERVES 4

Allow 1–1½ lb (450–675 g) meat for four people. With less meat, put in plenty of vegetables. It is incredibly quick and simple.

INGREDIENTS

1 lb (450 g) stewing steak
3 carrots
3 onions
1 small can tomato soup
1 oz (25 g) flour
1 stock cube
salt and freshly ground black pepper
½ teaspoon dried mixed herbs

HOW TO MAKE

Heat the oven to 325°F/160°C/gas mark 3. Cut the meat into 1 inch (2.5 cm) pieces. Chop the carrots and onions roughly and put in a casserole with the meat. Stir in the tomato soup.

Measure flour and crumble the stock cube into a bowl, fill the empty soup can with water and blend it into the flour. Add the seasoning and herbs and stir until smooth. Pour it over the meat and mix together.

Cook in the oven for about 3 hours, or until meat is tender. Serve with buttered noodles.

First Rate Cottage Pie

SERVES 6

This is a wonderful, upmarket version, of the family classic. For everyday you can leave out the port and green pepper, if you wish, but increase the stock if you omit the port. A good way to use up the weekend roast, or, if you prefer, use raw minced meat and increase the cooking time by 25 minutes. Fry with the onion and garlic first.

INGREDIENTS

3 tablespoons oil
1 large onion, chopped
1 fat clove garlic, crushed
1 green pepper, seeded and chopped
6 oz (175 g) button mushrooms, quartered
about 1 lb (450 g) cooked beef or lamb, minced
1 generous tablespoon flour
14 oz (400 g) can chopped tomatoes
½ pint (300 ml) good stock
1 tablespoon Worcestershire sauce
4 tablespoons port
1 sprig thyme
bay leaf
salt and freshly ground black pepper

TOPPING
2 lb (900 g) peeled potatoes
milk and butter for mashing
2 oz (50 g) mature Cheddar cheese, grated

HOW TO MAKE

Measure the oil into a large pan, add onion and garlic and fry gently for about 10 minutes until lightly browned. Add the pepper, mushrooms and meat and cook quickly for a few moments. Sprinkle in the flour, then add the tomatoes, stock, Worcestershire sauce, port, thyme and bay leaf. Season well, bring to the boil and simmer for about 15 minutes.

Remove the thyme and bay leaf and check the seasoning. Turn the mixture into a shallow 2½ pint (1.5 litre) pie dish and leave to cool.

Meanwhile, heat the oven to 425°F/220°C/gas mark 7. Cook and mash potatoes with the butter and milk. Season to taste. Spread the potato over the meat and sprinkle cheese on top. (At this stage the pie can be chilled in the refrigerator until ready to cook, if wished.)

Cook in oven for about 20–25 minutes, or until brown, hot and bubbling.

OXTAIL

SERVES 4–6

Oxtail has a very rich flavour and is inclined to be fatty. If possible, it is better to cook it the day before you need it, then let it get quite cold. The fat will then come to the surface so you can easily remove it. Take care to simmer the oxtail gently once it has come to the boil – fast boiling spoils the flavour and shrinks the meat. It does take a long time to cook, the meat should literally nearly fall off the bone.

INGREDIENTS

1 oxtail, about 2½ lb (1.1 kg) in weight, jointed
1 oz (25 g) flour
1 pint (600 ml) beef stock (see page 14)
2 onions, chopped
2 carrots, chopped
2 sticks celery, chopped
salt and freshly ground black pepper
¼ teaspoon cayenne pepper
1 bay leaf
little gravy browning (optional)

HOW TO MAKE

Trim any excess fat from oxtail. Heat a large non-stick frying pan and fry the oxtail on all sides, slowly at first to extract the fat then at a higher heat to brown. Lift it out with a slotted spoon and keep on one side.

Stir the flour into the fat remaining in the pan and cook for a minute. Blend in the stock and bring to the boil, stirring until the sauce has thickened.

Transfer the oxtail to an ovenproof casserole with the vegetables, seasoning, cayenne, and bay leaf. Add a little gravy browning, if liked. Cover with a lid and simmer very gently for about 3½–4 hours or until the meat can easily be removed from the bones.

Skim off any surplus fat. Taste and check the seasoning. Remove the bay leaf. Serve with bright green young cabbage.

BOBOTIE

SERVES 6–8

A South African dish and a very interesting variation on the minced beef theme. A spicy meat base topped with a rich, savoury, set sauce.

INGREDIENTS

2 lb (900 g) raw minced beef
2 large onions, chopped
1 thick slice white or brown bread, crusts removed
½ pint (300 ml) milk
1 tablespoon curry powder
1 tablespoon sugar
freshly ground black pepper
1 tablespoon turmeric
2 tablespoons lemon juice
1 oz (25 g) flaked almonds
3 oz (75 g) sultanas
3 tablespoons chutney
2 eggs
4 bay leaves

HOW TO MAKE

Heat the oven to 350°F/180°C/gas mark 4. Heat a large non-stick frying pan, spread out the minced beef in the pan and cook gently until the fat begins to run out from the meat, then add the onions and increase the heat to brown the meat and onions.

Soak the bread in the milk, then squeeze out the excess liquid and keep on one side. Crumble the bread into the meat and add all the remaining ingredients except the reserved milk, eggs and bay leaves.

Mix thoroughly, then turn this mixture into a greased 3 pint (1.7 litre) ovenproof dish and bake for 45 minutes.

Beat eggs and milk together and pour them over the meat. Arrange the bay leaves on top and return to the oven for a further 15 minutes until the topping is set.

COOK'S TIP
Buy lean red, finely ground minced beef. Cheap fatty mince is a false economy as the fat melts when cooked making the dish greasy, and the meat itself shrinks and can be tough. If you can't find lean mince, buy steak and mince your own.

STEAK, KIDNEY AND MUSHROOM PIE

SERVES 6

The best cut of beef to use in steak and kidney pie is skirt, which is sometimes difficult to get as there is only a limited amount on each side of beef, so it is best to order it from your butcher in advance. It is usually the same price as other stewing beef. Beef kidney is best; buy it in one large piece, then remove the white suet part yourself and cut it into pieces. Do not buy ready-mixed steak and kidney as it is not such good value.

INGREDIENTS

1 lb (450 g) skirt beef
8 oz (225 g) beef kidney
1 oz (25 g) flour
2 tablespoons oil
1 large onion, chopped
½ pint (300 ml) beef stock (see page 14)
salt and freshly ground black pepper
8 oz (225 g) mushrooms, sliced
7½ oz (212 g) packet of puff pastry, thawed

HOW TO MAKE

Cut the steak and kidney into 1 inch (2.5 cm) cubes, put them in a polythene bag with the flour and toss until well coated.

Melt the oil in a saucepan, add the meat and onion and fry until browned. Stir in stock and bring to the boil, stirring constantly. Season with salt and freshly ground pepper.

Partially cover the pan and simmer for 1½ hours, then stir in the mushrooms and continue cooking for a further 30 minutes or until the meat is almost tender. Taste and check seasoning. Turn into a 1½ pint (900 ml) pie dish and allow to become quite cold. Place a pie funnel in the centre.

Heat the oven to 425°F/220°C/gas mark 7.

Roll out the pastry on a lightly floured surface and cover the pie with it. Seal and crimp the edges, make a small slit in the centre to allow the steam to escape and use any pastry trimmings to decorate the top of the pie.

Brush with milk to glaze and cook in the oven for 30–35 minutes, or until the pastry is well risen and golden brown and the meat is hot through. If the pastry starts to get too brown, cover with foil.

COOK'S TIP

If freezing the Steak, Kidney and Mushroom Pie it is best to freeze it before glazing and cooking the pastry. Thaw completely before glazing and cooking as in the recipe.

PENANG BEEF CURRY

SERVES 12*

This curry is not overpoweringly strong, has a superb flavour, a rich deep colour and is surprisingly simple to make. If you like a really hot curry, add chilli powder with the spices – half a teaspoon of ground chilli is enough for most tastes. It freezes well so make more than you need; thaw slowly before reheating.

INGREDIENTS

3 tablespoons oil
3 large onions, chopped
2 fat cloves garlic, crushed
2 rounded tablespoons ground coriander
1 rounded teaspoon ground cumin
1 teaspoon ground turmeric
1 rounded teaspoon garam masala
piece of fresh root ginger, walnut-sized, finely chopped
8 oz (225 g) can tomatoes
2 tablespoons tomato purée
½ pint (300 ml) water
2 lb (900 g) lean chuck steak, cut into cubes

HOW TO MAKE

Heat the oil in a large pan and fry onions and garlic until golden brown. Add the spices and ginger and cook for a minute, then stir in the tomatoes, tomato purée and water.

Add the meat, cover with a lid, bring to the boil and simmer gently for about 2–2½ hours until the meat is tender.

*Serves 12 with one other meat or vegetable curry, or 6 on its own with rice and side dishes (see page 102).

COOK'S TIP
Fresh root ginger will keep for a week if wrapped and stored in the refrigerator. It can also be frozen then peeled and grated when needed without thawing. Always remove the skin before chopping, grating or slicing as required.

SPECIAL STEAK AND KIDNEY PUDDING

SERVES 6

This recipe is for a traditional steak and kidney pudding such as might have been served in the nineteenth century. The suet crust pastry is richer than I use normally, but it works well. Use skirt beef if possible as it gives the best results. If you like a lot of gravy make extra and serve with the pudding.

INGREDIENTS

1 lb (450 g) skirt beef
12 oz (350 g) beef kidney
1 medium onion, finely chopped
6 oz (175 g) mushrooms, sliced
salt and freshly ground black pepper
a few drops of Worcestershire sauce
¼ pint (150 ml) beef stock (see page 14)

SUET CRUST PASTRY
8 oz (225 g) self-raising flour
6 oz (175 g) shredded suet
salt
about 9–10 tablespoons cold water

HOW TO MAKE

Grease a 2 pint (1.2 litre) pudding basin. Cut the steak and kidney into ½ inch (1.25 cm) cubes, removing any fat. Use scissors to remove the core from the kidneys.

Put the steak and kidney in a bowl with the onion, mushrooms, salt, pepper and Worcestershire sauce and mix together well.

To make the pastry, put the flour, suet and a little salt into a bowl and gradually add the water. Mix to a soft but not sticky dough. Take one-third of the pastry and roll out on a lightly floured surface to a circle large enough to cover the top of the basin, set it aside. Roll out the remaining pastry and use it to line the basin.

Fill the basin with the meat mixture and add the stock. Dampen the edges of the pastry and cover with the pastry lid. Press the pastry edges together firmly to seal. Cover the pudding with a piece of greased greaseproof paper with a pleat in it, then a lid of foil.

Stand the basin in a saucepan and pour enough boiling water into the pan to come halfway up the sides of the basin.

Simmer for 3½–4 hours, topping up with more boiling water when necessary. When cooked, lift out of the pan, remove the foil and greaseproof paper. Wrap the basin in a napkin and serve from the basin at the table.

Right: *Tropical Chicken Kebabs (page 70–1)*

FRENCH BEEF CASSEROLE

SERVES 4–6

No cookery book would be complete without the classic Boeuf Bour-guignonne recipe.

INGREDIENTS

1½ lb (675 g) chuck steak
6 oz (175 g) streaky bacon
1 tablespoon flour
¼ pint (150 ml) beef stock (see page 14)
½ pint (300 ml) inexpensive Burgundy
1 bay leaf
½ level teaspoon dried mixed herbs
salt and freshly ground black pepper
12 small pickling onions
6 oz (175 g) button mushrooms
chopped parsley, for garnish

HOW TO MAKE

Cut beef into 1½ inch (4 cm) cubes. Cut the rind, excess fat and any bones from the bacon. Cut across into small strips.

Place rind and fat from bacon in a frying pan, gently heat and cook for 3–4 minutes until the fat runs out. Remove rinds from frying pan and add the bacon strips and beef and fry until brown. Lift them out of the pan with a slotted spoon and place in a 3 pint (1.7 litre) casserole.

Stir the flour into the frying pan and cook for a minute. Gradually blend in the stock, wine, bay leaf, herbs and seasoning. Bring to the boil, stirring, then pour over meat in the casserole. Cover with a lid or foil and cook for about 1½ hours.

Peel the onions, leaving them whole and add to the casserole with the mushrooms. Cook for another hour or until the meat is really tender. Taste and check the seasoning. Remove the bay leaf and skim any fat from top, if necessary. Sprinkle with chopped parsley and serve straight from the cooking dish.

Left: *Mild Vegetable Curry (page 152)*

LIVER AND SAGE

SERVES 4

Ask your butcher to slice the liver very thinly for you. You could use lamb's liver instead of calf's for a more economical dish.

INGREDIENTS

2 tablespoons flour
salt and freshly ground black pepper
1 lb (450 g) calves' liver, thinly sliced
2 tablespoons vegetable or sunflower oil
1 oz (25 g) butter
about 20 leaves of fresh sage
juice of 1 lemon

HOW TO MAKE

Put the flour and salt and pepper into a polythene bag. Add the slices of liver and shake until all coated with seasoned flour.

Heat a large frying pan with oil and half the butter. Fry the liver in two batches over a high heat, browning each side. It will only take a few minutes. To test when cooked, cut off an edge and if the liver is faintly pink in the middle it is done. If the liver is still bloody, cook for a little longer.

Remove the liver as it is cooked and keep hot. Melt the remaining butter in the frying pan and add the lemon juice and most of the sage leaves. Swirl the mixture quickly around the pan and then spoon over the liver. Decorate with the remaining sage leaves and serve at once.

Variation

Liver and Bacon   Follow the recipe above but leave out the sage and lemon juice, and serve the fried liver slices with a couple of rashers of grilled back bacon per person.

COOK'S TIP
Soaking liver overnight in milk will draw out any bitterness. Drain and dry before cooking, discarding the milk.

ORANGE SPICED LAMB

SERVES 8

Serve this delicious fruity casserole with boiled rice and a green salad.

INGREDIENTS

a little oil
2½ lb (1.1 kg) boneless shoulder lamb, cubed
8 oz (225 g) onions, chopped
2 oz (50 g) flour
¾ pint (450 ml) cider
¼ pint (150 ml) chicken stock (see page 14)
4 oz (100 g) dried apricots, cut into pieces
2 oranges, quartered and pips removed
2 tablespoons vinegar
1 teaspoon curry powder
1 tablespoon soy sauce
2 cloves garlic, crushed
4 oz (100 g) seedless raisins
1 oz (25 g) dark muscovado sugar
1 sprig thyme
2 teaspoons salt
freshly ground black pepper
chopped parsley, for garnish

HOW TO MAKE

Heat the oven to 325°F/160°C/gas mark 3. Heat a little oil in a large non-stick pan and fry the meat until browned all over. Lift out with a slotted spoon and put into a 4 pint (2.3 litre) casserole.

Add the onions to the pan and fry until lightly browned. Sprinkle in the flour and cook for 1 minute, then blend in the cider and stock. Add the remaining ingredients except the garnish, and bring to the boil, stirring continuously.

Pour the mixture over the meat, cover the casserole with a lid or piece of foil and cook in the oven for about 3 hours, until the meat is tender. Taste and check the seasoning, and discard the thyme and pieces of orange.

Sprinkle with chopped parsley just before serving.

KIDNEYS ALSACE

SERVES 4

Kidneys in a rich sauce make a delicious meal if served with plain boiled noodles and broccoli.

INGREDIENTS

12 pickling onions
9 pork chipolata sausages
8 lamb's kidneys
1 oz (25 g) butter
1 oz (25 g) flour
¼ pint (150 ml) red wine
¼ pint (150 ml) good stock
1 tablespoon tomato purée
salt and freshly ground black pepper

HOW TO MAKE

Peel the onions carefully, trimming only the minimum at the top and base so they stay whole. Place in a pan of cold water, bring to the boil and simmer for 5 minutes, then drain well.

Twist each sausage in half and cut. Peel the papery skin off the kidneys and cut them in half horizontally. Remove the tough cores and slice the remaining meat.

Melt the butter in a pan, add the kidney slices and sausages and fry quickly to brown. Lift out with a slotted spoon and keep warm. Sprinkle flour into pan, stir and cook for a minute.

Gradually blend in the wine and stock and bring to the boil, stirring continuously. Add the tomato purée and seasoning. Return the kidneys and sausages to the sauce with the onions. Cover and simmer gently for 15 minutes. Taste and adjust the seasoning if necessary and serve in a warm serving dish.

LANCASHIRE HOT POT

SERVES 4

If it is more convenient, prepare the vegetables ahead and put in a bowl of cold water. Leave overnight and assemble the dish on the day.

INGREDIENTS

1½ lb (675 g) potatoes, sliced
2 onions, chopped
6–8 carrots, sliced
3 sticks celery, sliced
2 lb (900 g) middle neck of lamb
2 lamb's kidneys
a little seasoned flour
salt and freshly ground black pepper
¾ pint (450 ml) chicken stock (see page 14)

HOW TO MAKE

If preparing the vegetables ahead, put half the potato slices in a bowl on their own to use for the top of the hot pot. Heat the oven to 350°F/180°C/gas mark 4.

Wipe the lamb and cut into even-sized pieces. Cut the kidneys in half, peel off the skin and snip out the core with a pair of scissors. Coat both the lamb and kidneys with seasoned flour.

Arrange layers of vegetables and meat in a large ovenproof dish of at least 4 pint (2.3 litre) capacity, seasoning well between each layer and finishing with a layer of potato slices neatly arranged on top.

Pour over the stock, cover with a piece of buttered greaseproof paper and a tight fitting lid and cook for 2 hours.

Remove the lid and paper and continue to cook, uncovered, for a further 30 minutes.

IRISH STEW

SERVES 4

True Irish stew is made using only lamb and potatoes but I include carrots too. If you dislike bones, make the stew with neck fillet of lamb, allow 1 lb (450 g) for four people and cut into neat 1 inch (2.5 cm) cubes. You can also use scrag end of neck lamb, which has a delicious flavour but is rather bony.

INGREDIENTS

2½ lb (1.1 kg) scrag end neck of lamb
2 large onions
8 oz (225 g) carrots (optional)
1½ lb (675 g) potatoes
salt and freshly ground black pepper
chopped parsley, for garnish

HOW TO MAKE

Heat the oven to 325°F/160°C/gas mark 3. Trim the lamb joints into neat pieces, trimming off any excess fat or gristle. Peel and slice onions, carrots and potatoes.

Arrange alternate layers of meat with layers of each vegetable in a 3 pint (1.75 litre) casserole, seasoning each layer with plenty of salt and pepper. Finish with a layer of potato, which should be neatly arranged to give an attractive appearance to the finished dish.

Pour in sufficient water to half-fill the casserole. Cover with a lid and bake in the oven for 2½ hours or until the meat is nearly tender.

Remove the lid, increase the oven temperature to 350°F/180°C/gas mark 4 and cook for a further 30 minutes, or until the potatoes are pale brown.

Serve with a green vegetable such as cabbage or sprouts.

LAMB CURRY

SERVES 12*

Take care to wash your hands straight away after handling chillies (or use rubber gloves). If you rub your eyes with your hand, it makes them sting like mad.

INGREDIENTS

1½ inch (4 cm) piece fresh root ginger, peeled, chopped
3 fat cloves garlic
2 green chillies
2 oz (50 g) unsalted cashew nuts
¼ teaspoon ground cloves
¼ teaspoon ground cardamom
2 teaspoons ground coriander
¼ teaspoon ground turmeric
6 tablespoons water
2 oz (50 g) butter
1 large onion, finely chopped
2 lb (900 g) lean lamb, cubed
½ pint (300 ml) natural yoghurt
1 tablespoon lemon juice
salt

HOW TO MAKE

Put the ginger, garlic, chillies, nuts and all the spices into a blender or food processor together with the water and purée until smooth.

Melt the butter in a large pan, add the onion and lamb and fry for about 5 minutes, stir in the spice mixture, yoghurt and lemon juice, stir well, cover and simmer gently for about 1 hour until the lamb is tender. Check seasoning. Serve with the accompaniments listed below.

*Serves 12 with one other curry, or 6 with rice and side dishes.

Accompaniments for curry

Rice   Use basmati or long grain rice and cook in plenty of salted water until just tender. Drain well. Allow 2 oz (50 g) uncooked rice per person.

Poppadums   Fried in a non-stick pan in about 1 inch (2.5 cm) of oil, served in a stacked pile on a plate.

Side dishes (sambals)
Cucumber, yoghurt and mint: Mix 1 tablespoon chopped mint with a 6 inch (15 cm) piece cucumber, peeled and diced, and ½ pint (300 ml) natural yoghurt. Season well.

Banana: 6 bananas, sliced and tossed in lemon juice.

Onion and green pepper: 1 mild onion, finely sliced, mixed with 1 green pepper, chopped.

Mango chutney: buy ready-made.

Hard-boiled egg: 8 small hard-boiled eggs, sliced.

Coconut: 4 oz (100 g) desiccated coconut.

Tomato: 8 tomatoes, sliced and scattered with thinly sliced onion.

Dhal: (see page 153).

ROAST MARINATED LAMB

SERVES 6

This is a top family favourite. To me, it is a real joy to put a roast in the oven and for it to come ready to serve, with the delicious gravy-cum-sauce made in the roasting tin underneath. Ask the butcher to bone the lamb out flat. It will form the shape of a butterfly. Alternatively use a rack of lamb and reduce the cooking time.

INGREDIENTS

1 leg lamb, about 3 lb (1.5 kg) boned

MARINADE
8 fl oz (250 ml) orange juice
3 tablespoons clear honey
3 tablespoons soy sauce
2 cloves garlic, crushed
2 heaped teaspoons dried rosemary
1 teaspoon ground ginger

HOW TO MAKE

Combine all the ingredients for the marinade. Take two large freezer bags and put one inside the other, then put the lamb and the marinade into the bag, seal and leave for at least 12 hours in the refrigerator, turning occasionally. (The lamb may be left to marinate for up to 3 days.)

When ready to cook, heat the oven to 350°F/180°C/gas mark 4. Reserving the marinade, place the lamb in a roasting tin and roast for 30 minutes. Cover with a piece of foil if the skin is getting too brown. Pour over the marinade. Cook for a further 30–40 minutes, until the marinade has changed colour and becomes a dark gravy, and when the lamb is pierced with a skewer the juices run clear.

To serve, lift the lamb on to a board and cut long, medium thick slices. Skim off any fat from the gravy and serve the gravy with the lamb.

APRICOT STUFFED LAMB

SERVES 8

Boning and stuffing a shoulder of lamb makes the joint go much further and makes carving so simple. Most butchers will remove the bones for you if they are not too busy.

INGREDIENTS

3½ lb (1.5 kg) shoulder of lamb, boned
salt and freshly ground black pepper

STUFFING
1 oz (25 g) butter
1 onion, chopped
4 oz (100 g) fresh brown breadcrumbs
1 tablespoon chopped fresh mint
2 oz (50 g) raisins
1 large cooking apple, peeled, cored and diced
7½ oz (213 g) can of apricots
1 egg, beaten

HOW TO MAKE

Open out the shoulder and season well with salt and pepper. Heat the oven to 375°F/190°C/gas mark 5.

To make the stuffing, melt the butter in a non-stick saucepan, add the onion, cover a cook gently for about 10 minutes, or until the onion is soft but not brown. Remove from the heat and add the breadcrumbs, mint, raisins and apple. Drain the apricots, reserving the juice for the gravy. Chop the fruit and add to the stuffing with the egg, mix well and season with salt and pepper to taste.

Use the stuffing to fill the cavity in the lamb, close with skewers to hold the stuffing in place and, if necessary, tie with fine string.

Place the shoulder in a roasting tin and roast in oven for about 1 hour 45 minutes (30 minutes to the 1 lb [450 g]). Remove from the oven and place on a warm serving dish.

Serve with gravy (see page 90) using the apricot syrup.

COOK'S TIP
When buying a joint for a special occasion, try to remember to buy it ahead of time so it can mature in the refrigerator for a few days. If you buy your weekend meat on, say, a Wednesday, there is likely to be more choice too.

WHOLEGRAIN MUSTARD PORK CHOPS

SERVES 4

This simple but tasty recipe can be easily adapted to serve any number.

INGREDIENTS

4 lean pork chops
wholegrain mustard
about 4 oz (100 g) demerara sugar
2 small oranges

HOW TO MAKE

Heat the oven to 400°F/200°C/gas mark 6. Trim chops of excess fat, then spread with mustard on both sides.

Spread out the sugar on a plate, then roll the chops in the sugar until well coated. Lay them in a greased shallow ovenproof dish.

Peel the oranges and then, holding them over a bowl to collect any juice, divide them into segments, removing all the pips and pith. Arrange the orange segments on top of the chops and pour over any juice.

Bake uncovered for 35 minutes or until tender, basting occasionally.

SPICY BARBECUED SPARE RIBS

SERVES 4

Spare rib chops are cheaper than loin chops and very good served this way. Trim off any excess fat before browning them.

INGREDIENTS

8 pork spare rib chops

SAUCE
2 tablespoons mango chutney juice
1 teaspoon curry powder
1 clove garlic, crushed
1 tablespoon Worcestershire sauce
3 tablespoons tomato ketchup
1 tablespoon soy sauce
salt and freshly ground black pepper

HOW TO MAKE

Heat the oven to 350°F/180°C/gas mark 4. Put the chops in a non-stick pan and fry gently until the fat begins to run, increase the heat and fry quickly for about 10 minutes until browned all over. Arrange in a single layer in a shallow ovenproof dish so that they just touch.

Mix together the mango juice, curry powder, garlic, Worcestershire sauce until well blended, then add the tomato ketchup and soy sauce. Season and pour over the chops, coating them evenly. Cover with foil.

Cook in the oven for about an hour until the meat is tender, removing the foil for the last 15 minutes. Serve with rice and a green salad.

GAMMON AND MUSTARD SAUCE

SERVES 4

The traditional accompaniment to gammon steaks is a slice of pineapple. This mustard-flavoured sauce makes a very pleasant change. Be sure to keep stirring until it thickens or you will have a lumpy sauce.

INGREDIENTS

2 oz (50 g) light brown soft sugar
1 oz (25 g) flour
2 teaspoons dry mustard
salt and freshly ground black pepper
½ pint (300 ml) good stock
4 tablespoons white wine vinegar
4 gammon steaks
a little butter
small sprigs of watercress, for garnish

HOW TO MAKE

Measure the sugar, flour, mustard, salt and pepper into a small saucepan. Add half the stock a little at a time, stirring constantly until blended to a smooth paste. Add the remaining stock and the vinegar.

Bring to the boil over a moderate heat, stirring constantly until the sauce has thickened. Reduce the heat and simmer for 10 minutes. Meanwhile, heat the grill to moderate.

Place the gammon steaks in the grill pan and dot with butter. Grill for about 5 minutes each side. Lift them out and arrange on a warm serving dish.

Stir any juices from the grill pan into the sauce. Taste and check the seasoning. Garnish the steaks with small sprigs of watercress. Serve the sauce separately.

Variation

Gammon with Mustard and Raisin Sauce   Add 2 oz (50 g) raisins to the sauce after it has thickened. Continue as above.

COOK'S TIP
Use scissors to make small cuts all round the edges of the rind or fat of a gammon steak before cooking. This will prevent it curling up as it cooks.

NORFOLK HOTPOT

SERVES 6

Both knuckle and forehock are inexpensive bacon joints. This hotpot takes time to make but is very good. Taste the bacon stock before using to make the sauce, and if it is too salty use a stock cube and water instead.

INGREDIENTS

1 knuckle or forehock of bacon
1 bay leaf
1 lb (450 g) onions, sliced
1 lb (450 g) potatoes, sliced

SAUCE
2 oz (50 g) butter
2 oz (50 g) flour
¾ pint (450 ml) milk
salt and freshly ground black pepper
2 oz (50 g) well-flavoured Cheddar cheese

HOW TO MAKE

Soak the bacon in a pan of cold water overnight, then throw away the water. Cover the bacon with fresh water and add the bay leaf. Cover the pan, bring to the boil and simmer gently for about 2 hours until tender. Lift bacon out of stock and allow to cool. Reserve ¾ pint (450 ml) of the stock to make the sauce with.

When cool, take the meat off the bone and discard the skin, fat and bones. Cut the meat into small cubes.

Bring a large pan of salted water to the boil, add the onions and potatoes and simmer for about 10 minutes, until barely tender. Drain and reserve about 15 of the largest potato slices for the top of the hotpot. Meanwhile, heat the oven to 375°F/190°C/gas mark 5.

Prepare the sauce. Melt the butter in a pan, stir in the flour and cook for a minute. Gradually blend in the milk and reserved stock and bring to the boil slowly, stirring until thickened. Taste and add seasoning.

Mix the sauce with the bacon, onion and potato, except the reserved slices. Check the seasoning, then pour into a 3 pint (1.75 litre) shallow casserole.

Top with the reserved potato slices and sprinkle with cheese. Bake in the oven for about 20 minutes, until crispy brown.

MICHAELMAS BACON BAKE

SERVES 4

This is the ideal way to use up the last cuts off a cooked bacon joint.

INGREDIENTS

12 oz (350 g) cooked bacon
1 pint (600 ml) cider
1 lb (450 g) potatoes, scrubbed
1 large onion, coarsely chopped
2 oz (50 g) butter
2 oz (50 g) flour
½ pint (300 ml) milk
6 oz (175 g) button mushrooms, sliced
3 hard-boiled eggs, roughly chopped
salt and freshly ground black pepper
2 oz (50 g) mature Cheddar cheese, grated
1 oz (25 g) Parmesan cheese, grated

HOW TO MAKE

Cut the bacon into cubes. Pour the cider into a pan, bring to the boil and then boil to reduce by half.

Meanwhile, boil the potatoes in their skins with the onion until tender, drain, set the onion to one side. Peel and slice the potatoes.

Melt the butter in a large pan, add the flour and cook for a minute. Gradually stir in the milk and cider and bring to the boil, stirring until thickened. Add the mushrooms and simmer for 5 minutes. Remove from heat, add the bacon, potato, onion and eggs and mix well. Season to taste.

Turn the mixture into a 3½ pint (2 litre) ovenproof dish and sprinkle with the cheeses. Place under a medium grill until golden brown and heated through.

If the pie has been made in advance, heat thoroughly in a fairly hot oven, 375°F/190°C/gas mark 5, for about 20–25 minutes.

Serve with French bread and a green salad.

COOK'S TIP
When cooking with bacon or gammon, remember not to add salt to the dish as the meat itself will be salty enough.

Pasta

Pasta originated in Italy but is now firmly established in everyday use almost world-wide. Made from a specially grown hard wheat, and available either dried in packets or fresh, pasta is nutritious, cheap and very versatile. It comes in a wide choice of shapes, colours and flavours. Fresh pasta is best used within a few days of purchase or it keeps well in the freezer. Dry pasta will keep for several months in the store cupboard.

Nutritionally, pasta provides carbo-hydrate in the diet as well as some protein, vitamins and minerals. Wholewheat pasta has a higher fibre content than that made with refined flour. Green pasta is flavoured with spinach, red with tomato. Other flavourings include garlic and basil. Every kind of shape is used in pasta production, from bows, shells and spirals to rings, tubes and wheels.

The following are some the most popular shapes:

Spaghetti Long straight strands varying in thickness, which cook quickly. Used in dishes like Spaghetti Bolognese (see page 116).

Lasagne Wide flat thin sheets of pasta, spinach-flavoured or plain, used layered between meat, fish or vegetables with a well-flavoured sauce. Available as traditional, which needs cooking before assembling the baked dish, or quick-cook which does not need pre-cooking.

Tagliatelle (noodles) Narrow flat ribbons in various lengths. Sometimes folded in nest-like shapes. They are very quick to cook.

Vermicelli Very fine strands mostly used in soups.

Cannelloni Large hollow tubes stuffed with savoury meat or vegetable mixtures, then cooked and served with a well-flavoured cheese sauce.

Ravioli Square pillows of pasta bought ready-stuffed with meat or vegetable and cheese fillings.

Macaroni and penne Various sized hollow tubes of pasta cut in short lengths.

Shells (conchiglie) Shell-shaped pasta in different sizes. Smaller sizes can be served with a sauce, the large size can be stuffed.

To cook pasta

Cook the pasta in boiling salted water in a large pan, adding 1 tablespoon of oil to the water to prevent it sticking together. Cooking time varies according to the type used. Manu-facturers generally give accurate timings. When cooked, pasta should be *al dente* i.e. not soggy but retaining a slight bite. Drain well and, if using hot, mix with the other ingredients immediately. If not using straight away drain well and rinse with warm water and drain well again (this removes excess starch which would make the pasta stick together). To serve cold in salads, drain, then cool under cold running water, drain again and mix with the other ingredients.

Quantity

Depending on how hungry you are, allow 2–3 oz (50–75 g) uncooked pasta per person for a main dish. To serve as an accompani-ment allow 2 oz (50 g) per person.

SIMPLE PASTA DISHES

Once cooked *al dente* and drained, pasta can be served with any number of flavourings or sauces. Here are a few suggestions for very quick and easy pasta dishes:

Parmesan Toss the pasta in a few tablespoons of olive oil and add freshly grated Parmesan cheese and a good grinding of black pepper. Add chopped fresh herbs if liked.

Pesto Toss the pasta in a little olive oil and plenty of Pesto Sauce (see page 227).

Tomato Toss the pasta in hot Tomato Sauce (page 232). Add chopped fresh basil and a little freshly grated Parmesan cheese for a traditional Milanese dish.

Blue Cheese Mix together equal quantities of single cream and yoghurt and stir into the pasta with some crumbled blue cheese.

TAGLIATELLE WITH GARLIC CREAM SAUCE

SERVES 4–6

This rich pasta dish needs only a crisp green salad to accompany it.

INGREDIENTS

1 lb (450 g) tagliatelle
a good knob of butter
1 large clove garlic, crushed
½ pint (300 ml) double cream
2 rounded tablespoons chopped parsley
salt and freshly ground black pepper

HOW TO MAKE

Cook the tagliatelle in plenty of fast boiling salted water until just tender as directed on the packet. Drain very well and rinse in hot water and then drain again.

Rinse out the saucepan, melt the butter, add the garlic and fry for 2–3 minutes. Stir the cream into the pan with the parsley, then add the tagliatelle and toss well until it is coated with the sauce. Taste and add salt and plenty of good black pepper. Turn into a warm dish and serve.

Variation

Tagliatelle with Garlic Mushroom Sauce Add 4 oz (100 g) sliced button mushrooms with the garlic.

SPAGHETTI CARBONARA

SERVES 6

Ideal for a supper after the cinema or theatre as everything can be prepared ahead – the garlic and bacon fried, tagliatelle weighed out and the eggs beaten with cheese – then the dish just needs assembling when you come home. Serve with a crisp green salad.

INGREDIENTS

6 oz (175 g) streaky bacon
1 clove garlic, crushed
1 lb (450 g) spaghetti
6 eggs
4 oz (100 g) Parmesan cheese, grated
salt and freshly ground black pepper
¼ pint (150 ml) single cream

HOW TO MAKE

Cook the bacon in a non-stick pan over a gentle heat until the fat begins to run out, then increase the heat. Add the garlic and fry quickly until the bacon is crisp.

Meanwhile, cook the spaghetti in a large pan of boiling salted water as directed on the packet.

Break the eggs into a bowl, add the cheese and plenty of seasoning and beat well until blended.

Drain the spaghetti thoroughly and return to the hot pan. Add the bacon and egg mixture and cook gently over a moderate heat, stirring all the time until the egg is lightly set. Stir in the cream and continue to cook until heated through. Serve straight away.

COOK'S TIP
Buy Parmesan cheese in a piece and grate it yourself when needed. Ready-grated Parmesan cheese bought in drums or packets is actually less economical and lacks flavour compared to the freshly-grated cheese.

TUNA TAGLIATELLE

SERVES 6

I fall back on this recipe time and time again when the refrigerator is bare. I've always a can of tuna, pasta, eggs, milk and cheese in the house. If time is short, I forget the breadcrumb topping and use cheese alone.

INGREDIENTS

8 oz (225 g) tagliatelle
1 onion, finely sliced
3½ oz (85 g) butter
2 oz (50 g) flour
1 pint (600 ml) milk
7 oz (200 g) can tuna in oil, drained
3 hard-boiled eggs, coarsely chopped
salt and freshly ground black pepper
4 oz (100 g) mature Cheddar cheese, grated
3 oz (75 g) wholemeal breadcrumbs

HOW TO MAKE

Heat the oven to 400°F/200°C/gas mark 6. Boil the tagliatelle and onion together in a pan of salted water for about 12 minutes, until the pasta is *al dente*. Drain well and rinse in hot water then drain again and set aside.

Melt 2 oz (50 g) of the butter in a pan, add the flour and cook for 1 minute, then gradually add the milk and bring to the boil, stirring until thickened. Stir in the tagliatelle and onion, the tuna, eggs, seasoning and cheese, and turn into a 3½ pint (2 litre) shallow ovenproof dish. Fry the breadcrumbs in the remaining butter until crisp, then sprinkle over the top.

Cook in the oven for about 45 minutes, until hot through and browned on the top.

COOK'S TIP
Tuna fish in oil has more flavour than tuna in brine, but also more calories.

PASTA IN LEEK AND MUSHROOM SAUCE

SERVES 4

This dish can be served as a 'vegetable' accompaniment or as a meal in itself with garlic or herb bread. If leeks are not in season, use two peeled and chopped Spanish onions instead.

INGREDIENTS

8 oz (225 g) pasta shells
3 oz (75 g) butter
2 large leeks, washed and sliced
6 oz (175 g) mushrooms, sliced
1½ oz (40 g) flour
½ pint (300 ml) chicken stock (see page 14)
¼ pint (150 ml) milk
salt and freshly ground black pepper
4 oz (100 g) well-flavoured Cheddar cheese

HOW TO MAKE

Heat the oven to 375°F/190°C/gas mark 5. Cook the pasta in boiling salted water according to instructions on packet. Drain and rinse under cold running water.

Meanwhile, melt half the butter in a pan and fry the leeks for about 10 minutes, until tender, then add the mushrooms and cook for a further few minutes. Lift out of the saucepan with a slotted spoon. Melt the remaining butter, sprinkle on the flour and cook for 1 minute, then gradually blend in the stock and milk. Bring to the boil, stirring until thickened.

Remove from the heat, stir in the pasta, leeks and mushrooms. Season to taste. Turn into a 2 pint (1.2 litre) ovenproof dish, sprinkle the cheese over the top, then cook in the oven for about 15–20 minutes, until the cheese has melted and is bubbling and the pasta has heated through.

Variation

For a more substantial dish add a small can of drained tuna with the leeks and mushrooms.

MID-SUMMER VEGETABLES NAPOLITAINE

SERVES 6

Such a simple pasta dish, but so good. If you prefer, use other small pasta shapes instead of penne, which are sometimes call quills.

INGREDIENTS

8 oz (225 g) calabrese or broccoli
6 oz (175 g) penne
1 tablespoon oil
knob of butter
1 large onion, chopped
2 fat cloves garlic, crushed
4 oz (100 g) button mushrooms, sliced
1 red pepper, seeded and sliced
8 oz (225 g) courgettes, sliced
salt and freshly ground black pepper
3 oz (75 g) well-flavoured Cheddar cheese, grated

SAUCE
2 oz (50 g) butter
2 oz (50 g) flour
1 pint (600 ml) milk
1 teaspoon Dijon mustard
freshly grated nutmeg
salt and freshly ground black pepper
1 egg, beaten

HOW TO MAKE

Heat the oven to 400°F/200°C/gas mark 6. Slice all the stalks from the calabrese or broccoli, boil them in salted water for 5 minutes, then add the broken-up heads and cook for a further 2 minutes. Drain in a colander and refresh under cold running water.

Meanwhile, cook the pasta in plenty of boiling salted water as directed on packet until *al dente*, then drain and rinse under cold water.

Heat the oil and butter in a large frying pan, add the onion and garlic and fry until tender. Add the mushrooms, pepper and courgettes and fry quickly for about 3 minutes. Remove from heat, stir in calabrese or broccoli and season well.

To make the sauce, melt the butter in a pan, add the flour and cook for 1 minute. Gradually blend in the milk and bring to the boil, stirring until thickened. Season with the mustard, nutmeg, salt and pepper.

Remove from the heat and stir in the egg, then the vegetables and pasta. Turn the mixture into a large shallow ovenproof dish. Scatter over the cheese. Cook in the oven for about 20–30 minutes, until golden brown.

PASTA WITH CLAM SAUCE

SERVES 4

Clam sauce is a classic Italian addition to cooked spaghetti, but can also be served with pasta shells, as here. Clams are now cultivated in Britain and sold live in their shells. They are available most of the year but at their best in autumn. Grated cheese is not usually offered with this dish.

INGREDIENTS

1 dozen clams
4 tablespoons olive oil
2 cloves garlic, crushed
14 oz (400 g) can chopped tomatoes, drained
1 tablespoon chopped parsley
salt and freshly ground black pepper
1 lb (450 g) pasta shells

HOW TO MAKE

Scrub clams and rinse well under cold running water to remove sand. Holding the clams in a cloth, insert a thin knife blade between the shell edges to open shells. Cut the clams into small pieces and set aside in a bowl with any juice from clams.

Heat the oil in a pan, add the garlic and cook until pale golden. Add the clam juice, strained tomatoes, chopped parsley and seasoning to taste. Simmer until thick and pulpy.

Meanwhile, cook the pasta in boiling salted water according to packet instructions, drain, then toss in a little olive oil to prevent sticking and transfer to a warm serving dish.

Add the clams to the tomato mixture, increase the heat and cook for 2 minutes – longer will toughen the clams. Pour over pasta and serve at once.

Variation

Pasta with Scallops   Scallops are delicious cooked this way too. Use either 1 dozen small queen scallops or 4 or 5 of the larger king scallops, which will need cutting into four.

SPAGHETTI BOLOGNESE

SERVES 4–6

The sauce freezes well and is useful as a stuffing for vegetables. Don't be tempted to skimp on the simmering time; it needs an hour for the flavour to develop and the mince to become tender.

INGREDIENTS

2 tablespoons oil
8 oz (225 g) onions, chopped
2 sticks celery, sliced
1 lb (450 g) good quality minced beef
1 oz (25 g) flour
2 cloves garlic, crushed
2½ oz (62 g) can tomato purée
¼ pint (150 ml) beef stock (see page 14)
¼ pint (150 ml) red wine
14 oz (400 g) can peeled tomatoes
1 tablespoon redcurrant jelly
salt and freshly ground black pepper
1 lb (450 g) spaghetti
grated Parmesan cheese, for serving

HOW TO MAKE

Heat the oil in a pan, add the onions, celery and beef and fry for 5 minutes. Sprinkle in the flour, add the garlic and tomato purée and cook for 1 minute. Add the stock, wine, tomatoes, redcurrant jelly and seasoning and bring to the boil, stirring until thickened. Reduce the heat, partially cover the pan and simmer gently for 1 hour.

Cook the spaghetti in a pan of boiling salted water until *al dente*. Strain it in a colander and rinse out the saucepan. Add a little oil or a large knob of butter, return the pasta to the pan and toss gently.

Serve the spaghetti on to plates and ladle the sauce on top. Hand the Parmesan cheese separately.

LASAGNE

SERVES 6–8

An Italian classic. Layers of pasta, meat sauce, white sauce and cheese, crispy brown on top. Use just well-flavoured Cheddar cheese if cooking it for everyday. This is a marvellous dish for the freezer.

INGREDIENTS

6 oz (175 g) quick-cook lasagne
1 oz (25 g) Parmesan cheese, grated
4 oz (100 g) Gruyère cheese, grated

MEAT SAUCE
2 oz (50 g) bacon, chopped
2 lb (900 g) lean minced beef
1½ oz (40 g) flour
6 sticks celery, chopped
12 oz (350 g) onion, chopped
½ pint (300 ml) beef stock (see page 14)
2 fat cloves garlic, crushed
14 oz (400 g) can chopped tomatoes
4 tablespoons tomato purée
1 teaspoon sugar
1 teaspoon chopped basil
salt and freshly ground black pepper

WHITE SAUCE
2 oz (50 g) butter
1½ oz (40 g) flour
1 pint (600 ml) milk
1 teaspoon Dijon mustard
freshly grated nutmeg

HOW TO MAKE

First prepare the meat sauce. Put the bacon in a large non-stick frying pan and fry gently until the fat begins to run. Then add the mince. Increase the heat and fry quickly until browned. Sprinkle on the flour and blend in. Stir in all remaining ingredients, bring to the boil and cover with a lid. Simmer for about 1 hour, until the meat is tender.

Meanwhile, make the white sauce. Melt the butter in a pan, add the flour and cook for 1 minute. Gradually blend in the milk and bring to the boil, stirring until thickened. Remove from the heat and stir in the mustard and nutmeg. Season to taste.

Heat the oven to 375°F/190°C/gas mark 5. In a 9 × 12 inch (23 × 30 cm) shallow ovenproof dish, put layers of meat sauce, lasagne and white sauce, then grated cheese. Repeat the layers, finishing with cheese on top. Do not overlap the pasta sheets; if necessary, break the pieces to fit into the dish.

Cook, uncovered, in the oven for about 45–60 minutes, until cooked through, bubbling and crispy brown on top.

Rice

Rice is available as long grain, medium grain or short grain, and may also be described as brown, wholegrain or natural, meaning the grains retain the outer bran layers, which makes them nutritionally superior to white polished rice, but they do require longer cooking time. All rice contains carbohydrate, protein, vitamins and minerals but no fat.

Easy-cook, pre-cooked and pre-fluffed rice have been steam treated before packaging and have the advantage of needing a shorter cooking time.

Frozen partly cooked rice is also available and this can either be finished off in the traditional way or in a microwave cooker following the instructions on the packet.

Cooked rice can be stored covered in the refrigerator for up to 1 week. However if mixed or cooked with other foods it will keep for only a day.

Types of rice

Long grain rice   Use for savoury dishes such as Kedgeree (see page 121) and Nasi Goreng (see page 123). When cooked the grains are separate and fluffy. The two main types are Patna which is a good all purpose grain, and Basmati, an Indian grain used to accompany curries.

Medium grain rice   Use in both sweet and savoury dishes. It absorbs more moisture during cooking than long grain rice, with a stickier end result.

Italian short grain (risotto) rice   Used in risotto dishes such as Risotto Milanese (see page 122).

Short grain or pudding rice   Used in sweet dishes such as rice pudding. It absorbs a lot of liquid during cooking and becomes very sticky.

Brown or whole grain rice   Rice without the husk removed. It is more nutritious than white rice and has a nutty texture and flavour. It takes about 15–20 minutes longer to cook, but refer to instructions on the packet. It is available in both long and short grain varieties.

Easy-cook rice   Part cooked rice that requires less cooking time than ordinary rice. It should be cooked according to the manufacturer's instructions.

Wild rice   This is not really a type of rice though it is always used like one. It is a dark brown slim grass seed. Cook as for long grain rice. It has a special flavour and looks attractive mixed with plain boiled rice. It is expensive to buy, but only a little is needed.

It takes about twice as long to cook as ordinary rice and needs rinsing first. Boil the wild rice in a large saucepan of water for about 15 minutes before adding the other rice and continuing to cook according to instructions.

Quantity

To serve with curry and as an accompaniment to main dishes, allow 1–2 oz (25–50 g) uncooked rice per person. When the rice forms an integral part of the dish, allow 2–3 oz (50–75 g) uncooked rice per person, depending on the other main ingredients in the dish.

PLAIN RICE

SERVES 4

Rinse the grains in a sieve under cold running water to remove the excess starch before cooking.

INGREDIENTS

8 oz (225 g) long grain rice
salt

HOW TO MAKE

Boiling method
Bring a large pan of salted water to the boil, then add the rice. Stir briefly to prevent the grains sticking on the base of the pan, then cook for 12–15 minutes, until tender but not soggy. Drain well, rinse with hot water and drain again.

Baking method
Rice can also be cooked in the oven in an ovenproof dish. Use double the volume of water to rice, allowing enough room in the dish for the rice to swell to approximately double. Bring the salted water to the boil, add rice and stir. Cover with a well fitting lid or foil and bake in the oven at 350°F/180°C/gas mark 4 for about 40 minutes, until all the liquid has been absorbed and the grains are tender.

Microwave method
Cooking rice in a microwave oven doesn't cut down on time but it produces nice separate grains perfectly cooked. Measure rice and 1 pint (600 ml) boiling water into a large glass dish. Add a knob of butter, stir, cover and cook on HIGH for about 13–15 minutes, or follow manufacturer's instructions. Leave to stand for about 10 minutes or until all the water has been absorbed. Add salt to taste. Fluff up with a fork.

Variations

Any number of ingredients can be added to the rice as it cooks to flavour it. Here are some traditional ones:

Yellow Rice   Add a pinch of saffron or turmeric.

Lemon Rice   Add a thick slice of lemon. Remove when the rice is cooked.

Vegetable Rice   Add a handful of frozen mixed diced vegetables – no need to thaw before using.

Cardamom Rice   Add a few whole cardamom pods. Remove before serving.

EGG-FRIED RICE

SERVES 4

This is a good way of using up leftover cooked rice and makes a tasty accompaniment to chicken, pork or cold meats.

INGREDIENTS

5 oz (150 g) long grain rice
2 tablespoons oil
6 spring onions, trimmed and sliced thinly on the diagonal
6 baby sweetcorns, halved
2 cloves garlic, crushed
1 tablespoon light soy sauce
salt and freshly ground black pepper
3 eggs, beaten

HOW TO MAKE

Cook the rice in plenty of boiling salted water for 12–15 minutes until just tender. Drain.

Heat the oil in a wok or heavy based saucepan and fry the spring onion, baby sweetcorn and garlic, stirring continuously for 1 minute. Add the rice and stir continuously until the rice is hot.

Add the soy sauce, salt and pepper. Keep stirring and add the beaten egg. Continue stirring vigorously until the eggs are well mixed with the rice and cooked. Serve at once.

PORTUGUESE RICE

SERVES 4

In this recipe the rice is cooked by the absorption method. The rice is simmered in stock until all the liquid has been absorbed. Portuguese Rice goes particularly well with grills and chops.

INGREDIENTS

3 rashers streaky bacon, cut into strips
3 oz (75 g) onion, chopped
a little olive oil
6 oz (175 g) long grain brown rice
¾ pint (450 ml) hot chicken stock (see page 14)
1 oz (25 g) raisins
2 tablespoons soy sauce
freshly ground black pepper

HOW TO MAKE

Place the bacon in a pan and heat until beginning to sizzle. Add the onion and oil and cook for about 10 minutes. Add the rice and stir it into the onion. Pour in the hot stock, bring to the boil, cover and simmer for about 20 minutes, until all the liquid has been absorbed and the rice is tender. Stir in the raisins, soy sauce and pepper.

HADDOCK KEDGEREE

SERVES 4

Serve this Anglo-Indian dish as a tasty and satisfying breakfast, brunch or supper dish.

INGREDIENTS

6 oz (175 g) long grain rice
2 hard-boiled eggs
12 oz (350 g) smoked haddock fillet
2 oz (50 g) butter
juice of 1/2 lemon
salt
cayenne pepper
1/4 pint (150 ml) single cream
sprigs of parsley, for garnish

HOW TO MAKE

Cook the rice in boiling salted water for 12–15 minutes, until tender. Rinse well, drain and keep warm. Cut a few wedges of egg and reserve as garnish, then chop the rest coarsely.

Meanwhile, poach the haddock in a little water for about 10 minutes. Drain and remove all skin and bones, then flake the fish. Heat the oven to 350°F/180°C/gas mark 4.

Put the fish into a large bowl, add the rice, chopped egg, butter, lemon, seasoning and cream. Pile the kedgeree into a buttered serving dish and bake in the oven for 15–20 minutes, gently stirring with a fork from time to time until piping hot all through. Decorate with parsley sprigs and the reserved egg wedges.

COOK'S TIP
Some smoked haddock is artificially coloured bright yellow with dye, so look out for smoked haddock that is pale in colour or is labelled as 'un-dyed'.

RISOTTO MILANESE

SERVES 4

Long grain rice can be used if Italian is not available. Frying the rice first adds to the flavour. When cooked the rice should be creamy but retain a slight bite.

INGREDIENTS

2 oz (50 g) butter
1 small onion, chopped
8 oz (225 g) Italian risotto rice
¼ pint (150 ml) dry white wine
1 pint (600 ml) hot chicken stock (see page 14)
salt and freshly ground black pepper
1 oz (25 g) Parmesan cheese

HOW TO MAKE

Melt 1 oz (25 g) butter in a pan and fry the onion over a low heat until soft but not brown. Add the rice to the pan and cook for about 2 minutes. Pour on the wine and simmer for a few minutes, then add the stock and seasoning. Bring to the boil, cover and let the risotto simmer for about 20 minutes, or until the rice is tender and all the liquid has been absorbed.

Add the remaining butter and the grated cheese. Stir with a fork to mix in, taste and check seasoning, then serve on a hot dish.

CHICKEN LIVER RISOTTO

SERVES 4

A wonderful way of using up the last mushrooms and bacon in the refrigerator. Chicken livers are surprisingly inexpensive.

INGREDIENTS

2½ oz (65 g) butter
1 tablespoon oil
1 onion, chopped
4 oz (100 g) bacon, chopped
1 clove garlic, crushed
8 oz (225 g) Italian risotto rice
1 pint (600 ml) hot chicken stock (see page 14)
4 oz (100 g) button mushrooms, sliced
8 oz (225 g) chicken livers, sliced
4 oz (100 g) canned sweetcorn, drained
salt and freshly ground black pepper
1 oz (25 g) Parmesan cheese
chopped parsley, for garnish

HOW TO MAKE   Heat 2 oz (50 g) butter and the oil in a pan, add the onion, bacon and garlic and fry over a low heat until the onion is soft. Stir in the rice and cook for 1–2 minutes. Stir in the stock and mushrooms and bring to the boil. Cover and simmer for 25 minutes.

Fry the chicken livers in the remaining butter for a few minutes, stirring. Add to the rice mixture with the sweetcorn and simmer for a further 5 minutes. Season well. Transfer to a warm serving dish, stir in the cheese and sprinkle with chopped parsley.

NASI GORENG

SERVES 6 OR 12   A Malay rice dish with prawns and strips of omelette. It is best to cook the rice well ahead. This quantity will serve 6 on its own or 12 with a vegetable curry and side dishes.

INGREDIENTS

12 oz (350 g) long grain rice
3 eggs, beaten
salt and freshly ground black pepper
good knob of butter
about 6 tablespoons oil
2 large onions, chopped
3 cloves garlic, crushed
1/2 teaspoon chilli powder
2 heaped teaspoons curry powder
6 tablespoons soy sauce
6 oz (175 g) peeled prawns
6 spring onions, chopped

HOW TO MAKE   Cook the rice in plenty of boiling salted water for 12–15 minutes until just tender. Drain and cool, preferably overnight.

Mix the eggs with seasoning in a bowl. Melt the butter in a non-stick frying pan and add half the egg mixture to make a thin pancake-like omelette, cook on one side, then turn over to cook on other side. Set aside and repeat with the remaining mixture.

Heat the oil in a large non-stick pan, add the onion and garlic and fry, without colouring, until tender. Add the chilli powder and curry powder, cook for a few moments, than add the soy sauce, rice and seasoning. Reheat the rice, tossing it to prevent sticking.

Meanwhile, roll the two flat omelettes together and shred finely. Add to the rice with the prawns and spring onions. When piping hot, pile on a flat dish, sprinkle with more spring onion and serve with prawn crackers.

Salads

SALAD VEGETABLES

Buy salad ingredients as fresh as possible, the salad greens should look crisp and unblemished. Store in the salad or 'crisper' drawer in the refrigerator, or in polythene bags. If the refrigerator is full, keep them in the coldest part of the kitchen or larder in a large heavy saucepan or crock with a lid. If salads are a little limp, drop the whole head of lettuce, bunch of parsley, celery, cucumber or watercress into very cold water then, holding the root end or stems, shake off the surplus water and put the salad in a polythene bag in the refrigerator for a few hours and it will become crisp.

The following is just a selection of salad vegetables. Many of the vegetables listed at the beginning of the chapter 'Vegetables and Pulses', can also be used in salads, as can many varieties of fruit and nuts. Rice and pasta also make the base of more substantial salads.

Alfalfa

Looks a little like fine cress. Store in a polythene bag in the refrigerator and use within 2 days.

Preparation: Eat raw with salads to add colour and flavour. Especially good with eggs in sandwiches and in omlettes with mushrooms. Use alfalfa to garnish dishes as you would use cress.

Avocados

Test for ripeness by pressing the narrow end with your thumb. The avocado should be just soft. Unripe avocados will ripen at room temperature within a few days of purchase. Ripe avocados can be stored in the fridge for a couple of days.

Preparation: The flesh discolours on contact with air, so don't peel or cut until required. Lemon juice sprinkled on the flesh slows down the process. Cut the avocado in half lengthways through to the stone. Gently twist the two halves in opposite directions and they should come apart, leaving the stone in one half which can be prised out. The cavity may be stuffed with prawns or pâté, or the skin removed and the flesh sliced or chopped for use in salads.

Celery

Choose fresh-looking white or green celery. Any leaves should be crisp.

Preparation and cooking: Break off the stalks, trim, wash and use sliced in salads, or serve the heart with cheese. The very outside stalks and leaves can be used in stocks, soups and stews.

Corn salad (sometimes known as lamb's lettuce)

Looks like a small open spinach plant crossed with a Cos lettuce. Tastes similar.

Preparation: Trim off the end, wash and serve in mixed salad.

Cucumber

Choose really firm ones. Check by feeling down the complete cucumber.

Preparation and cooking: For salads, peel, if liked, with a potato peeler and slice. For cooking, boil in salted water for 30 seconds, then serve with buttered peas.

Endive

This is like a curly-leaved firm lettuce with a slightly bitter flavour. It keeps very well, and longer than English lettuce, in the refrigerator in a polythene bag. It will last for up to 10 days.

Preparation: Cut off the end of the stalk and any dark tough outer leaves, then shred and use in salads.

Lettuces, green and red

There are many varieties of lettuce. The most widely available is the soft-leaved round lettuce. It is the cheapest and most popular, but also the most perishable. Webbs and Cos are tougher lettuces. The one that keeps best is the paler, dense, crisp Iceberg lettuce, popular in America. Lollo rosso has a pretty frilled edge and makes salads look attractive, while oak leaf lettuce has unusually shaped leaves

Preparation: Take off and wash the amount you need, store the rest in a polythene bag in the refrigerator.

Radicchio

Sometimes called red Verona chicory, looks like a small red coloured cabbage with open round lettuce-shaped leaves.

Preparation: Wash, trim stalk and tear the leaves to serve in mixed salad.

Radishes

Choose salad radishes which are bright in colour. They will keep for a few days in the refrigerator.

Preparation: Top and tail and wash. Eat raw or use as a garnish. To make radish flowers, make four or five cuts lengthways in the radish, or cut petals all round the outside. Soak the radishes in cold water and they will open into flowers.

Rape and cress

Used to be sold as mustard and cress but has contained rape and cress for many years because mustard seeds look like small snails. Usually 85 per cent rape and 15 per cent cress, and it's often difficult to see the cress as it grows shorter.

Preparation: Just snip off what you want from the tray with scissors; the rest will keep in the refrigerator for a couple of days. Wash, then use in salads or as a garnish.

Spring onions and salad onions

Keep in the refrigerator in a polythene bag; use as soon as possible.

Preparation: Cut off root and outer leaves. Serve in salads, whole or sliced. Use scissors to snip tops.

Tomatoes

Varieties vary with the time of year, ranging in size from the baby cherry tomato to the large beef or beefsteak tomato which are ideal for stuffing.

Preparation: Remove stalks, if any, use large ones sliced or stuffed and small ones sliced or whole, hot or cold. To skin tomatoes put in boiling water for a few seconds and the skins will then peel off easily.

Watercress

Keep watercress cool once you get it home, otherwise it will quickly turn yellow. Stand the bunches stalks downwards in a jug of cold water, almost immersing the leaves. If keeping for more than one day, stand the jug in the refrigerator. If refrigerator space is short, plunge the watercress into cold water, shake well, then chill in a polythene bag.

Preparation: Take off ends of stalks, wash carefully, changing the water. Serve as salad, or in sandwiches, or as a garnish for savoury dishes. Watercress when cooked or puréed makes a delicious soup or sauce to go with fish.

MAYONNAISE

MAKES ABOUT
1¾ PINTS
(1 LITRE)

This is foolproof and makes a delicious mayonnaise. Because it is made from whole eggs, it is a little less rich than using just yolks. If liked, substitute half the sunflower oil with olive oil. If you haven't got a blender or food processor, whisk together the eggs, vinegar, sugar and seasonings then gradually whisk in the oil until thick, and lastly add the lemon juice. Bought mayonnaise can be livened up with added lemon juice or spoonful of Greek yoghurt before serving.

INGREDIENTS

2 eggs at room temperature
1 tablespoon wine vinegar
1 teaspoon caster sugar
1 teaspoon dry mustard
salt and freshly ground black pepper
1½ pints (900 ml) sunflower oil
juice of 1 large lemon

HOW TO MAKE

Put all the ingredients except the oil and lemon juice into a blender or food processor. Process briefly to blend, then add the oil in a slow steady stream through the funnel until the mixture is very thick and all the oil has been incorporated. Switch on again and add all the lemon juice. Taste and check the seasoning.

If you want a thinner mayonnaise, add a little water or milk in the same way. Turn out and keep for up to 2 weeks in the refrigerator.

Variations

Tomato Mayonnaise Add about 2 tablespoons tomato purée and a little Worcestershire sauce to the blender or processor with the last amount of oil, then check the seasoning.

Aioli Aioli is the classic French garlic mayonnaise. Add two (or more if you like) crushed cloves of garlic to the blender or processor with the other ingredients.

Watercress Mayonnaise After pouring out the mayonnaise, put one washed and chopped bunch of watercress into the blender or processor and process briefly, then mix into the mayonnaise. Check the seasoning.

Avocado Mayonnaise After turning out the mayonnaise, add 1 peeled and stoned avocado to the blender or processor with 1 tablespoon of lemon juice. Process briefly and add ½ pint (300 ml) of the made mayonnaise, then process very briefly to mix. Check the seasoning.

Tartare Sauce After turning out the mayonnaise, add to the blender or processor 1 rounded dessertspoon each of chopped gherkins and capers, and a few sprigs of parsley. Process briefly and add ½ pint (300 ml) of the made mayonnaise. Process very briefly to mix. Check the seasoning.

Herb Mayonnaise   After turning out the mayonnaise, add to the blender or processor a generous handful of mixed fresh herbs, or your favourite herb, washed and drained. Process briefly and add ½ pint (300 ml) of the made mayonnaise. Process briefly to mix. Check the seasoning.

Curry Mayonnaise   Add 2–3 teaspoons curry powder and a little mango chutney juice with the ingredients.

FRENCH DRESSING

MAKES A GOOD
¾ PINT
(450 ML)

Well worth making in a food processor as it emulsifies and lasts better made this way, also it is quite marvellous when you are preparing vast quantities of salad for a party. If you are making it by hand, use a whisk and add the oil slowly.

INGREDIENTS

1 clove garlic, crushed
1 teaspoon dry mustard
salt and freshly ground black pepper
2 tablespoons caster sugar
½ pint (300 ml) sunflower oil
¼ pint (150 ml) white or red wine vinegar

HOW TO MAKE

Put all the ingredients into a food processor and process to combine – a longer time makes a thicker dressing if that is how you like it. Keep for up to 1 month in the fridge.

Variations

Any of the following can be added before processing:

Garlic Dressing   Add 3–4 cloves garlic, peeled and crushed.

Herb Dressing   Add 3–4 tablespoons freshly chopped herbs, such as parsley, marjoram, chervil and chives.

Basil Dressing   Add 2 tablespoons chopped fresh basil. Good with tomatoes and summer salads.

Tarragon Dressing   Add 2 tablespoons chopped fresh tarragon. Serve with salads to accompany chicken or fish.

Mint Dressing   Add 3–4 tablespoons chopped fresh mint. Serve with new potato or tomato salad.

TABOULEH

SERVES 4

Tabouleh is traditionally served in a bowl lined with cooked vine leaves or raw lettuce leaves (the inner leaves of a Cos lettuce are best, or chinese leaves). The salad is then scooped up in other leaves served in a separate bowl. Cracked wheat (also called bulgur or bulgar wheat) can be bought from most good delicatessens and health food shops.

INGREDIENTS

4 oz (100 g) cracked wheat
3 spring onions, chopped
2 firm tomatoes, skinned, seeded and diced
salt and freshly ground black pepper
2 tablespoons freshly chopped parsley
1 tablespoon freshly chopped mint
3 tablespoons French dressing (see page 127)
juice of ½ lemon

TO SERVE
lettuce leaves
cucumber slices, tomato wedges and parsley sprigs

HOW TO MAKE

Measure the cracked wheat into a bowl, cover with water and leave to stand for about 30 minutes. Drain very thoroughly, squeezing out as much liquid as possible. Return to a dry clean bowl and stir in the remaining ingredients. Taste to check seasoning, adding more lemon juice if necessary to give a distinctive lemon flavour to the salad.

Line a serving dish with lettuce leaves, spoon the salad into the centre and decorate with the cucumber, tomato and parsley. Serve with a separate bowl of fresh crisp lettuce leaves.

Right: *Spanish Omelette (page 42)*

Facing page 129: *Egg-fried Rice (page 120)*

ENDIVE, ORANGE AND WALNUT SALAD

SERVES 4–6

A refreshing, crunchy side salad with a nutty-flavoured dressing.

INGREDIENTS

6 heads endive
2 oranges
1 oz (25 g) broken shelled walnuts
1 tablespoon sugar
salt and freshly ground black pepper
3 tablespoons walnut oil
small bunch watercress

HOW TO MAKE

Break the leaves off the endive, cutting the larger ones in half. Place in a bowl. Peel one and a half oranges and cut into slices or segments, removing all the pips and pith. Add to the endive in the bowl with the walnuts.

Squeeze the juice from the remaining orange half into a separate bowl and add the sugar and salt and pepper. Whisk in the walnut oil. Pour over the salad and toss. Decorate with sprigs of watercress.

TOMATO AND AVOCADO SALAD

SERVES 4

For a more substantial meal, add sliced cold chicken and some chopped spring onion, or lightly cooked French beans and slices of mozzarella cheese.

INGREDIENTS

1 large avocado pear
1 tablespoon lemon juice
1 lb (450 g) firm tomatoes, skinned, sliced
About 5 tablespoons French dressing (see page 127)

HOW TO MAKE

About 30 minutes before serving, peel the avocado, cut in half and remove the stone. Cut the flesh into slices and sprinkle with lemon juice to prevent discoloration.

Arrange the tomato slices on an attractive serving dish with the avocado slices on top, radiating outwards from the centre. Chill in the refrigerator for about 20 minutes. Spoon over the dressing just before serving.

POTATO SALAD

SERVES 4–6

New or waxy potatoes are best for salads as they retain their shape rather than breaking up. If you like added crunch, add 4 sticks of celery, chopped.

INGREDIENTS

1 ½ lb (675 g) new or waxy potatoes
¼ pint (150 ml) mayonnaise (see page 126)
4 tablespoons single cream
salt and freshly ground black pepper
3 tablespoons chopped herbs, such as chervil, parsley or basil

HOW TO MAKE

Cook the potatoes in boiling water with their skins still on. Drain. When cool enough to handle, skin and slice thickly, or leave whole if small and new.

Thin the mayonnaise with the cream, then pour it over the warm potatoes. Season well with salt and pepper and sprinkle on the herbs. Toss gently to coat evenly.

This salad is best served unchilled when freshly made.

COLESLAW

SERVES 8

This classic recipe is a favourite for parties and buffets. If you're making a large quantity, use a food processor to chop the cabbage and onion and to grate the carrots.

INGREDIENTS

1 small, firm white cabbage about 1 ½ lb (675 g)
¼ pint (150 ml) French dressing (see page 127)
salt and freshly ground black pepper
1 teaspoon Dijon mustard
1 small onion, finely chopped
2 carrots
5–6 tablespoons mayonnaise (see page 126)

HOW TO MAKE

Cut the cabbage into quarters, trim away the tough stalk, then finely slice into strips. Place in a large bowl with the French dressing, seasoning, mustard and onion. Toss well. Cover with clingfilm and leave in the refrigerator until needed, preferably overnight.

Next day, grate the carrots coarsely and stir into the cabbage, with the mayonnaise. If time allows, leave to stand in the refrigerator for an hour before checking the seasoning. Pile into a large serving dish to serve.

FETA CHEESE SALAD

SERVES 4

Feta is a pure white crumbly Greek cheese, with a distinctive salty taste. This is an ideal salad to serve as a starter.

INGREDIENTS

½ crisp lettuce
½ cucumber, thickly sliced
½ green pepper, seeded and cubed
4 oz (100 g) Feta cheese
2 oz (50 g) fat black olives
5 tablespoons French dressing (see page 127), made with good
*   quality olive oil*
1 tablespoon chopped parsley and marjoram

HOW TO MAKE

Place all the salad ingredients in an attractive salad bowl or on a plate. Cut the Feta cheese into triangles and add to the salad bowl. Scatter on the olives. Spoon over the dressing and sprinkle with herbs.

SPECIAL MUSHROOM SALAD

SERVES 6

Try and get hold of tiny white button mushrooms for this dish, as they look so pretty. If unavailable use ordinary button mushrooms cut into quarters.

INGREDIENTS

5 tablespoons water
4 tablespoons oil
salt and freshly ground black pepper
½ teaspoon ground coriander
12 oz (350 g) button mushrooms
4 fl oz (100 ml) Madeira
2 sticks celery, chopped

HOW TO MAKE

Put the water, oil, seasoning, coriander and whole mushrooms in a saucepan. Bring to the boil and simmer gently, without a lid, for about 5 minutes, tossing frequently.

Lift the mushrooms out of the pan with a slotted spoon and put in a bowl. Add the Madeira to the liquid left in the saucepan and boil rapidly until the liquid has reduced to a syrup. Pour over the mushrooms.

Allow to cool, then cover with clingfilm and chill in the refrigerator overnight. Just before serving, stir in the celery, then transfer the salad to a serving dish.

WALDORF SALAD

SERVES 6

You can peel the apples if you prefer, but red apples make the salad look pretty if the skin is left on.

INGREDIENTS

1 small head of celery
8 dessert apples
juice of ½ lemon
½ pint (300 ml) mayonnaise (see page 126)
¼ pint (150 ml) whipping cream, whipped
salt and freshly ground black pepper
6 oz (175 g) walnut pieces

HOW TO MAKE

Chop the celery. Quarter, core and dice apples, place them in a bowl with lemon juice and turn in the juice to coat each piece to prevent discoloration. Put the mayonnaise, cream and seasoning into a bowl and mix well together. Add the celery and apples and mix to coat with mayonnaise.

Chill in the refrigerator until required. Just before serving, add the walnuts, turn into a serving dish and serve with a selection of other salads.

CELERIAC REMOULADE

SERVES 4

You need to blanch the celeriac as soon as it is cut or it will quickly discolour.

INGREDIENTS

1 good-size head of celeriac
juice of 1 lemon
4 tablespoons good thick mayonnaise (see page 126)
salt and freshly ground black pepper
leafy green herbs, for garnish

HOW TO MAKE

Thickly peel the celeriac and cut into longish matchsticks. Blanch them in boiling salted water for 1 minute, then refresh under cold running water. Drain well, put into a bowl with the lemon juice, turning the celeriac in the lemon juice to prevent discoloration. Mix in the mayonnaise and season.

Turn on to a pretty serving plate and decorate with leafy green herbs.

MEXICAN SALAD

SERVES 4–6

A great change from the usual rice or potato salad. It is essential to soak the beans overnight first, then drain and cook in fresh water. Don't add any salt at this stage as it tends to toughen the beans.

INGREDIENTS

1 lb (450 g) mixed dried beans, such as haricot, red kidney, black
*   eye and aduki*
1 clove garlic, crushed
a little finely chopped onion
4 sticks celery, finely chopped
6 tablespoons French dressing (see page 127)
salt and freshly ground black pepper
chopped parsley

HOW TO MAKE

Put the beans in a bowl, cover with cold water and leave to soak overnight.
    Drain well and put in a saucepan, cover with cold water and bring to the boil. Simmer for 1 hour, or until tender. Rinse under hot water and while they are still warm put in a bowl and add all the other ingredients except the parsley. Toss well, season and then cover. Leave in a cool place to marinate overnight. Sprinkle with parsley before serving.

SPINACH AND BACON SALAD

SERVES 4

This salad is very popular in America. Remember croûtons freeze well, so if you have this salad often keep some extra croûtons in the freezer.

INGREDIENTS

8 oz (225 g) fresh young spinach
2 large slices thick-cut white bread
sunflower oil for frying
1 clove garlic, crushed
8 rashers thin streaky bacon
about 8 tablespoons French dressing (see page 127)

HOW TO MAKE

Wash well and dry spinach leaves, trim stalks and shred any large leaves into fine strips. Divide between four pretty shell-shaped side plates and set aside.
    Cut the crusts from the bread and cut the slices into small cubes. Heat the oil in frying pan and fry the bread cubes until golden on all sides. Add the crushed garlic and stir to distribute evenly among the croûtons (bread cubes). Remove with a slotted spoon and drain on absorbent kitchen paper.
    Add the bacon rashers to the pan and fry for about 5 minutes, until crisp and golden. Drain on absorbent kitchen paper. Snip into small pieces, then divide between the four plates of spinach. Spoon the French dressing over the salad. Season, toss slightly, scatter the croûtons on top and serve at once.

SALAD NIÇOISE

SERVES 4

This salad needs careful tossing otherwise the eggs and tuna become too mixed and loose their shape. Leave out the onion if you have an aversion to eating it raw. The cucumber and tomatoes can be skinned if you prefer (see pages 124–5).

INGREDIENTS

3 tomatoes, quartered
½ cucumber, thinly sliced
½ Spanish onion, chopped
about 5 tablespoons French dressing (see page 127)
1 Cos lettuce
7 oz (200 g) can tuna fish, drained and flaked
2 oz (50 g) can anchovy fillets, drained and halved lengthways
2 oz (50 g) black olives
2 hard-boiled eggs
chopped parsley

HOW TO MAKE

Place the tomatoes, cucumber and onion in a large roomy bowl. Spoon over the French dressing and mix lightly.

Arrange the lettuce leaves in the bottom of a salad bowl or serving dish and spoon the vegetables on top. Arrange the tuna fish, anchovy fillets and black olives on top. Cut the eggs in half lengthways, then into quarters and arrange on top. Sprinkle with parsley.

Variation

To make the salad go further, add 8 oz (225 g) French beans, cooked and cut into short lengths, and 1 small green pepper, quartered, seeded and thinly sliced.

COOK'S TIP

If you dislike the saltiness or oiliness of anchovy fillets, wash in hot water and dry on kitchen paper. Soaking them in milk for a few hours has the same effect. Anchovies don't travel well and can only be eaten fresh, not frozen, which is why we only ever see them in tins in this country.

Vegetables and Pulses

Vegetables are an essential part of our diet, and no one has ever told us to eat less of them.

Generally vegetables are best cooked *al dente* rather than overcooked and soft. In recent years we have taken to cooking them in a minimum amount of water, if boiling, to conserve flavour and vitamins. Stir-frying is also immensely popular as a quick and healthy method of cooking vegetables. It's not essential to have a wok as any large pan will do. The important thing is to have an intense heat under the pan, and well prepared vegetables of even thickness.

Another modern method of cooking vegetables is in a microwave. The microwave cooks vegetables in small quantities well, but if cooking 1 lb (450 g) or more, then conventional cooking methods are quicker and better.

The following A–Z list of vegetables and how to prepare them includes the most popular ones available throughout the year, as well as some more unusual varieties that have recently become more widely available. Many of the recipes that follow on pages 142–155 can be served as vegetarian main courses.

Artichokes

Globe Artichokes Over recent years these have become more popular, usually as a first course, hot or cold, with either melted butter or a sauce such as hollandaise or mayonnaise. Large succulent ones come from France in summer.

To prepare: Cut off stalk. Boil in salted water for 20–40 minutes, until tender. Drain well, serve hot or cold, 1 per person.

To eat: Pull leaves off and dip the inner fleshy end into melted butter or sauce and eat by using teeth to 'scrape' off the fleshy bit.

When all the leaves have been removed, take out the hairy 'choke' and discard. The base or 'fond', the nicest part, can then be eaten with a knife and fork with more sauce.

Jerusalem Artichokes Knobbly, cream coloured root vegetables with a soft smoky flavour, which make excellent soup or purée or they can be sliced and tossed in butter or served with parsley sauce. Avoid larger roots, which can be woody.

To prepare: Scrub well, cook in boiling salted water for about 8 minutes when the skins will peel off easily. Drain in a colander, then rinse under cold running water until cool enough to handle. Peel off the skins, slice artichokes and return to pan with a little fresh water. Cover with a lid, bring to the boil and simmer for about 10 minutes, until just tender.

Asparagus

An expensive vegetable but with little waste. It has a delicate flavour and is best served simply with melted butter, a mayonnaise-based sauce or hollandaise. Usually served hot. Asparagus also makes delicious soups and salads, and is a luxurious vegetable accompaniment to summer meals.

Thin whispy stalks of asparagus called sprue are sometimes sold, these are cheaper and usually tender enough for the whole stalk to be eaten.

To prepare: Wash stalks well in plenty of cold water to remove any gritty sand from the asparagus bed. Trim some of the thick woody end. Tie in bundles and cook in a special asparagus pan or a deep saucepan in boiling salted water, stalk end down, for about 15–20 minutes depending on thickness. Can also be steamed. Drain well.

Aubergine (Egg plant)

Widely available in many colours from mottled off-white to deep purple. To me, it seems a shame to use anything but the deep purple coloured aubergines. Freshest when shiny looking. Use sliced in moussaka or ratatouille. Can also be halved lengthwise and stuffed with minced meat or chopped vegetables. The peel is eaten as well as the flesh.

To prepare: Cut off the stalk and halve or slice. Some people like to sprinkle the cut surfaces with salt to draw out excess moisture and any bitter juices, rinsing the surfaces after 30 minutes. I find this isn't necessary. Can be baked, fried or grilled.

Beans and peas

French green beans, runner or stick beans, broad beans, garden peas and mange-tout all add variety as they come into season.
To prepare:
French beans   Top and tail and remove side strings. Leave very small beans whole or cut into 1 or 2 inch (2.5–5 cm) lengths.

Runner beans   Top, tail and remove side strings. Slice diagonally fairly finely.

Mange-tout   Top and tail, remove any side strings.

Peas and broad beans   Shell.

To cook: Cook all the beans or peas in boiling salted water until just tender but still crisp. Whole green beans take about 6–8 minutes, 3–5 if cut, runner beans about 3–5 minutes, broad beans about 5–6 minutes, fresh peas 5–8 minutes, mange-tout about 1–3 minutes. Drain and serve with a little butter and freshly ground black pepper. Broad beans are traditionally served with hot parsley sauce.

Bean sprouts

Specially sprouted mung beans can be stir fried or eaten raw in salads. Buy and use within a day or two. Keep in the refrigerator.

Rinse in cold water and add to salads, or cook for 1 minute in stir fry dishes.

Beetroot

Sold cooked or raw. It can be served hot with white sauce or cold sliced in vinegar or incorporated into a salad.

To prepare: Scrub to remove soil. Trim leaves to within an inch or so of the top. Take care not to damage the skin or juices will 'bleed' into the cooking water. Simmer until soft, about 2 hours depending on the size. Peel when cool.

Broccoli

Three main types, purple or white sprouting is smallest of all broccoli, usually home-grown, with several single heads on one steam. Calabrese (broccoli spears) has a larger head, usually on one stem. Cape broccoli is like a cauliflower but coloured purple and the head is more open. Serve boiled or steamed until just tender with melted butter and freshly ground black pepper.

To prepare: Trim ends of stalks; wash. Slice thick end of broccoli or calabrese stalk and cook for 2 minutes in boiling salted water, add rest of broccoli and cook until just tender. Purple sprouting takes about 5 minutes, calabrese about 6 minutes and cape broccoli about 7 minutes.

Brussels sprouts

Usually sold by weight but occasionally sold on the stick, which includes the top. Sprouts keep very well if sold on the stick (2 weeks in a cold place). Serve hot, boiled or steamed with a little butter and freshly ground black pepper, add fried chestnut pieces or almonds for a special occasion. Can also be added raw and finely shredded to salads.

To prepare: Remove sprout end and any damaged or discoloured leaves. Make a knife cut in the base of the sprout to speed up the cooking time. Bring a pan of salted water to the boil, just enough to almost cover the sprouts, add sprouts and cook for about 5–8 minutes until just tender. Drain well.

Cabbage and kale

This wonderful vegetable comes in many forms all the year round – thinnings from main crop sold as spring greens before the heart has grown; spring cabbages with a small heart; summer cabbages firm and green; winter cabbages, red or white, coarser and stronger in flavour; curly kale, non-hearting variety with very curly leaves and strong leaf stem.

To prepare: Wash all the varieties in cold water. Remove damaged or discoloured leaves and any coarse stalks. Shred leaves and cook quickly in boiling salted water for a few minutes until just tender with a hint of crispness. Drain, toss in butter and freshly ground black pepper.

Carrots

Available all the year round as maincrop are lifted and stored through winter. Served raw, grated in salads, puréed, boiled or steamed, or as a base for soups.

To prepare: Early baby carrots need only washing to remove soil, older carrots may be scraped or peeled, then cut lengthwise or in rounds. Cook by steaming, or in boiling salted water for about 10 minutes, until tender but retaining a definite bite. Drain, toss in butter and freshly ground black pepper.

Cauliflower

Available throughout the year. Sprigs can be broken off to have raw for salads, or the cauliflower can be cooked and served hot. Choose compact, firm heads without blemishes.

To prepare: Wash in cold water, remove tough outer leaves and stalks, cut into four or more wedges or leave whole or divided into florets (the smaller flower heads). Cook by steaming, or in boiling salted water for about 10–15 minutes, until just tender but with a

hint of crispness. Can be served with a plain white or well-flavoured cheese sauce.

Celeriac

A largely knobbly root with a distinctive celery flavour. It is usually served cooked, then puréed and added to an equal quantity of mashed potato. To serve as salad, peel, cut into matchsticks or tiny cubes, blanch in boiling water for 30 seconds, refresh in cold water and toss in mayonnaise.

To prepare: Peel off the brownish skin. The white flesh will discolour if not cooked immediately or put in water to which a tablespoon or two of lemon juice has been added. Cut into cubes or strips and steam or cook in boiling salted water for about 15 minutes until tender. Drain, then toss in butter and freshly ground black pepper.

Chicory

Sold as a complete head of compact leaves. It should be pale yellow rather than green which can be bitter. Serve the raw leaves whole or sliced in salads. To serve as a vegetable leave whole and cook in a good chicken stock with seasoning for flavour. Bring to the boil, then simmer, covered, for about 25–30 minutes, until tender.

To prepare: Cut the base from the head of chicory and separate the leaves. Wash in cold water. If using raw in salads, sprinkle with lemon juice to prevent discoloration.

Chinese leaves

Available throughout the year, these leaves can be shredded raw for salads, or stir fried and served hot. If added to a stir fry, eat at once as it quickly becomes limp.

To prepare: Remove any tattered leaves, then wash in cold water. Shred as much as you want and cook in a large frying pan or wok with a little oil or butter, over a fairly high heat. Add a dash or two of soy sauce and cook until the leaves are tender but not soggy.

Corn on the cob

When it is in season in summer, look for ears of corn that are pale yellow and well filled with plump shiny pieces of corn. Golden coloured corn is over-ripe and crinkly corn is usually tough and dry. Serve hot with melted butter and seasoning, eat in the fingers or speared with corn picks.

To prepare: Remove outer leaves and silky threads, trim stalk. Cook in boiling water for about 10 minutes, until tender.

Baby sweet corn A special variety of imported corn, grown specially to mature when the small ear is only about 2½ inch (6 cm) long. Cooked and eaten whole or sliced raw into salads.

To prepare: Wash and cook whole in boiling salted water for about 4–5 minutes until tender but slightly crisp. Also can be blanched and added to a stir fry.

Courgettes

Available all the year round but much cheaper in summer when homegrown ones are available. Both green and yellow varieties should be firm and shiny. Serve hot, cooked whole or sliced in boiling salted water, or sautéed in butter.

To prepare: Wipe, trim off each end and leave whole if small, otherwise slice. Cook in boiling salted water, whole about 5 minutes, sliced about 2 minutes, or steam for about 5 minutes. Drain well, toss in butter and freshly ground black pepper. To sauté, keep turning in a little hot butter and seasoning until just tender with a hint of crispness. Older large courgettes can be used in the same way as marrows.

Florence fennel

Available all the year round, has a pronounced aniseed flavour. Served raw in salads to give a nice flavour or served hot with a sauce or cheese topping.

To prepare: Trim leafy stems and root end. Chop, slice or grate for salads, adding a squeeze of lemon juice or a salad dressing, to prevent discoloration. Cut into quarters, cook in boiling salted water with a little lemon juice for about 30 minutes, until tender. Leave whole or slice, then pour on a well-flavoured white sauce or add some grated cheese and brown under the grill. Can also be finished by sautéeing in butter when cooked and sliced. The leaves make an attractive garnish for salads.

Kohlrabi

Looks rather like a turnip but it is a swollen stalk, not a root. Buy smallish kohlrabi up to 2 inches (5 cm) in diameter, as larger ones tend to be tough. They are either white or purple. Can be served raw, thinly sliced for salads, or cooked or fried to serve hot.

To prepare: Trim the base, cut off the leaves and stalks and peel the globe thinly, then slice or dice. Cook in boiling salted water for about 20 minutes, until tender. Drain and serve with butter or white sauce flavoured with parsley or chives.

Leeks

A relative of the onion, leeks make good soups, can be added to casseroles and flans or served hot with a white sauce or cooked and served with French dressing (see page 127).

To prepare: Trim any root off plus the top and any damaged leaves. If serving sliced, wash the slices in several changes of cold water. If cooking whole, cut through to within 2 inches (5 cm) of the base and soak in warm water for 10 minutes to loosen the dirt, then wash under cold running water to remove any soil. Older tougher leeks will take longer to cook than thin young ones. Cook in boiling salted water until tender: whole about 10 minutes, sliced about 5 minutes. Drain very well. Serve with a well-flavoured white sauce or butter and freshly ground black pepper.

Marrow

Marrows are available in late summer and autumn and will keep for 1–2 weeks in a cool place. Very large marrows yield less flesh as they are full of seeds and can be fibrous. Marrow can be added to vegetable quiches, or ratatouille, stuffed with minced meat, or simply served as a hot vegetable with a good white or cheese sauce. Young marrows have the best flavour.

To prepare: Peel, cut in half and remove the seeds. Cut into slices or cubes, cook by steaming, or boiling in salted water for about 3–5 minutes, until just tender. Drain very well. Serve with butter and freshly ground black pepper or a well-flavoured sauce.

Mushrooms

Numerous unusual mushroom are now widely available. Of the cultivated variety, the smallest are pure white button mushrooms with tight caps. Cup mushrooms are slightly more mature with a cap partially opened, and flat mushrooms have the cap completely opened out and flat. Always buy firm, fresh looking mushrooms. Use for soups, stuffings, sauces, casseroles, or serve raw in salads, or hot or cold as a first course.

To prepare: Wipe with a damp cloth; if very dirty, wash but do not soak. Do not peel. To cook, fry in a little butter or oil, either whole or sliced, until tender.

Okra

Green podded vegetable with ridges which looks like a chilli. Do not buy pods with brown marks on as they indicate staleness. Serve hot as a vegetable or in a stir fry.

To prepare: Wash, then top and tail, taking care not to pierce them or they will become slimy when cooked. Cook whole in a little boiling salted water for about 3–5 minutes, until just tender. Do not overcook or they will become slimy. Drain, then toss in butter and freshly ground black pepper.

Onions

Many varieties are available with lots of different uses. Onions are used in soups, salads, stuffings, sauces, casseroles, stir fries, as well as a vegetable in their own right, either boiled, baked, braised, stuffed or fried. Generally, globe onions are mostly used for casseroles and cooking, the larger milder Spanish onions, for frying and using raw, and spring onions for salads and stir fries. Italian red onions are oblong-shaped, mild and sweet in flavour, but lose their colour when cooked, so look better raw in salads and for decoration. Shallots are small onions with a strong flavour and are used mainly in casseroles; they are available in late summer and autumn. Use onion skins to flavour and colour stocks.

To prepare: Cut a thin slice from top to root end of the onion and peel away outer skins. To boil whole, cook for about 30–40 minutes; bake for 1–1½ hours; braise for 30–40 minutes; fry slices gently in butter or oil until tender.

Parsnips

Available from September onwards through the winter, but have a better flavour after some frosty weather. Parsnips have a sweet taste, and can be used in soups, as a vegetable purée, or roasted or sautéed.

To prepare: Trim both ends and peel thinly. Young ones can be left whole to bake or boil. Large sizes can be cut into halves, quarters or slices, removing the inner core if woody. Cook in boiling salted water for 15–20 minutes until tender, or steam. To roast or bake, partly cook by boiling in salted water for a few minutes, then drain and roast or bake in the oven or fry in butter in a frying pan.

Peppers

Now grown in the UK as well as imported, these colourful vegetables ranging from red and green to yellow, orange and black, have many uses. They can be sliced raw in salads, stuffed with savoury mixtures, or added to stir fries and casseroles. Choose peppers that are shiny and show no signs of shrivelling.

To prepare: Remove stalk, cut out seeds and core. Slice or dice for salads or adding to stir fries and casseroles. Cut in half for stuffing.

Potatoes

A vast choice is available and most supermarkets or stall holders will give information as to the variety best suited to your needs. Potatoes are a very versatile vegetable widely used in soups, as a salad ingredient and boiled, baked, creamed, roasted, steamed and sautéed.

To prepare: For **baked potatoes in their jackets** simply scrub well, remove any discoloured bits, prick with a fork or pierce through with a skewer (which can be left in to speed up cooking) then bake in a hot oven at 400°F/200°C/gas mark 6 for about 1 hour. If shorter of time, cut each large potato in half and bake for 30 minutes.

Peel potatoes thinly for **boiling, steaming, roasting** etc. Cook in boiling salted water until tender for creamed potatoes, then mash with butter, milk and seasoning. For **roast potatoes**, bring to the boil then drain, then roast in hot fat in the oven. For **frying**, first steam them in their skins until almost tender. Peel when cool enough to handle, slice thickly and fry in butter or oil until golden brown.

Pumpkin

A relative of the marrow, quite widely available in the autumn. Can be used as a vegetable or fruit. Whole large varieties may weigh up to 15 lb (6–7 kg). Also sold in slices by weight. Can be baked around a Sunday roast, or stuffed, added to casseroles or used in a variety of sweet pies and puddings.

To prepare: Cut in half and scoop out seeds, peel and cut into pieces. Use for pies or as a vegetable cooked in the same way as marrow.

Salsify and scorzonera

Two long rooted vegetables which are closely related. Salsify has a white skin and scorzonera a brownish black skin. Can be used in soups, casseroles, raw in salads, and boiled.

To prepare: Wash well and scrub off all dirt. Do not peel. Boil in salted water with a tablespoon of lemon juice added to prevent discolouring, for about 30 minutes, depending on size, until just tender. Drain. When cool enough to handle, peel and cut into slices. Serve in a white sauce or fry slices in butter and scatter with fresh garden herbs.

Spinach

Summer spinach has bright green leaves and a fine texture. Winter spinach, also known as spinach beet or perpetual spinach, is darker, coarser and stronger tasting. Spinach is used in soups, terrines, light stuffings, quiches and roulades, or raw in salads.

To prepare: Wash well to remove dirt and grit in several changes of water. Remove coarse stalks, especially from winter spinach. Summer spinach is best cooked carefully in a pan with just the water that clings to the leaves after washing. Cook winter spinach in a little boiling salted water for about 5–10 minutes, until tender. Drain both very well, if necessary pressing down leaves in a colander with the back of a wooden spoon or potato masher. Chop finely, return to the pan with a little butter and freshly ground black pepper.

Swede

Winter root vegetable with orange flesh. Large swedes can be tough, so choose smaller sizes and serve mashed with butter and seasoning.

To prepare: Peel thickly and cut into slices or chunks. Cook in boiling salted water for about 20–25 minutes, until tender. Drain, mash well with butter and plenty of seasoning.

Sweet potato

Bulbous pink-skinned tubers, not related to our native potato, with a sweet-flavoured flesh. Use to boil, bake, fry or roast. Choose smaller ones that are firm to touch as the large ones tend to be fibrous.

To prepare: Wash, then either boil or bake in their skins until tender, then peel, slice or mash. Toss in butter and season well. Alternatively, roast as for potatoes.

Turnip

Early turnips are available from April to July. They have green and white skins and should be small, firm and thin skinned. They have a slight mustard flavour and can be used in soups, casseroles, and as a vegetable cooked whole or puréed with potato or carrots. Maincrop turnips have thicker skins and coarser flesh. They are best used in soups and casseroles.

To prepare: Remove top and root, peel early variety thinly, leave whole if small, or cut into chunks if large, then cook in boiling salted water for about 20–30 minutes, depending on age. Drain, toss in a little butter and season with salt and freshly ground black pepper. Purée with an equal quantity of mashed potato. Young turnips can be served raw, thinly sliced or grated as an addition to salads.

Dried beans, lentils and peas

Pulse is the term which includes all the dried beans, peas and lentils. There are many varieties in different shapes, sizes and colours. Pulses are very versatile and can be used in all sorts of savoury dishes where their nutritional value adds to the diet since they are a valuable source of protein, fibre, vitamins and minerals. They play a particularly important part in a vegetarian diet.

Pulses contain almost no fat. They are sold in packets with a shelf life of up to 9 months and are best bought in small quantities.

To prepare: Wash thoroughly and pick out any damaged seeds or pieces of stone and grit. All pulses with the exception of lentils need soaking, preferably overnight, before cooking. If time does not allow for this, the quick soaking method can be used; place the pulses in a pan with cold water, bring to the boil, simmer for 2 minutes, then leave to soak in the water for 2–3 hours. Cook according to the instructions for the individual pulse.

Allow double the volume of water to beans and do not add salt until cooked, or the beans will be tough. Do not cook dark coloured beans with pale beans in the same pan otherwise the pales ones will take colour from the dark ones. Times given are for cooking after soaking.

Aduki beans Small reddish brown beans with a sweet flavour. Boiling time approximately 30 minutes.

Black beans Oval with shiny black skin and white flesh. Used in soups and as an alternative to red kidney beans. Boiling time approximately 1 hour.

Black-eyed beans Creamy white with a black spot, good with pork casseroles. Boiling time approximately 45 minutes.

Butter beans Large, oval beans with floury texture. Cook gently if required whole. Boiling time approximately 50 minutes.

Cannellini beans White beans often referred to in Italian cooking. Boiling time approximately 1½ hours.

Chick peas Round, beige peas, main ingredient in the Greek dip hummus. Boiling time approximately 1½ hours.

Flageolet beans Pale green oval beans with delicate flavour. Can be used cold in salads with other varieties. Boiling time approximately 1¼ hours.

Haricot beans White oval beans more readily known as baked beans. Boiling time approximately 1¼ hours.

Indian dhals Indian lentils, numerous varieties available in Asian and Indian supermarkets and health stores. Boiling time approximately 1 hour.

Lentils Need no soaking. Come in various colours: red, green or brown are available. Red split lentils cook very quickly to a purée and can be used in soups and casseroles. Brown whole lentils cook quickly but keep their shape; use them in casseroles and salads. Boiling time approximately 30 minutes.

Mung beans Small round green beans, good in stuffings and savoury roasts. The seeds when sprouted are called bean sprouts. Boiling time approximately 30 minutes.

Peas Green or yellow, split or whole, used in soups and purées. Boiling time approximately 45 minutes.

Red kidney beans Dark red with white flesh, used in casseroles and bean salads. Very important to boil them for at least 10 minutes at the start of the cooking time as they contain a substance which can be dangerous if they are not cooked properly. Should be thoroughly cooked before adding to any dish. Boiling time approximately 1 hour. To save time buy canned ready-cooked.

Soya beans Round pale brown beans. Most nutritional of all pulses as they contain first class protein. For this reason they are very popular with vegetarians.

BAKED ONIONS

SERVES 6

A simple and delicious recipe. The flavour retained by cooking the onions in their skins is quite wonderful. Choose six medium-sized onions, all about the same size.

INGREDIENTS

6 onions, with the skin left on

HOW TO MAKE

Heat the oven to 400°F/200°C/gas mark 6. Wipe the onions and place in a small roasting tin. Cook in the oven for about 1½ hours.

Serve with roast and grilled meat and just scoop the onion out of its skin as you would a jacket potato.

FENNEL WITH LEMON BUTTER

SERVES 6

When raw, fennel has a distinct aniseed flavour, which is more subtle when it is cooked. This dish would make a good first course for a summer meal, or could be served as an accompaniment to fish or chicken dishes.

INGREDIENTS

4 large fennel heads
salt and freshly ground black pepper
butter
juice of 1 lemon

HOW TO MAKE

Heat the oven to 350°F/180°C/gas mark 4. Cut each fennel into six wedges and arrange in an ovenproof dish. Season well. Dot with butter and pour over the lemon juice. Cover with a lid or piece of foil and bake in the oven for about 1 hour until the fennel is tender.

PURÉED VEGETABLES

Vegetable purées make an attractive alternative to plain boiled vegetables and they have the added advantage that they can be made ahead and reheated in the oven in a buttered dish covered with buttered foil. Cream can be added as well as butter, if liked.

Celeriac Purée
Cook equal quantities of celeriac and potato in boiling salted water. Drain well, then purée in a blender or food processor. Season to taste with salt and freshly ground black pepper and serve with a good knob of butter melting on top.

Sprout Purée
Cook Brussels sprouts in boiling salted water until just tender. Drain well, then purée with 2 tablespoons milk, salt and pepper in a blender or food processor. Heat a little butter in the bottom of a pan and reheat the purée in this before serving.

Swede and Carrot Purée
Cook equal quantities of carrot and swede in boiling salted water until tender. Drain well, then purée with salt and pepper and a knob of butter in a blender or food processor until smooth. Serve with more butter melting on top.

Parsnip Purée
Cook parsnips in boiling salted water until tender. Drain and purée with salt, pepper, butter and a little curry powder, if liked, in a blender or food processor.

BAKED PARSNIPS WITH FRESH GINGER AND CREAM

SERVES 4

This unusual vegetable dish is particularly good served with baked ham or game. It would make a good main dish for a vegetarian. The quantity here would serve 2 as a main course.

INGREDIENTS

1 lb (450 g) parsnips
1 inch (2.5 cm) piece of fresh root ginger, peeled
knob of butter
salt and freshly ground black pepper
¼ pint (150 ml) double cream

HOW TO MAKE

Heat the oven to 375°F/190°C/gas mark 5. Cut the parsnips into 1 inch (2.5 cm) cubes, blanch for 2 minutes in boiling salted water, then drain. Finely chop or grate the ginger. Melt the butter in a pan, gently soften the ginger, then add the parsnip cubes, tossing to coat in butter. Season well.

Turn into a shallow ovenproof dish and pour the cream over the top. Bake in the oven for about 25–30 minutes, until tender.

LYONNAISE POTATOES

SERVES 6

An excellent way of cooking potatoes when you have friends for supper. They cook by themselves and need no attention at all, and you can serve them in the dish in which they are cooked.

INGREDIENTS

3–4 oz (75–100 g) butter
1 lb (500 g) onions, sliced
2 lb (900 g) potatoes, peeled and sliced
salt and freshly ground black pepper

HOW TO MAKE

Heat the oven to 375°C/190°C/gas mark 5. Melt 2 oz (50 g) butter in a pan and fry the onions for about 5 minutes without browning. Generously butter a 2½–3 pint (1.5–1.75 litre) ovenproof dish with some of the remaining butter and arrange the potatoes and onions in alternate layers, seasoning well between each layer and finishing with a potato layer neatly overlapping.

Melt the remaining butter and pour over the top layer of potatoes, making sure they are well coated. Bake in the oven for 1¾–2 hours. If using a shallow dish, allow about 1½ hours cooking time.

GARLIC CREAM POTATOES

SERVES 4–6

Potatoes served this way are wonderful, especially with something without sauce or gravy, such as lamb chops or steak. See the variation (below) for the classic Gratin Dauphinoise. For a less rich version use single cream instead of double.

INGREDIENTS

2 lb (900 g) potatoes
salt and freshly ground black pepper
2 fat cloves garlic, crushed
½ pint (300 ml) double cream

HOW TO MAKE

Heat the oven to 400°F/200°C/gas mark 6. Generously butter a 3 pint (1.75 litre) shallow ovenproof dish. Peel and slice the potatoes. Arrange half the potatoes over the bottom of the dish and season well. Mix the garlic in the cream. Stir well and pour half on to the potatoes in the dish.

Cover with the remaining potato slices, season well and pour over the remaining cream. Cover with foil and cook in the oven for about 1 hour 20 minutes, removing the foil after 30 minutes. The top should be just beginning to brown. Serve piping hot.

Variation

Gratin Dauphinoise Make as above but grate 2 oz (50 g) Gruyère cheese and scatter over each layer of potatoes.

COOK'S TIP
Raw sliced potatoes discolour very quickly, so dishes like Lyonnaise Potatoes and Garlic Cream Potatoes should be put in the oven as soon as they are prepared. If it is absolutely vital to prepare them up to the cooking stage in advance, first blanch the sliced potatoes very briefly and rinse under cold water, then continue with the recipe.

RED CABBAGE WITH APPLE

SERVES 4–6

The traditional partner to red cabbage is apple. Together they make an ideal accompaniment for fatty meats or pork chops and other grills.

INGREDIENTS

1 small red cabbage
12 oz (350 g) cooking apples, sliced
¼ pint (150 ml) water
1½ oz (40 g) sugar
salt
3 cloves
5 tablespoons wine vinegar
2 oz (50 g) butter
1 tablespoon redcurrant jelly

HOW TO MAKE

Finely shred cabbage and put in saucepan with the apples and water. Add the sugar, salt and cloves, cover and simmer gently for about 40 minutes or until the cabbage is just tender. Strain off the liquid and remove the cloves. Return the cabbage to the pan and add the vinegar, butter and redcurrant jelly, stirring until the butter has melted. Taste and check the seasoning.

GREEN BEANS IN TOMATO SAUCE

SERVES 8

This is a classic way of serving beans in Greece. I prefer to cook the whole beans in boiling salted water until just tender but still crisp – *al dente* – then serve them with the sauce.

INGREDIENTS

2 lb (900 g) French beans, trimmed
1 tablespoon oil
1 onion, finely chopped
1 fat clove garlic, crushed
14 oz (400 g) can chopped tomatoes
salt and freshly ground black pepper
a little sugar

HOW TO MAKE

Heat the oven to 275°F/140°C/gas mark 1. Put the beans in a pan of boiling salted water, bring back to the boil and boil for 1 minute. Drain and then keep warm in an ovenproof dish.

Heat the oil in a saucepan, add the onion, garlic and tomatoes and simmer, uncovered, until reduced to a thick pulp. Add the seasoning and sugar and pour over the beans. Cook in the oven for about 20 minutes.

NOUVELLE RATATOUILLE

SERVES 6

I call this version 'Nouvelle' because the vegetables are still slightly crisp and bright in colour when cooked, rather than mushy and dull as they become when cooked for longer, as in the traditional way of making ratatouille. If you have a glut of fresh tomatoes and wish to use them to make ratatouille, skin them first (see page 125).

INGREDIENTS

2 red peppers
1 yellow pepper
1 lb (450 g) aubergines
5 tablespoons olive oil
2 onions, chopped
2 cloves garlic, crushed
1½ lb (675 g) canned chopped tomatoes
salt and freshly ground black pepper
12 oz (350 g) small courgettes, thinly sliced

HOW TO MAKE

Cut the peppers in half, remove stalks and seeds and slice thinly. Cut the stalks from the aubergines and cut into slices. Blanch in boiling water for 2 minutes, then drain well.

Heat the oil in a large pan, add the onions and garlic and fry gently with the lid on until the onion is transparent but not soft. Add the aubergines and cook for 5 minutes, then stir in the peppers and tomatoes. Season. Finally, add the courgettes, tossing well and cooking fast until the courgettes are just becoming tender. Serve immediately.

COOK'S TIP
When frying onions, be careful to note whether the recipe requires them to be transparent but not soft, or brown, as this will affect the flavour of the finished dish. Onions contain sugar and turn golden brown when fried because the sugar caramelises.

Rösti

SERVES 4–6

Wonderful fried, grated potatoes. Allow the par-boiled potatoes to cool before grating so they are firm and easy to grate.

INGREDIENTS

2 lb (900 g) large potatoes
freshly ground black pepper
4 tablespoons oil
1 oz (25 g) butter

HOW TO MAKE

Scrub potatoes and boil for about 10 minutes, or until the point of a knife can be inserted for about 1 inch (2.5 cm) before meeting resistance. Drain, cool and then peel, leave in a cool place overnight or chill for several hours.

Grate potatoes coarsely into a bowl, season well with pepper and mix. Heat half the butter and oil in a non-stick frying pan and add the grated potato, flattening it with a fish slice or palette knife. Cook very slowly over a low heat for about 20 minutes, until the base is golden brown. Turn out on to a large plate.

Melt the remaining butter and oil in the pan, slide potato cake off the plate into the pan to brown the other side, very slowly as before. Turn on to a warm serving dish and cut in to wedges to serve.

Cheesy leeks with ham

SERVES 4

This recipe is a light meal in itself. For a more substantial dish add cooked ham or bacon. Serve with crusty French bread.

INGREDIENTS

4 leeks
4 slices cooked lean ham

SAUCE
1 oz (25 g) butter
1 oz (25 g) flour
¼ pint (150 ml) milk
3 oz (75 g) mature Cheddar cheese, grated
1 teaspoon Dijon mustard
salt and freshly ground black pepper

HOW TO MAKE

Trim the coarse green ends from the leeks. Wash thoroughly under cold running water, cutting partially through the leek to help remove the grit if they are very dirty. Cook in boiling salted water under tender. Drain, reserving ¼ pint (150 ml) of the cooking liquid for the sauce. Wrap each leek in a slice of ham and arrange in a shallow ovenproof dish.

Melt the butter in a saucepan, add the flour and cook for 1 minute. Gradually blend in the milk and reserved cooking water and bring to the boil, stirring until thickened.

Remove from the heat and stir in two-thirds of the cheese, the mustard and seasoning. Pour the sauce over leeks and sprinkle with remaining cheese. Brown under grill until heated through and bubbling.

MR Mc GREGOR'S BAKE

SERVES 4

Make this when courgettes, tomatoes and peppers are at their cheapest in the shops or at their most plentiful in the garden.

INGREDIENTS

VEGETABLE BASE
1 tablespoon oil
a good knob of butter
8 oz (225 g) onions, chopped
2 cloves garlic, crushed
2 peppers, seeded and chopped
1 lb (450 g) courgettes, sliced
1 lb (450 g) tomatoes, skinned and sliced
salt and freshly ground black pepper

SAUCE TOPPING
a good 1½ oz (40 g) butter
1½ oz (40 g) flour
¾ pint (450 ml) milk
1 teaspoon Dijon mustard
a little grated nutmeg
1 egg, beaten
3 oz (75 g) Cheddar cheese, grated

HOW TO MAKE

Heat the oven to 400°F/200°C/gas mark 6. Heat the oil and butter in a large non-stick pan, then fry the onions gently until tender. Increase the heat and stir fry the garlic and other vegetables except the tomatoes and season well.

Turn the mixture into a large ovenproof shallow dish, about 3 pint (1.7 litre) capacity. Top with the tomato slices and season well.

To make the sauce, melt the butter, add the flour and cook for 1 minute. Gradually blend in the milk and bring to the boil, stirring continuously until thickened, then season well with mustard, salt, pepper and nutmeg. Remove the pan from the heat and stir in the egg.

Pour the sauce over the vegetables and sprinkle with cheese. Bake in the oven for 20 minutes. Serve at once with crusty bread.

BAKED MARROW

SERVES 4

Marrow can be a rather uninteresting watery vegetable. This recipe, however, certainly makes the most of it and is something I look forward to making every summer.

INGREDIENTS

1 lb (450 g) raw minced beef
1 onion, chopped
¼ pint (150 ml) beef stock (see page 14)
2 tablespoons fresh breadcrumbs
salt and freshly ground black pepper
1 medium marrow or overgrown courgette
1 teaspoon Dijon mustard
freshly grated nutmeg
¾ pint (450 ml) white sauce (see page 228)
4 oz (100 g) well-flavoured Cheddar cheese

HOW TO MAKE

Turn the minced beef into a non-stick pan on a low heat to draw out the natural fat, then increase the heat and fry quickly with the onion. Add the stock, bring to the boil, cover and simmer for 20 minutes. Remove from the heat, stir in the breadcrumbs and season well. Meanwhile heat the oven to 425°F/220°C/gas mark 7.

Peel the marrow with a potato peeler, cut into about 8 rings, scoop out and discard the seeds from each ring. Blanch the marrow rings in boiling salted water for about 5 minutes, so they still remain just crisp; drain well.

Butter a shallow oblong dish and arrange the marrow rings in the dish. Spoon the mince into the rings, piling it up on top. Stir Dijon mustard and nutmeg into the white sauce, spoon it over rings, and scatter the cheese on top. Bake in the oven for about 30–40 minutes, or until golden brown and bubbling.

Serve with garlic bread.

COOK'S TIP
Breadcrumbs take no time to make in a processor. Make in bulk and keep a supply in the freezer.

BAKED STUFFED PEPPERS

SERVES 4

Fried chicken livers can be used instead of bacon, or for a vegetarian version leave out the bacon and double up on the mushrooms.

INGREDIENTS

4 red or green peppers
large knob of butter
1 medium onion, chopped
4 oz (100 g) streaky bacon, snipped
4 oz (100 g) button mushrooms, sliced
4 oz (100 g) long grain brown rice, cooked
2 tablespoons chopped parsley
salt and freshly ground black pepper

CHEESE SAUCE
1½ oz (40 g) butter
1½ oz (40 g) flour
¾ pint (450 ml) milk
1 teaspoon Dijon mustard
grated nutmeg
6 oz (175 g) full-flavoured Cheddar cheese, grated
1 egg, beaten

HOW TO MAKE

Heat the oven to 350°F/180°C/gas mark 4. Cut each pepper in half lengthways, remove stem and seeds and arrange the halves in a shallow ovenproof dish so they just fit snugly.

Melt the butter in a large non-stick frying pan and fry the onion until soft. Add the bacon and cook for a few minutes, then add the mushrooms and cook for 1–2 minutes. Stir in the cooked rice and chopped parsley. Season well and divide between the pepper halves.

To make the cheese sauce, melt the butter in a saucepan, stir in the flour and cook for 1 minute. Gradually blend in the milk and bring to the boil, stirring until thickened and smooth. Remove from the heat and stir in the mustard and nutmeg. Season well. Add about half the cheese and the beaten egg. Mix well together. Pour the sauce over and around the peppers. Sprinkle with the remaining cheese and bake in the oven for about 1 hour, until the peppers are tender.

MILD VEGETABLE CURRY

SERVES 4

A delicious combination of tasty vegetables in an authentic curry sauce. A dessertspoon of chopped stem ginger will give the curry extra zip. Serve with garlic bread or crusty rolls. If you want to serve it with rice, replace the potatoes with another root vegetable.

INGREDIENTS

1 tablespoon sunflower oil
1 medium onion, peeled and roughly chopped
1 clove garlic, peeled and crushed
1 teaspoon curry powder
8 oz (225 g) carrots, sliced
8 oz (225 g) young courgettes, sliced
~~*4 sticks celery, sliced*~~
2 lb (450 g) potatoes, peeled and diced
2 oz (50 g) red lentils
1 tablespoon tomato purée
¾ pint (450 ml) vegetable stock
1 tablespoon mango chutney
1 teaspoon ground turmeric
salt and freshly ground black pepper
1 teaspoon cornflour

HOW TO MAKE

Heat the oil in a large saucepan and lightly fry the onion with the garlic and curry powder for 2 minutes.

Add the remaining vegetables and lentils and stir in the tomato purée, vegetable stock, mango chutney and turmeric.

Season well and bring to the boil. Cover and simmer for about 10–15 minutes, stirring occasionally until the vegetables are just tender.

Strain off the stock. Mix 2 tablespoons cold water with the cornflour to make a smooth paste. Pour on the hot stock and mix well. Transfer the vegetables to a plate and keep warm. Meanwhile return the stock to the pan and bring to the boil, stirring until thickened. Return the vegetables to the stock, check the seasoning and serve.

COOK'S TIP
If French bread or rolls are not crisp and fresh enough, sprinkle with water and place in a hot oven for 7 minutes. Serve warm.

DHAL

SERVES 8 WITH
CURRY

A sort of lentil purée, Dhal is a traditional curry accompaniment. This would also make a perfect alternative to potatoes or pasta to serve with grilled or roast meat. You might even persuade your family to enjoy lentils this way. Dhal freezes well.

INGREDIENTS

8 oz (225 g) red lentils
1 bay leaf
2 tablespoons oil
1 large carrot, chopped
1 large green pepper, seeded and chopped
1 large onion, chopped
1/2 inch (1.25 cm) piece fresh root ginger, peeled and finely chopped
1/2 teaspoon ground cinnamon
1/2 teaspoon ground cumin
1/2 teaspoon ground coriander
14 oz (400 g) can chopped tomatoes
salt and freshly ground black pepper

HOW TO MAKE

Rinse the lentils well under cold running water, removing any stones or grit. Drain. Place the lentils in a pan with sufficient cold water to cover. Bring to the boil and add the bay leaf, then simmer, covered, for about 30 minutes, or until the lentils are tender. Drain and remove the bay leaf.

Heat the oil in a large pan, add the vegetables and fry for about 5 minutes, stirring. Add lentils, spices and tomatoes and cook gently until the carrot is soft. Turn into a blender or food processor and process for about 30 seconds – it does not need to be completely smooth, some texture is nice. Rinse out the pan, return mixture to the pan and reheat. Taste for seasoning. Serve hot with curries.

COOK'S TIP
A set of four plastic measuring spoons is invaluable for measuring small quantities of ingredients, like spices. When filled until level they measure one tablespoon, one teaspoon, half a teaspoon and a quarter of a teaspoon.

BAKED STUFFED AUBERGINES

SERVES 6

A vegetarian dish that will appeal to non-vegetarians as well. Use cooked brown rice instead of bulgar wheat, if preferred. Depending on what you are serving this with you may want a sauce to accompany it, such as Instant Yoghurt Sauce (page 226) or Tomato Sauce (page 232).

INGREDIENTS

3 aubergines
oil
salt and freshly ground black pepper
2 onions, chopped
14 oz (400 g) can chopped tomatoes
1 clove garlic, crushed
2 oz (50 g) bulgar wheat
1 tablespoon parsley, chopped
1 oz (25 g) chopped almonds
1 oz (25 g) raisins
2 oz (50 g) well-flavoured Cheddar cheese, grated

HOW TO MAKE

Cut the leaf stem from aubergines, then cook whole for 10 minutes in boiling salted water. Drain and leave to cool. When cool enough to handle, cut in half lengthways and scoop out the flesh, leaving about ½ inch (1.25 cm) thickness in the shell so they don't collapse.

Chop the flesh and set to one side. Brush the outer skins with oil and arrange in an ovenproof dish so they just touch. Season.

Heat 2 tablespoons oil in a non-stick frying pan, add the onions and fry until soft. Add the tomatoes and garlic and cook for about 10 minutes, until most of the liquid has evaporated.

Meanwhile, heat the oven to 350°F/180°C/gas mark 4. Prepare the bulgar wheat according to the packet instructions by pouring on boiling water to just cover wheat, then leave to stand for 10 minutes. Drain well. Remove pan from heat, stir in the tomato mixture, chopped aubergine, parsley, almonds, raisins, bulgar wheat and plenty of seasoning. Mix well. Spoon into aubergine shells and sprinkle the cheese over the top. Bake in the oven for about 20 minutes, until thoroughly heated.

GERMAN ONION TART

SERVES 6–8

If you haven't time to make the yeast base for this tart, use a shortcrust pastry base and bake blind first (see page 43).

INGREDIENTS

DOUGH
6 tablespoons lukewarm water
½ teaspoon sugar
½ oz (15 g) dried yeast
8 oz (225 g) strong flour
2 oz (50 g) butter, melted and cooled
1 egg yolk
½ teaspoon salt

FILLING
1½ oz (40 g) butter
1½ lb (675 g) large mild onions, sliced
3 eggs
¼ pint (150 ml) soured cream
1½ oz (40 g) plain flour
freshly ground black pepper
4 oz (100 g) streaky bacon

HOW TO MAKE

To make the dough, measure the lukewarm water into a bowl, stir in the sugar and sprinkle on the yeast. Leave to stand for about 10 minutes until it is frothy. Stir 4 tablespoons of the flour into the yeast mixture, cover and leave in a warm place for about 15 minutes.

Sift the remaining flour into a bowl, make a well in the centre, stir in the yeast mixture, cooled melted butter, egg yolk and salt. Beat well with a wooden spoon until well mixed. Add a little more milk if the dough looks very dry. Knead well until the dough leaves the sides of the bowl clean. Cover the bowl with a damp cloth and leave in a warm place until the dough has doubled its size.

Meanwhile, make the filling. Melt the butter in a large frying pan, add the onions and fry gently for about 20 minutes, until soft but not brown. Heat the oven to 400°F/200°C/gas mark 6.

Remove the onions from the heat and allow to cool. Blend together eggs, soured cream and flour, season with salt and plenty of pepper and mix with the onions.

Roll out the yeast dough and line a deep 9 inch (23 cm) flan tin. Pour in the filling and smooth the top. Cut bacon into small pieces and sprinkle over top.

Bake in the oven for about 35 minutes, until the top is golden brown and set and the bread crust crisp. Serve warm.

Desserts and Puddings

Puddings needn't be rich and extravagant. What could be nicer than ripe fresh pineapple, or any fresh fruit in season, made into a colourful fruit salad and served with a mixture of cream and yoghurt or *crème fraiche*? And what could be simpler than a selection of beautiful fresh cheeses accompanied by some sweet and juicy grapes?

Homegrown fruit such as rhubarb, gooseberries, currants, apples and plums needn't always be made into crumbles and pies. They are delicious baked with a light sponge topping (see page 160) for a change, or turned into mousses and fools.

Two great standby desserts are Crème Brûlée and Caramel Custard. Both are cooked in a bain-marie – a roasting tin half filled with boiling water. It is essential with both to see that they are not overcooked, but are just set. I always use single rather than double cream for crème brulée as it makes a much lighter custard.

Home-made ice cream is always a popular dessert. My version is dead simple to make and doesn't use an ice cream machine. It is simply a meringue mixture with yolks and flavourings folded in and then frozen. There's no need for whipping halfway through the freezing time, as with traditional ice cream making methods. The basic recipe is vanilla, but the variations are limitless, and I give a selection on page 189.

When entertaining choose a dessert that can be made ahead and kept in the refrigerator until needed, or simply heated through. Consider the richness, texture and colour of the other courses you will be serving when choosing a dessert.

The recipes in this chapter have been grouped according to type, so you will find for example, all the pies and tarts together, and all the custard-based recipes (like Crème Brûlée, Bread and Butter Pudding and Trifle) together.

Simple Fresh Fruit Desserts

SPECIAL FRESH FRUIT SALAD

SERVES 8–10

I am not a great one for making a sugar syrup; I find that it works well simply layering the fruits early in the day, or the day before, with caster sugar. Use about 2 oz (50 g) sugar to each prepared 1 lb (450 g) of fruit – or less if you like it very sharp. First prepare all the citrus fruit, then any fruit that might discolour such as pears, or grapes – the cut side can go brown. Blend the fruits carefully, but well.

INGREDIENTS

1 grapefruit, peeled and segmented
1 melon, peeled, seeded and cut in to cubes
2 eating pears, peeled, cored and sliced
juice of 1 lemon
6–8 oz (175–225 g) caster sugar
8 oz (225 g) black grapes, halved and seeded
2 kiwi fruit, sliced and peeled
1 mango, peeled and cut in to wedges from the stone
few strawberries or raspberries if in season

HOW TO MAKE

Place the fruit in layers in a bowl, sprinkling with lemon juice and sugar between each layer. Continue until all the fruit has been used, finishing with a layer of sugar.

Cover the bowl with a plate or piece of clingfilm and leave overnight in the refrigerator.

Turn into a glass serving dish, mixing lightly so that all the fruits are blended evenly. Serve with plenty of cream.

PEARS IN RED WINE

SERVES 6

Best served well chilled. The pears need to be ripe and unblemished.

INGREDIENTS

6 oz (175 g) granulated sugar
¼ pint (150 ml) water
¼ pint (150 ml) red wine
strip of lemon rind
small piece of cinnamon stick
6 ripe dessert pears
1 rounded teaspoon arrowroot
1 oz (25 g) flaked almonds, toasted

HOW TO MAKE

Measure the sugar, water, wine, lemon rind and cinnamon into a pan and heat gently until the sugar has dissolved, stirring occasionally. Bring to the boil and simmer for 1 minute.

Peel the pears but leave on the stalks; remove the eye from the base. Place the pears in the syrup, cover and gently poach for about 25–30 minutes, until the pears are tender. Carefully lift out the pears with a slotted spoon and arrange in a glass serving dish.

Strain the syrup. Blend the arrowroot with a little cold water in a saucepan, gradually stir in the strained syrup and heat gently, stirring until thickened. Bring to the boil, cook for 2 minutes, then spoon over the pears and leave to cool. When cold, refrigerate until ready to serve. Sprinkle with almonds and serve with thick cream.

CARAMELISED ORANGES

SERVES 6

When satsumas are in the shops you can use them for this recipe. Leave them whole, rather than slicing them like the oranges.

INGREDIENTS

6 thin-skinned oranges
4 oz (100 g) granulated sugar
5 tablespoons water
2 tablespoons brandy or orange liqueur

HOW TO MAKE

Thinly peel the rind from two oranges with a potato peeler, then cut peel into very fine strips. Place them in a small saucepan, cover with cold water, bring to the boil and simmer for about 20 minutes until tender. Drain the strip and reserve.

Slice both ends from the oranges then, standing the fruit on a board, preferably with a channel to catch the juice, slice down and around each fruit to remove all the peel and pith. Slice oranges into rounds, removing any pips, then re-assemble into the original shape and secure with a cocktail stick. Place in an ovenproof dish. Keep all the juice from the oranges and put it in a measuring jug with the brandy or liqueur. Make up to ¼ pint (150 ml) with water.

Measure the sugar and 5 tablespoons of water into a small heavy-based pan and heat slowly, stirring until all the sugar has dissolved. Bring to the boil and cook rapidly until the caramel is a nice dark brown. Remove from the heat and add the orange juice mixture. Be careful as it will splutter. Return the pan to the heat and warm enough to mix the juice and the caramel. Pour over oranges, leave to cool, then chill thoroughly overnight.

Next day transfer to a glass serving dish and pour over the syrup, sprinkle with strips of orange rind and serve with lightly whipped cream.

COOK'S TIP
When buying oranges or any other citrus fruit, choose ones that are heavy for their size as they will be more juicy.

BAKED APPLES

SERVES 4

Bramleys are the best apples to use for baking. Choose unblemished ones.

INGREDIENTS

4 medium cooking apples
mincemeat

HOW TO MAKE

Heat the oven to 400°F/200°C/gas mark 6. Core the apples and make a shallow cut through the skin around the middle of each apple.

Place the apples in a shallow ovenproof dish and fill the centre of each one with mincemeat. Bake in the oven for about 40 minutes, until the apples are soft.

Serve hot with custard or thick cream.

Variations

Use demerara sugar instead of mincemeat or any dried fruits, such as chopped dates or dried apricots, or a mixture of fruit and nuts.

FRUIT CRUMBLE

SERVES 4

It is useful to make a larger amount of crumble topping and keep it in the freezer for a quick pudding.

INGREDIENTS

4 oz (100 g) flour
2 oz (50 g) butter, cut into pieces
3–4 oz (75–100 g) sugar
1 lb (450 g) fruit, such as sliced apples, rhubarb, plums or
* gooseberries*

HOW TO MAKE

Heat the oven to 400°F/200°C/gas mark 6. Measure the flour into a bowl, add the butter and rub in until the mixture resembles fine breadcrumbs. Stir in 1 oz (25 g) sugar.

Place the fruit in a 2 pint (1.2 litre) shallow ovenproof dish or pie dish. Sprinkle with 2–3 oz (50–75 g) sugar depending on the fruit. Spoon over the crumble mixture, press down slightly and bake in the oven for about 30–40 minutes, until the fruit is tender and crumble top pale golden brown. Serve hot with custard.

PLUM AND ALMOND PUDDING

SERVES 4

If fresh plums aren't in season, or to save time, use a 14 oz (400 g) can of plum halves instead of fresh plums. I like to serve this lovely pudding with real custard (see page 235) or Greek yoghurt.

INGREDIENTS

FILLING
1 lb (450 g) Victoria plums
3 oz (75 g) caster sugar
1 tablespoon water

SPONGE TOPPING
4 oz (100 g) caster sugar
4 oz (100 g) soft margarine
2 eggs, beaten
4 oz (100 g) self-raising flour
½ teaspoon almond essence
1 tablespoon flaked almonds
icing sugar to decorate

HOW TO MAKE

To make the filling place the fresh plums, sugar and water in a saucepan and stew lightly. Remove from the heat and allow to cool. Halve the plums and remove the stones.

Grease a 2 pint (1.2 litre) shallow ovenproof dish. Arrange the plum halves on the bottom and pour over any juice. Heat the oven to 350°F/180°C/gas mark 4.

To make the sponge topping, measure the sugar, margarine, eggs, flour and almond essence into a bowl and cream together until smooth. Spoon over the plums and spread the surface level. Sprinkle on the flaked almonds. Bake for about 35–45 minutes until risen and golden. Sift a little icing sugar over the top and serve hot.

Variation

Eve's Pudding   Instead of plums for the filling use apples. Peel and core 1 lb (450 g) cooking apples and slice into the prepared dish. Sprinkle with 3 oz (75 g) demerara sugar. Make the sponge topping as above, but leave out the almond essence and the flaked almonds.

Right: *Plum and Almond Pudding (above)*

SUMMER PUDDING

SERVES 8

A simple recipe to make when there's a glut of these fruits. Serve with lots of thick cream or Greek yoghurt.

INGREDIENTS

6 to 8 large fairly thick slices white bread, crusts removed
8 oz (225 g) rhubarb, cut into ½ inch (1.25 cm) lengths
8 oz (225 g) blackberries
4 oz (100 g) blackcurrants
8 oz (225 g) redcurrants
12 oz (350 g) granulated sugar
6 tablespoons water
8 oz (225 g) small strawberries, hulled
8 oz (225 g) raspberries, hulled
thick cream to serve

HOW TO MAKE

Put one slice of bread aside for the top and use the remainder to line the base and sides of a 2½ pint (1.5 litre) basin (or use a round, fairly shallow dish).

Put the rhubarb, blackberries and currants into a saucepan, and add the sugar and water. Bring to the boil and simmer for a few minutes until barely tender, stirring. Add the strawberries and raspberries and cook for a further minute.

Turn the fruits into the basin, saving a small bowlful to spoon over the top of the pudding when serving. Lay the reserved slice of bread on top of the fruits and bend over the tops of the bread slices at the sides towards the centre. Place a saucer on top, pressing down a little until the juices rise to the top of the basin.

Leave the pudding to soak until cold, then put in the refrigerator overnight. Turn out just before serving and top with the reserved fruits.

Left: *Pear and Chocolate Soufflé (page 188)*

APPLE CAKE

SERVES 6

An excellent way of using up windfall apples, much nicer than apple pie. Delicious served with cream. If you are fond of almonds sprinkle the cake mixture with 1 oz (25 g) flaked almonds before baking.

INGREDIENTS

8 oz (225 g) self-raising flour
1½ level teaspoons baking powder
8 oz (225 g) caster sugar
2 large eggs
1 teaspoon almond essence
5 oz (150 g) margarine, melted
1 lb (450 g) cooking apples, peeled, cored and sliced
caster sugar for sprinkling

HOW TO MAKE

Heat the oven to 325°F/160°C/gas mark 3. Line an 8 inch (20 cm) loose-bottomed cake tin with baking parchment or greased greaseproof paper.

Sieve the flour and baking powder into a bowl with the sugar. Beat the eggs and almond essence together, then stir into the flour with the margarine. Mix well. Spoon half of this mixture into the tin, arrange the apple slices on top and spoon the remaining mixture over the apples in blobs.

Bake in the oven for about 1½ hours, until golden brown and shrinking away from the sides of the tin. Leave to cool for about 15 minutes, then turn out, sprinkle with caster sugar and serve warm with cream.

Batter Puddings

PANCAKES

SERVES 8

The skill in making pancakes is getting them thin. If the first pancake you cook is too thick, thin the batter down with a little water.

INGREDIENTS

4 oz (100 g) flour
1 egg
½ pint (300 ml) milk (or milk and water mixed)
oil for cooking

HOW TO MAKE

Measure flour into a bowl. Make a well in the centre, add egg and a little milk. Mix to a smooth paste and gradually whisk in remaining milk.

Lightly oil a non-stick omelette pan, allow to become very hot, pour in a film of batter and cook until golden, turn over and briefly cook the other side.

Serve immediately with lemon and sugar.

Variation

Savoury Pancakes   The same batter can be used for savoury pancakes with a fish, meat or vegetarian filling. Use up all the batter and stack the pancakes to one side. Fill, then re-heat when required. Spread the filling on the pancakes, roll up and top with grated cheese or a cheese sauce and heat through until bubbling. Also see Cod and Mushroom Pancakes (page 58).

APPLE FRITTERS

SERVES 4

This batter can also be used to coat chunks of banana, when it is best to use slightly under-ripe fruit.

INGREDIENTS

1 lb (450 g) cooking apples
4 oz (100 g) plain flour
1 egg, separated
¼ pint (150 ml) milk
deep fat or oil for frying
caster sugar
cinnamon

HOW TO MAKE

Peel and quarter the apples and remove the cores. If the apples are very large cut the quarters in half. (If liked the apples could be peeled and cut across in rings.)

Put the flour in a bowl and make a well in the centre. Blend the egg yolk with the milk and then add to the flour to make a smooth thick batter. Whisk the egg white until stiff and then fold into the batter.

Heat the oil or fat in a large pan, dip the fruit into the batter, one piece at a time, and then fry until golden brown. Lift out with a slotted spoon and drain on kitchen paper. Toss in a mixture of caster sugar with a little cinnamon added and then serve at once.

Pies and Tarts

BLACKBERRY AND APPLE PIE

SERVES 4–6

Use any seasonal fruit for this pie. Adjust the quantity of sugar according to the tartness of the fruit.

INGREDIENTS

8 oz (225 g) cooking apples, peeled, cored and sliced
4 oz (100 g) blackberries
about 2 oz (50 g) sugar
1 tablespoon water
1 tablespoon cornflour

PASTRY
8 oz (225 g) flour
2 oz (50 g) block margarine
2 oz (50 g) lard
about 3 tablespoons cold water

HOW TO MAKE

Put the apples, blackberries, sugar and water into a saucepan and simmer gently until the apple is tender. Blend the cornflour with a little cold water and stir into the fruit. Cook for 2 minutes, or until the mixture has thickened. Leave to cool.

To make the pastry, measure flour into a large bowl, add the fats cut into small pieces, and rub in with fingertips until the mixture resembles fine breadcrumbs. Add the cold water and work to a firm dough. If the fruit has not cooled, wrap pastry in foil and chill.

Heat the oven to 425°F/220°C/gas mark 7. Divide the pastry in half, roll out one piece and use to line the base of an 8 inch (20 cm) enamel or foil pie plate. Spoon the fruit on to the pastry. Dampen the edge with a little water. Roll out the remaining pastry and use to cover fruit. Seal edges firmly and decorate (see below).

Make two small slits in the top of the pie with a sharp knife to allow steam to escape. Brush with a little milk and bake in the oven for about 45 minutes, until the pastry is golden brown and crisp.

COOK'S TIP
The easiest way to decorate the edges of a pie is to press all round the edge with the back of a floured fork.

VERY SPECIAL MINCE PIES

SERVES 10 AT LEAST!

A different and easier way of making a large mince pie. The attractive topping makes it less heavy and, as a bonus, you get plenty of mincemeat in each slice!

INGREDIENTS

PASTRY BASE
6 oz (175 g) flour
4 oz (100 g) block margarine, cut into pieces
1 tablespoon icing sugar
2–3 tablespoons cold water

FILLING
about 1 lb (450 g) mincemeat

TOPPING
4 oz (100 g) margarine, just melted
4 oz (100 g) self-raising flour
2 oz (50 g) semolina
2 oz (50 g) caster sugar

HOW TO MAKE

Lightly grease a 13 × 9 inch (33 × 23 cm) Swiss roll tin.

For the pastry base, measure the flour into a bowl and rub in the margarine until the mixture resembles fine breadcrumbs. Stir in the sugar and sufficient water to mix to a firm dough. Wrap in clingfilm and chill if time allows. Meanwhile, heat the oven to 400°F/200°C/gas mark 6.

Roll out the pastry on a lightly floured surface and use to line the tin. Spread generously with the mincemeat.

For the topping, measure all the ingredients into a bowl and knead together to form a soft dough. Using a coarse grater, grate this mixture on top of the mincemeat. If it is too soft to grate, then chill in the refrigerator for about 15 minutes.

Bake in the oven for about 40 minutes, until pale golden brown. If it begins to get too brown, then lay a piece of foil over the top. Allow to cool, then serve in slices.

COOK'S TIP
The secrets of successful pastry making are cold hands, chilled fat, cold (or iced) water and a cool rolling-out surface (marble is best). Chill the dough for 30 minutes before baking if time allows, as this prevents shrinkage of the pastry as it cooks. See page 166 more pastry-making tips.

OLD ENGLISH TREACLE TART

SERVES 6–8

Treacle tart is a favourite recipe that is easy to prepare and always popular. Serve with real custard (see page 235), cream or Vanilla Ice Cream (see pages 188–9).

INGREDIENTS

6 oz (175 g) flour
3 oz (75 g) block margarine, cut into pieces
about 2 tablespoons cold water
about 9 good tablespoons golden syrup
about 5 oz (150 g) fresh breadcrumbs
grated rind and juice of 1 lemon

HOW TO MAKE

Measure flour into a bowl and rub in the margarine until the mixture resembles fine breadcrumbs. Add sufficient water to mix to a firm dough. Roll out thinly on a lightly floured surface and use to line a 9 inch (23 cm) loose-bottomed flan tin. Leave to chill in the refrigerator for 30 minutes.

Meanwhile, heat the oven to 400°F/200°C/gas mark 6. Heat the syrup in a large pan until runny, then stir in the breadcrumbs, lemon rind and juice. Pour into the pastry case, don't worry if the mixture looks runny at this stage, the breadcrumbs will absorb the syrup.

Bake in the oven for 10 minutes, then reduce the temperature to 350°F/180°C/gas mark 4 and bake for a further 25–30 minutes, until the tart is cooked. Leave to cool in the tin for a few minutes, then lift out to serve.

COOK'S TIP
When rubbing fat into flour for pastry, use a large mixing bowl and first cut the fat into small pieces with a knife. Then use your fingertips and thumbs to lightly rub the flour and fat together. Raise your hands above the bowl as you do so, to help trap air into the mixture as it falls back into the bowl. Use a light touch and don't over handle the dough at any stage.

BAKEWELL TART

SERVES 8

This makes a delicious tart – although it contains only almond essence, it tastes very almondy.

INGREDIENTS

PASTRY
6 oz (175 g) flour
3 oz (75 g) margarine, cut into small pieces
about 2 tablespoons cold water

FILLING
4 oz (100 g) margarine
4 oz (100 g) caster sugar
4 oz (100 g) ground rice or semolina
½ teaspoon almond essence
1 egg, beaten
about 2 tablespoons apricot jam
a few flaked almonds

HOW TO MAKE

First make the pastry. Measure the flour into a large bowl, add the margarine and rub in until the mixture resembles breadcrumbs. Mix to a stiff dough with the water: add all the water at once and mix with a round-bladed knife, then gather the lump of pastry together. Rest the pastry, wrapped in clingfilm, in the refrigerator for 30 minutes. Meanwhile, heat the oven to 400°F/200°C/gas mark 6.

Put a baking sheet in the oven on the shelf just above the centre. Roll out the pastry on a floured surface and use to line an 8–9 inch (20–23 cm) flan tin. Prick the base well.

To make the filling, melt the margarine in a pan and add the sugar, ground rice or semolina, almond essence and egg. Spread the base of the flan with the jam, then pour in the filling. Sprinkle the top with flaked almonds.

Bake in the oven for about 35 minutes, until the pastry is pale golden brown at the edges and the filling golden brown too. Remove from the oven and leave to cool in the flan tin for a few minutes. Serve cut into wedges.

TARTE TATIN

SERVES 6

This French apple tart has a wonderful crisp base as it is cooked upside down.

INGREDIENTS

2 oz (50 g) butter, cut into pieces
2 oz (50 g) light muscovado sugar
2 lb (900 g) Cox's eating apples, peeled cored and thickly sliced
finely grated rind and juice of 1 lemon

PASTRY
4 oz (100 g) flour
3 oz (75 g) butter
1 egg yolk
scant tablespoon water
1/2 oz (15 g) icing sugar

HOW TO MAKE

Lightly grease an 8 inch (20 cm) sandwich tin. Measure butter and sugar into a heavy pan and melt together without boiling, until sugar has dissolved, stirring occasionally. Pour into the base of the tin. Mix the apples, lemon juice and rind together, then turn into the sandwich tin. Either leave apple pieces as they are or arrange in a circle. Leave to cool. Meanwhile, heat the oven to 425°F/220°C/gas mark 7.

For the pastry, measure the flour into a large bowl, and rub in the butter until it resembles fine breadcrumbs. Add the egg yolk, water and icing sugar and mix to a firm dough. Roll out on a lightly floured surface and use to cover the apples. Trim the surplus pastry.

Bake in the oven for 20–25 minutes, until the pastry is crisp and golden brown. Remove from the oven: the pastry will have shrunk a little. Tip the juices from the tin into a small pan and reduce to a caramelised sauce for about 3–4 minutes. Turn the tart out on to a plate, with the pastry at the bottom, and pour the sauce over the apples.

Serve warm with lots of cream or natural yoghurt.

Steamed Puddings

STEAMED TREACLE SPONGE

SERVES 4

A satisfying nursery pudding that is so good on a chilly winter day. Children love this. Serve with lots of custard (see page 235) or cream.

INGREDIENTS

4 oz (100 g) soft margarine
4 oz (100 g) caster sugar
2 eggs, beaten
6 oz (175 g) self-raising flour
1 teaspoon baking powder
a little milk, to mix
about 2 good tablespoons golden syrup

HOW TO MAKE

Grease a 1½ pint (900 ml) pudding basin. Put the margarine, sugar, eggs, flour and baking powder into a large roomy bowl and beat well until thoroughly blended. Add enough milk for a dropping consistency. Spoon the golden syrup into the pudding basin, then add the sponge mixture and cover with a lid of greased foil with a pleat in it to allow the pudding to rise.

Steam in a steamer, or use a large saucepan with enough boiling water to come halfway up the basin, for 1½ hours.

Keep the water boiling in the pan, topping up when needed with more boiling water. If using a saucepan, stand the basin on an old saucer, upturned, to keep the basin off the bottom.

Turn out on to a warm plate and serve with custard.

Variations

Chocolate Sponge Pudding Omit the syrup and blend 4 tablespoons sieved cocoa into the flour. Serve with chocolate sauce (see page 234).

Jam Sponge Pudding Omit the syrup and use jam instead. Plum is especially good.

Lemon or Orange Sponge Add the grated rind of 1 lemon or orange to the basic mixture and omit the syrup.

CHRISTMAS PLUM PUDDING

SERVES 8

Turn the pudding out before serving lunch, leave the basin on top to keep it moist. If you wish to flame the pudding, heat both a spoon and the brandy or rum, *then* pour over the pudding and set alight at once. Serve with Brandy Butter (page 235), if liked.

INGREDIENTS

2 oz (50 g) self-raising flour
1 teaspoon mixed spice
12 oz (350 g) mixed dried fruit
3 oz (75 g) fresh breadcrumbs
3 oz (75 g) prepared suet
1 small cooking apple
1 oz (25 g) almonds
1 rounded tablespoon marmalade
3 oz (75 g) grated carrot
4 oz (100 g) soft brown sugar
2 eggs, beaten

HOW TO MAKE

Grease a 1½ pint (900 ml) pudding basin.

Sift together the flour and spice. Measure the dried fruit into a large bowl with the breadcrumbs and suet. Peel and coarsely grate the apple. Roughly chop the almonds and add to the bowl with the apple, marmalade and carrot. Stir in the flour and sugar and mix well together. Stir in the eggs and mix thoroughly. Turn into the greased basin, cover with greaseproof paper and a lid of foil with a pleat in it to allow the pudding to rise.

Steam in a steamer or a large saucepan with enough boiling water to come halfway up the basin for 6 hours. Keep the water boiling in the pan, topping up as necessary during cooking. Lift out of the pan, keeping the greaseproof and foil on. Cover with fresh foil and store in a cool place until required.

Simmer for a further 3 hours on Christmas Day.

COOK'S TIP
When steaming puddings, put a few glass marbles in the bottom of the double pan. They will rattle and warn you that the pan has boiled dry.

Mousses and Creams

PASSION PUDDING

SERVES 6

Otherwise known as Barbados Cream – I have called it both these names over the past few years! The easiest pudding to make – it takes all of 5 minutes – and not as wicked as cream alone. Individual dishes are a good idea when you have a choice of desserts: I make these in ramekins or syllabub cups.

INGREDIENTS

½ pint (300 ml) double cream
1 pint (600 ml) natural yoghurt
soft brown sugar

HOW TO MAKE

Lightly whip the cream, blend in the yoghurt and turn into a 1½ pint (900 ml) glass dish or six small ramekin dishes. Sprinkle with a ¼ inch (0.5 cm) layer of sugar.

Put in the refrigerator and chill overnight. Sprinkle again with sugar before serving well chilled.

REFRESHING LEMON MOUSSE

SERVES 6–8

This is a deliciously light mousse as it contains no cream.

INGREDIENTS

4 eggs, separated
4 oz (100 g) caster sugar
grated rind and juice of 2 large lemons
½ oz (15 g) powdered gelatine
3 tablespoons cold water
whipped cream, lemon slices and mint, for decoration

HOW TO MAKE

Put the egg yolks in a bowl with the sugar and beat until well blended and creamy, then add the lemon rind and juice. Put the whites in a separate bowl ready for whisking.

Sprinkle the gelatine over the water in a small bowl and leave for about 3 minutes to become spongy. Set the bowl over a pan of simmering water until the gelatine has dissolved, then allow to cool slightly. Stir into the yolk mixture. Leave to cool, but not set.

Whisk the egg whites, using an electric whisk, until stiff, then fold into the lemon mixture. Pour into a 2 pint (1.2 litre) glass dish and chill in the refrigerator until set. Decorate with whipped cream, lemon slices and mint.

WILD BRAMBLE MOUSSE

SERVES 6–8

Frozen blackberries are equally as good as fresh ones.

INGREDIENTS

1½ lb (675 g) blackberries
6 oz (175 g) caster sugar
juice of ½ large lemon
½ oz (15 g) powdered gelatine
3 tablespoons cold water
¼ pint (150 ml) double cream
2 egg whites
¼ pint (150 ml) whipping cream
few blackberries, for decoration

HOW TO MAKE

Put the blackberries in a pan with the sugar and lemon juice. Cover and cook over a low heat for about 15 minutes until the blackberries are soft and the juice is beginning to run out. Purée in a blender or food processor, then sieve to remove the seeds. Pour the purée into a large bowl.

Sprinkle the gelatine over the water in a small bowl and leave to stand for about 3 minutes to become spongy. Set the bowl over a pan of simmering water until the gelatine has dissolved, then allow to cool slightly. Stir the gelatine into the large bowl of fruit purée and leave on one side until cold and just beginning to thicken.

Lightly whip the double cream until it forms soft peaks and whisk the egg whites with an electric whisk until they form peaks. Fold them both into the slightly thickened purée until blended. Spoon the mixture into individual ramekin dishes or stemmed glasses and chill until set.

Decorate with whipped cream and blackberries.

Variations

You can use other fruit such as strawberries, raspberries or loganberries. If making a mousse from strawberries or raspberries there is no need to cook the fruit first, though the raspberry purée will need sieving to remove the pips.

If making a moulded mousse to turn out, increase the gelatine by half again so that the mousse will hold its shape. To turn out quickly, dip the dish into very hot water to loosen the mousse, then invert on to a wet plate, so that if the mousse is not quite central you can gently ease it over the the centre of the plate.

CHOCOLATE MOUSSE

SERVES 6–8

There really is no need to use whipped cream in this mousse. Evaporated milk gives light richness and the evaporated milk flavour is masked by the chocolate.

INGREDIENTS

½ oz (15 g) powdered gelatine
grated rind and juice of 1 orange
8 oz (225 g) plain chocolate
4 eggs, separated
2 tablespoons orange liqueur or brandy
4 oz (100 g) caster sugar
1 small can evaporated milk, chilled
whipped cream, for decoration

HOW TO MAKE

Sprinkle the gelatine over the orange juice in a small bowl and leave for about 3 minutes to become spongy. Set the bowl over a pan of simmering water until the gelatine has dissolved. Break the chocolate into a bowl and place over a pan of hot water. Leave until melted. Add the egg yolks and orange rind, remove from the heat and stir well.

Add the gelatine to the chocolate mixture, then the liqueur or brandy. Stir well to mix and leave until cool but not set. Whisk the egg whites until frothy, then add the sugar a teaspoon at a time, whisking between each addition until it is like a meringue.

Whisk the evaporated milk until the whisk leaves a trail when it is lifted out. Fold the chocolate into the egg whites and then fold in the evaporated milk, using a metal spoon and or balloon whisk in a figure-of-eight movement to ensure thorough mixing without knocking all the air out.

Turn the mixture into a 2½ pint (1.5 litre) dish, chill until set, then decorate with whipped cream.

COOK'S TIP
Always melt chocolate in a bowl set over a pan of simmering water. The water should not be boiling, and should not touch the bottom of the bowl. If chocolate is heated too rapidly it will burn or 'scramble', for which there is no remedy.

POTS OF CHOCOLATE

SERVES 6

Rich chocolate mousse served in tiny chocolate pots or ramekins.

INGREDIENTS

12 oz (350 g) plain chocolate
6 eggs, separated
2 tablespoons rum or brandy
¼ pint (150 ml) double cream

HOW TO MAKE

Break the chocolate into a bowl, and place over a pan of simmering water. Heat until the chocolate melts, stirring occasionally. Remove from the heat and beat in the egg yolks and rum or brandy.

Whisk the egg whites until stiff and fold into the chocolate mixture. Spoon into six individual pots or ramekins and chill in the refrigerator for at least 3 hours until set. Whip the cream until stiff and put into a piping bag fitted with a ½ inch (1.25 cm) star nozzle, then pipe on to the mousses.

LEMON SYLLABUB

SERVES 4

To make a less rich syllabub, use half whipped double cream and half Greek yoghurt. Serve with shortbread biscuits.

INGREDIENTS

½ pint (300 ml) double cream, whipped
finely grated rind and juice of 1 lemon
1 tablespoon brandy
1 tablespoon sherry
2 oz (50 g) caster sugar

HOW TO MAKE

Place all the ingredients in a bowl and mix together. Serve in small glasses or syllabub cups.

Variation

Fresh Kiwi Syllabub   For an attractive and refreshing variation on the basic syllabub, peel and slice 3 kiwi fruit and use the slices to line four tall glasses (this takes a little time). Prepare the syllabub mixture as described above and spoon it into the glasses.

Cheesecakes

LEMON CHEESECAKE

SERVES 6–8

This cheesecake is very quick to make. Decorate the top with fruits that are in season – grapes, sliced kiwi fruit, strawberries – or sugared lemon slices.

INGREDIENTS

3 oz (75 g) digestive biscuits
1½ oz (40 g) butter
1 oz (25 g) demerara sugar
8 oz (225 g) rich cream cheese
14 oz (400 g) can condensed milk
grated rind and juice of 3 lemons
¼ pint (150 ml) soured cream
fresh seasonal fruit, for decoration

HOW TO MAKE

Place the biscuits in a polythene bag and crush with a rolling pin. Melt the butter in a pan, add the sugar and biscuit crumbs and mix well. Turn into an 8 inch (20 cm) loose-bottomed cake tin and press firmly on to the base with the back of a spoon.

Put the cream cheese into a bowl and cream well until soft, then beat in the condensed milk until smooth. Mix in the lemon rind and juice. Pour over the biscuit base, smooth the top and chill in the refrigerator until set, preferably overnight.

Loosen the sides of the tin, press up the base and lift the cheesecake on to a flat dish. Spread the top with the soured cream and decorate with fruit.

COOK'S TIP
Biscuit bases are a good way of using up broken biscuits from the bottom of the biscuit tin. If they've gone a bit soft, crisp them first by placing on a baking tray in a warm oven for a few minutes. To keep biscuits dry, place a sugar cube in the biscuit tin. This will absorb any moisture.

GRAPEFRUIT CHEESECAKE

SERVES 8

This cheesecake is sharp, rich and creamy. To turn out, dip the tin in a bowl of very hot water for a moment, then put a serving plate on top of the tin and invert. Lift the tin off the cheesecake, peel off the circle of greaseproof paper and decorate as suggested in the recipe. This method means that you get a crisp base to the cheesecake and you do not need to buy a springform tin.

INGREDIENTS

½ oz (15 g) powdered gelatine
3 tablespoons cold water
1 lb (450 g) cream cheese
grated rind and juice of 2 grapefruit
3 oz (75 g) caster sugar
½ pint (300 ml) whipping cream
4 oz (100 g) ginger biscuits
2 oz (50 g) butter
1 oz (25 g) demerara sugar
black and white seedless grapes, for decoration

HOW TO MAKE

Sprinkle the gelatine over the water in a small bowl and leave to stand for 3 minutes to become spongy. Set the bowl over a pan of simmering water until the gelatine has dissolved. Remove from the heat and leave to cool.

Cream the cheese until soft, then gradually beat in the grapefruit rind and juice and the caster sugar. Stir in the cooled gelatine. Whisk the cream until it is thick, but not stiff, and fold into the cheese.

Place a circle of greaseproof paper in the bottom of a lightly oiled 8 inch (20 cm) cake tin and turn the cheesecake mixture into the tin. Transfer to the refrigerator.

Place the biscuits in a polythene bag and crush with a rolling pin. Melt the butter in a pan and stir in the biscuit crumbs and demerara sugar. Press this mixture over the cheesecake and return to the refrigerator for several hours, preferably overnight.

Turn out the cheesecake on to a serving plate and remove the greaseproof paper. Decorate the top with halved black and white grapes.

CONTINENTAL CHEESECAKE

SERVES 6–8

Wonderful cooked cheesecake.

INGREDIENTS

3 oz (75 g) digestive biscuits
1½ oz (40 g) butter, melted
1 oz (25 g) demerara sugar
2 oz (50 g) soft margarine
6 oz (175 g) caster sugar
1 lb (450 g) curd cheese
1 oz (25 g) flour
finely grated rind and juice of 1 lemon
3 eggs, separated
6 oz (175 g) sultanas
5 fl oz (150 ml) double cream, lightly whipped
icing sugar, for decoration

HOW TO MAKE

Heat the oven to 325°F/160°C/gas mark 3. Lightly grease a 9 inch (23 cm) loose-bottomed cake tin and line with baking parchment or greased greaseproof paper.

Place the biscuits in a polythene bag and crush with a rolling pin. Melt the butter in a pan, add the sugar and biscuit crumbs and mix well. Spread over the base of the tin and press down firmly with the back of a metal spoon. Leave to set.

Put the margarine, sugar, curd cheese, flour, lemon rind and juice and egg yolks into a large bowl. Beat until smooth. Add the sultanas. Fold in the cream. Whisk the egg whites until stiff and fold into mixture. Pour on to the crust.

Bake in the oven for about 1 hour until set. Turn off the oven and leave the cheesecake in the oven to cool for an hour. Run a knife round the edge of the tin, push the base up through the cake tin, and remove side paper.

Transfer to a serving plate and dust with sieved icing sugar to serve.

COOK'S TIP
To get maximum juice from a lemon or orange, it helps if the fruit is warm, or at least at room temperature rather than straight from the refrigerator. If you have a microwave, cut the fruit in half, put the cut sides on a plate and microwave for a few seconds. The juice will be plentiful.

Custard-based Desserts

SICILIAN CREAM

SERVES 6

This is a simplified Cordon Bleu recipe. If you like a lighter topping, use half cream and half plain yoghurt.

INGREDIENTS

6 oz (175 g) apricot jam
3 large eggs
1 tablespoon caster sugar
¾ pint (450 ml) milk
a few drops of vanilla essence
½ pint (300 ml) double cream, whipped

HOW TO MAKE

Heat the oven to 325°F/160°C/gas mark 3. Spread the jam in the base of a 2 pint (1.2 litre) soufflé dish.

Whisk two whole eggs and one egg yolk in a small bowl with the sugar. Heat the milk until just warm, but do not boil. Pour it on to the egg mixture and add a little vanilla essence to taste. Strain into the dish on top of the jam.

Cover with a lid of foil and stand in a baking tin half-filled with hot water and bake in the oven for 1¾ hours, or until the custard is set. Lift out the dish and leave to cool, then chill overnight in the refrigerator.

Whisk the egg white until stiff and then fold into the cream and spread over the custard.

CARAMEL CUSTARDS

SERVES 8

I always think that individual caramel custards are best. Leave them in the ramekin dishes or cups until the last moment before turning out, otherwise the caramel topping loses its shine and colour. Serve very cold. To make a large crème caramel, use a 1¾ pint (1 litre) soufflé dish and bake in the oven for about 1½ hours. If you have no vanilla sugar, use 2 oz (50 g) caster sugar and add a few drops of vanilla essence to the custard.

INGREDIENTS

4 oz (100 g) granulated sugar
4 tablespoons water
5 eggs
2 oz (50 g) vanilla sugar (see page 188)
1¼ pints (750 ml) milk

HOW TO MAKE

Heat the oven to 300°F/150°C/gas mark 2. To make the caramel, put the granulated sugar and water in a heavy saucepan and dissolve over a low heat. Bring to the boil and boil until the syrup is a pale golden brown. Remove from the heat and quickly pour into eight small ramekins.

For the custard, first mix the eggs and vanilla sugar together. Warm the milk in a saucepan over a low heat until it is hand-hot, then pour it on to the egg mixture, stirring constantly.

Butter the sides of the ramekins above the caramel. Strain the custard into the ramekins and place in a roasting tin half-filled with hot water. Bake in the oven for 45 minutes or until set.

Remove the caramel custards from the oven and leave to cool and set for at least 12 hours or overnight in the refrigerator. Turn out on to individual dishes to serve.

CRÈME BRÛLÉE

SERVES 4–6

Make the rich cream custard a day ahead, then chill overnight. Next day, sprinkle with a thick layer of demerara sugar and brown under the grill a couple of hours before serving. Chill well again. If preferred, bake in six individual soufflé dishes.

INGREDIENTS

1 egg
3 egg yolks
¾ pint (450 ml) single cream
1½ oz (40 g) caster sugar
a few drops of vanilla essence
2–3 oz (50–75 g) demerara sugar

HOW TO MAKE

Heat the oven to 300°F/150°C/gas mark 2. Blend the whole egg, egg yolks, cream, caster sugar and vanilla essence together and turn into 2 pint (1.2 litre) soufflé dish or other ovenproof dish. Stand the dish in a roasting tin containing 1 inch (2.5 cm) hot water and bake in the oven for about 1 hour, or until just firm. Remove from the oven and cool, then leave in the refrigerator overnight.

About 2 hours before serving, sprinkle the top with the demerara sugar and brown under a hot grill for 3–4 minutes, until the sugar has melted and become crisp. Watch carefully to make sure it does not burn.

Chill again before serving.

Variation

Add thinly sliced apples or apricots, if preferred, and a little sugar to the dish before pouring on the cream and egg mixture.

WICKEDLY RICH BRÛLÉE

SERVES 6

If you can't get seedless grapes, use large black grapes cut in half and scoop out the pips.

INGREDIENTS

1 lb (450 g) seedless black grapes, halved
4 oz (100 g) demerara sugar
½ pint (300 ml) double cream
½ pint (300 ml) Greek-style yoghurt

HOW TO MAKE

Arrange the grapes in the bottom of a 2 pint (1.2 litre) ovenproof dish and sprinkle with about half the sugar. Put the cream into a roomy bowl and lightly beat until beginning to thicken, add the yoghurt and mix together. Spoon the mixture over the grapes and chill for at least 6 hours, preferably overnight.

About 3 hours before serving, sprinkle on the remaining demerara sugar in a thick layer and put under a hot grill until the sugar melts and caramelises to a golden brown. Watch carefully to make sure it does not burn. Return to refrigerator until ready to serve.

THE BEST BREAD AND BUTTER PUDDING

SERVES 6

A long time favourite in our house. It is best left to stand before baking though if the bread is fresh it seems to work well without.

INGREDIENTS

about 3 oz (75 g) butter
9 thin slices white bread, crusts removed
4 oz (100 g) sultanas and currants, mixed
grated rind of 1 lemon
about 3 oz (75 g) demerara sugar
¾ pint (450 ml) milk
2 eggs

HOW TO MAKE

Thoroughly butter a 2½ pint (1.5 litre) ovenproof dish. Melt the butter in a saucepan and dip the bread into it, coating one side with it (this is easier than spreading the bread with butter).

Cut each slice in three and arrange half the bread over the base of the dish, butter side down. Cover with the fruit, lemon rind and half the sugar. Top with the rest of the bread, butter side uppermost, then sprinkle with the remaining sugar.

Blend the milk and eggs together and pour over the pudding. Leave to stand for about an hour.

Heat the oven to 350°F/180°C/gas mark 4. Bake the pudding in the oven for about 40 minutes, until pale golden brown and set.

BOOSEY TRIFLE

SERVES 6

Trifle is something that has gone very much out of fashion these days, but I welcome it back. It is best made in a shallow glass dish. If time is short, make thick custard using custard powder and the top of the milk, then whisk well in a blender or food processor – the result will be beautifully creamy and the colour and texture lighter.

INGREDIENTS

8 oz (225 g) can pears
6 individual sponge cakes, split in half
strawberry jam
2 oz (50 g) ratafia biscuits
12 maraschino cherries, chopped
5 tablespoons sherry
1/4 pint (150 ml) whipping cream
1/2 oz (15 g) blanched almonds, split and lightly toasted

CUSTARD
3 egg yolks
1 oz (25 g) caster sugar
1 heaped teaspoon cornflour
1/2 pint (300 ml) milk

HOW TO MAKE

Drain the pears, reserving the juice, then cut the fruit into small pieces. Sandwich the sponge cakes together with the strawberry jam. Put with the pears on the bottom of a shallow 2 pint (1.2 litre) serving dish and top with the ratafia biscuits. Sprinkle over the chopped cherries, pear juice, maraschino syrup and sherry.

For the custard, mix together the egg yolks, sugar and cornflour. Warm the milk in a saucepan over a low heat until it is hand-hot, then pour it on to the yolk mixture, stirring constantly. Return the mixture to the saucepan and cook gently, stirring until it thickens. Do not allow to boil, otherwise the custard will curdle. Allow to cool, then pour over the sponge cakes and chill until set.

Lightly whip the cream until it is thick, then spread it over the custard. Spike with the almonds and serve.

COOK'S TIP
To blanch almonds, place in a pan of boiling water for 1–2 minutes. Drain and when cool enough to handle, squeeze one end of the nut and it will slip out of its skin.

Meringues and Meringue-based Desserts

MERINGUES

MAKES 12 MERINGUES

Often a problem. I promise this is a foolproof method and I guarantee success. Use non-stick silicone paper, which can be bought from any good stationer and may be brushed off after use and used again and again. I like meringues to be off-white in colour so that they look home-make, not stark white like many of the shop-bought variety. If you like more toffee-flavoured ones, use half caster and half light muscovado sugar.

INGREDIENTS

4 egg whites, at room temperature
8 oz (225 g) caster sugar
whipping cream

HOW TO MAKE

Heat the oven to 200°F/100°C/gas mark ¼. Line two baking sheets with silicone paper.

Place the egg whites in a large bowl and whisk in high speed with an electric whisk or use a hand rotary whisk, until they form soft peaks. Add the sugar, a teaspoonful at a time, whisking well after each addition, still on full speed, until all the sugar has been added.

Using two dessert spoons, spoon the meringue out on to the baking sheets, putting 12 meringues on each tray. Bake in the oven for 3–4 hours, until the meringues are firm and dry and will lift easily from the silicone paper. (They will be very pale off-white, or slightly darker if you have used muscovado sugar.) Whip the cream until it is thick and use it to sandwich the meringues together when they are cool.

COOK'S TIP

To make a larger or smaller quantity of meringues than specified in the recipe (for example if you have leftover whites), allow 2 oz (50 g) sugar per egg white. If you lose count of how many egg whites you have, 4 egg whites are about ¼ pint (150 ml). Left-over whites can be stored in a covered container in the refrigerator for 3 weeks, or frozen for up to 6 months.

QUEEN OF PUDDINGS

SERVES 6

This old-fashioned pudding is well worth making. Essentially it is a baked custard base topped with jam and soft meringue.

INGREDIENTS

1 pint (600 ml) milk
1 oz (25 g) butter
2 oz (50 g) caster sugar
finely grated rind of 1 lemon
4 egg yolks
3 oz (75 g) fresh white breadcrumbs
3 tablespoons strawberry jam

TOPPING
4 egg whites
6 oz (175 g) caster sugar

HOW TO MAKE

Heat the oven to 350°F/180°C/gas mark 4. Well grease a 2 pint (1.2 litre) pie dish.

Warm the milk in a saucepan, add the butter, the 2 oz (50 g) sugar and lemon rind and heat until the sugar has dissolved and the butter melted, stirring occasionally. Whisk the egg yolks in a small bowl and gradually whisk in the warmed milk.

Put the breadcrumbs in the pie dish and pour over the warm milk. Leave to stand for about 15 minutes, then bake in the oven for about 30 minutes, until just set. Remove from oven and spread with warmed jam. Do not turn off the oven.

Whisk the egg whites until stiff then whisk in the sugar a teaspoonful at a time. Pile the meringue on to the pudding, spreading it right up to the dish edges and forming it into peaks. Return to the oven for about 10–15 minutes, until the meringue is pale golden brown. Serve at once with cream.

RASPBERRY CREAM PAVLOVA

SERVES 6

This is really not difficult and does not take too long to make. It needs just an hour, undisturbed, in the oven, then turn off the heat and forget it until it is quite cold. Do not open the oven door and peep. The vinegar and cornflour make the centre gooey.

INGREDIENTS

3 egg whites
6 oz (175 g) caster sugar
1 teaspoon vinegar
1 teaspoon cornflour

FILLING
½ pint (300 ml) whipping cream, whipped
8 oz (225 g) fresh raspberries
a little caster sugar

HOW TO MAKE

Heat the oven to 325°F/160°C/gas mark 3. Lay sheet of silicone paper on a baking sheet and mark an 8 inch (20 cm) circle on it.

Whisk the egg whites with a electric or hand rotary whisk until stiff, then whisk in the sugar a teaspoonful at a time. Blend the vinegar with the cornflour and whisk into the egg whites with the last spoonful of sugar. Spread out the meringue to cover the circle on the baking sheet, building up the sides so that they are higher than the centre.

Put the meringue case in the middle of the oven, turn the heat down to 300°F/150°C/gas mark 2, and bake for 1 hour. The pavlova will be a pale creamy colour rather than white. Turn the oven off and leave the pavlova undisturbed to become quite cold.

Lift the pavlova off the paper and transfer it to a serving plate. To make the filling, put the cream and the raspberries in a bowl, lightly fold them together and sweeten to taste with a little sugar. Pile the cream and raspberry mixture into the centre of the pavlova and leave to stand for 1 hour in a cool place, or the refrigerator, before serving.

COOK'S TIP
Leftover egg yolks can be stored in the refrigerator in a small container. Float a dessert spoon of water over the top of the unbroken yolk to prevent a skin forming, and cover the container. Use within one week by adding to homemade mayonnaise, lemon curd or hollandaise sauce, or use to enrich sauces (but don't boil after adding any egg yolk). Spare egg yolks can also be used up in scrambled egg or omelette mixtures.

CHOCOLATE MERINGUE SLICES

EACH CAKE
SERVES 6

This oblong meringue cake, which just melts in the mouth, is a great change from normal meringues. Both the shape and the 'softening' time make the cake much easier to slice than conventional meringue circles. Make the meringues up to a week ahead, if this suits you. Wrap in foil until you need to fill them.

INGREDIENTS

4 egg whites
8 oz (225 g) caster sugar

FILLING
½ pint (300 ml) double cream, whipped

TOPPING
1½ oz (40 g) soft margarine
1 oz (25 g) cocoa, sieved
2 tablespoons milk
4 oz (100 g) icing sugar, sieved
2 oz (50 g) plain chocolate, broken into small pieces

HOW TO MAKE

Heat the oven to 200°F/100°C/gas mark ¼. Line two large baking trays with non-stick silicone paper.

Whisk the egg whites until stiff, then gradually whisk in the sugar, a teaspoonful at a time, with the whisk still on full speed, until really stiff. Spread the meringue mixture into four oblongs about 12 × 4 inches (30 × 10 cm) and bake for about 3 hours until firm and a pale cream colour.

For the topping, heat the margarine in a small pan, stir in the cocoa and cook for 1 minute. Remove from the heat and stir in the milk and icing sugar. Beat until smooth and leave to cool until a spreading consistency.

Spread the chocolate topping over two of the meringues, on the rough side. Turn over the two remaining oblongs and spread the whipped cream on the flat sides. Sandwich the chocolate and cream pieces together, to give two cakes.

Melt the chocolate in a bowl over a pan of hot water, then turn into a polythene bag. Snip one corner off the bag to give a small hole, and drizzle the chocolate in a zig-zag pattern over the meringue. Leave for at least 4 hours for the meringue to soften, then serve in slices.

LEMON MERINGUE PIE

SERVES 6

The base for this family favourite is rich shortcrust pastry made with an egg yolk and sweetened with sugar.

INGREDIENTS

PASTRY
4 oz (100 g) flour
1 oz (25 g) butter, cut into pieces
1 oz (25 g) lard, cut into pieces
1 egg yolk
1 teaspoon caster sugar
1 teaspoon cold water

LEMON FILLING
finely grated rind and juice of 2 large lemons
1½ oz (40 g) cornflour
½ pint (300 ml) water
2 egg yolks
3 oz (75 g) caster sugar

MERINGUE TOPPING
3 egg whites
5 oz (150 g) caster sugar

HOW TO MAKE

To make the pastry, put the flour in a bowl, add the fats and rub in until the mixture resembles fine breadcrumbs. Mix the egg yolk, sugar and water together and stir into dry ingredients to bind them together. Roll out on a lightly floured surface and line an 8 inch (20 cm) flan tin. Chill for 30 minutes. Meanwhile, heat the oven to 425°F/220°C/gas mark 7.

Heat a thick baking sheet in the oven. Line the pastry case with foil or greaseproof paper and weigh down with baking beans. Bake on the baking sheet for 15 minutes, then remove the paper and beans and return the flan to the oven for a further 5 minutes to cook the base.

Meanwhile, prepare the filling. Put the lemon rind and juice in a bowl with the cornflour, add 2 tablespoons of the water and blend to a smooth paste. Bring the remaining water to the boil and pour on to the cornflour mixture. Return it to the pan and bring to the boil, stirring. Simmer for 3 minutes until thick, stirring all the time. Remove from the heat and add the egg yolks and sugar, beating well. Heat for a moment to thicken the sauce, then allow to cool slightly. Pour into the pastry case.

To make the topping, whisk the egg whites until they form stiff peaks, add the sugar a teaspoonful at a time, whisking well between each addition. Spoon the meringue over the filling, spreading it right up to the edge of the pastry. Lower the oven temperature to 325°F/160°C/gas mark 3 and cook the pie for about 30 minutes, until the meringue turns a pale golden brown. Serve warm.

Soufflés

LEMON SOUFFLÉ PUDDING

SERVES 6–8

A delicious light and easy pudding, much more special than it sounds. The top is a spongy mousse and underneath a sharp lemon sauce. For a smaller size, halve the quantities and bake in a 1½ pint (900 ml) dish for about 30 minutes. It is also good cold, served with cream.

INGREDIENTS

1 oz (25 g) butter
8 oz (225 g) caster sugar
4 eggs, separated
grated rind and juice of 2 large lemons
2 oz (50 g) flour
16 fl oz (750 ml) milk

HOW TO MAKE

Heat the oven to 400°F/200°C/gas mark 6. Grease a 2½ pint (1.5 litre) ovenproof dish. Beat the butter and sugar together in a bowl, then beat in the egg yolks, lemon rind and juice and flour, then lastly beat in the milk. Alternatively, put the egg yolks, lemon rind and juice, butter, sugar and flour into a food processor and blend well, then add the milk through the funnel with the machine running.

Beat the egg whites until firm and fold into the liquid. Pour into the greased dish.

Place the dish in a roasting tin, pour boiling water into the tin to come halfway up the dish and bake in the oven for 45 minutes.

Serve piping hot.

Variation

Summer Soufflé Pudding Put uncooked red fruit such as blackberries, black or redcurrants, or a tin of raspberries drained of their liquid, in the bottom of the greased ovenproof dish. Continue with the recipe.

PEAR AND CHOCOLATE SOUFFLÉ

SERVES 4–6

I like to serve individual soufflés, but if you prefer to make one large soufflé use a 2 pint (1.2 litre) soufflé dish and bake for about 45 minutes. For a really wicked dessert, serve the soufflés with Chocolate Sauce (see page 234).

INGREDIENTS

1 ripe pear, peeled, cored and diced
1½ (40 g) butter
1½ (40 g) plain flour
½ pint (300 ml) milk
3 oz (75 g) plain chocolate
2 oz (50 g) caster sugar
3 eggs, separated
icing sugar to decorate

HOW TO MAKE

Butter 4–6 ramekin dishes. Divide the diced pear between the dishes. Heat the oven to 400°F/200°C/gas mark 6 and place a baking tray large enough to take the ramekin dishes in the oven.

Melt the butter in a saucepan then add the flour. Cook for 1 minute without colouring. Gradually add the milk, stirring all the time. Keep stirring until the mixture has thickened. Remove from the heat. Melt the chocolate in a bowl over hot water.

Add the sugar, melted chocolate and egg yolks to the milk mixture and mix in until smooth. Whisk the egg whites until stiff and fold into the mixture. Fill the ramekin dishes almost to the top with soufflé mixture and place on the hot baking tray. Bake for 20–25 minutes until well risen and firm to the touch. Dust lightly with icing sugar and serve at once.

Iced Desserts

VANILLA ICE CREAM

SERVES 8–10

A really good easy recipe and there's no need to use an ice cream maker. Ice cream can be used as a base for sundaes or parfaits, or it can be served with hot puddings and pies instead of custard or cream. Remove the ice cream from the freezer 5–10 minutes before serving and leave to stand at room temperature. To make vanilla sugar, just store two or three vanilla pods in a screw-top jar of caster sugar. If you have not already done this, just add 1 teaspoon vanilla essence with the cream.

INGREDIENTS

4 eggs, separated
4 oz (100 g) vanilla sugar
½ pint (300 ml) double cream

HOW TO MAKE

Using an electric hand whisk, whisk the egg whites until stiff, then whisk in the sugar a teaspoonful at a time. Place the yolks in a separate bowl and whisk until well blended.

Whisk the cream until it forms soft peaks (add the vanilla essence at this stage if no vanilla sugar is available), then fold into the egg white mixture with the egg yolks.

Turn the ice cream into a 2½ pint (1.5 litre) plastic container, cover and freeze overnight.

Variations

If you are making one of these variations on the basic ice cream recipe, omit the vanilla sugar or vanilla essence and use plain caster sugar. Add the extra ingredients after folding in the cream and egg yolks.

Very Special Ginger Ice Cream   Add 1 teaspoon ground ginger and 4 oz (100 g) stem ginger, chopped, to the basic ice cream.

Brandy Ice Cream   At Christmas time flavour the ice cream with 2 tablespoons brandy and serve with Christmas pudding and mince pies.

Coffee and Rum Ice Cream   Add 2 tablespoons coffee essence and 2 tablespoons rum to the basic ice cream. If liked, soak 3 oz (75 g) chopped raisins in rum for 3 hours or more first.

Fresh Lemon or Lime Ice Cream   Add the grated rind and juice of 2 lemons or limes to the basic ice cream.

Mango Ice Cream   Add the lightly mashed flesh of a peeled and stoned mango to the basic ice cream.

Passion Fruit Ice Cream   Add the flesh and pips of 3 passion fruit to the basic ice cream.

Raspberry or Strawberry Ice Cream   Add ¼ pint (150 ml) strawberry purée or ¼ pint (150 ml) sieved raspberry purée to the basic ice cream.

Tutti Frutti   Soak 4 oz (100 g) mixed chopped glacé pineapple, raisins, dried apricots, cherries and angelica overnight in 4 tablespoons brandy to plump them. Fold into the basic ice cream. Serve with almond biscuits, a swirl of cream and a sprinkling of nuts.

Blackcurrant Ice Cream   Add about 3 tablespoons of blackcurrant cordial and 3 tablespoons cassis to the basic ice cream.

ORANGE SORBET

SERVES 4

Frozen concentrated orange is extremely good for this recipe and, as each can is said to contain 11 oranges, it's good value, too.

INGREDIENTS

3 oz (75 g) caster sugar
½ pint (300 ml) water
6½ fl oz (184 g) can concentrated frozen orange juice, undiluted
1 egg white

HOW TO MAKE

Put the sugar and water in a pan and heat slowly until the sugar has dissolved. Leave to cool and then stir in the orange juice and blend well. Pour into a 1 pint (600 ml) container. Freeze for about 30 minutes, or until barely firm, then turn into a bowl and mash down.

Whisk the egg white until stiff, then fold it into the orange mixture. Return to the freezer in the container with a lid on and then freeze until firm.

Leave to thaw in the refrigerator for 30 minutes before serving.

ICED LEMON FLUMMERY

SERVES 8–12

Quite my most favourite of all cold puddings. Desserts in individual dishes make serving so much simpler. Keep these ices in the freezer then, 10 minutes before serving, take them out and decorate.

INGREDIENTS

½ pint (300 ml) double cream
grated rind and juice of 2 lemons
12 oz (350 g) caster sugar
1 pint (600 ml) milk
¼ pint (150 ml) whipping cream, whipped
sprigs of fresh mint or lemon balm

HOW TO MAKE

Pour the double cream into a bowl and whisk until it forms soft peaks. Stir in the lemon rind and juice, sugar and milk and mix well until thoroughly blended. Pour into a 2½ pint (1.5 litre) plastic container, cover with a lid and freeze for at least 6 hours, until firm.

Cut into chunks and process in a blender or food processor, until smooth and creamy. Pour into individual ramekin dishes and return to the freezer overnight.

To serve, pipe a small blob of whipped cream on top of each ramekin and decorate with a sprig of mint or lemon balm.

Cakes, Biscuits and Bread

There are five main cake- and biscuit-making techniques, and the cakes and biscuits in this chapter have been grouped according to method.

All-in-one My all-in-one cakes are exactly that. Everything goes into the bowl at the same time, saving time and washing up. I use self-raising flour *and* baking powder for many of these cakes. The speed of the method means that there is not much air beaten into the mixture, and the baking powder gives that necessary lift.

Creaming For cakes made by the creaming method, the fat and sugar are beaten together until light and fluffy before the other ingredients are folded or beaten in.

Rubbing-in This method is used for plainer mixtures and scones, and involves rubbing the fat into the flour until it resembles fine breadcrumbs. The dough is then bound together with the liquid ingredients.

Melting-fat With the melting-fat method, for example when making gingerbread, take care not to heat the ingredients too much but just enough to melt the fat without actually cooking anything. If it gets too hot the flour will form lumps in the mixture. If you do notice lumps, however, this can be corrected by running the mixture through a sieve straight into the baking tin.

Whisking Whisked sponges and roulades are not difficult to make. An electric mixer helps and saves time. Take care not to over-whisk the mixture – there should just be a faint trail when the mixer is lifted out. As they don't contain any fat, these cakes are best eaten within a day, though they do freeze well.

Preparing ingredients

For successful baking results it is essential to weigh ingredients accurately, particularly with small quantities. And as with any recipe, follow only one set of measure – imperial or metric – as they are not interchangeable.

Ingredients should be at room temperature for baking, so if using remove eggs, milk and fat from the refrigerator in advance.

Lining cake tins

If a cake tin has a loose base, all you need to do is grease the base and sides. For tins without a loose base, you'll need to grease *and* line the bottom of the tin with greaseproof paper. If a cake mix is rich – a rich fruit cake for example – you'll need to grease and line both base and sides.

Bases For both round and square tins – and indeed any other shaped tin – put the base of the tin on a piece of greaseproof paper and draw in pencil round it. Cut out, just inside the pencilled line. Grease the base and sides of the tin, then insert the disc, square or whatever into the tin. Grease all surfaces again.

Sides Cut strips of greaseproof paper which are 1–1½ inches (2.5–4 cm) wider than the depth or height of the tin. The strips should be long enough to go completely around the sides of the tin, whether round or square. Fold over a good ½ inch (1.25 cm) along one whole length of the strip. Open out the fold and cut slanting lines through the narrow fold bit, precisely to the fold line. Fit this strip into the tin, with the slashed strip folding over on to the bottom of the tin. Then fit in the base disc or square *over* the slashes, and the tin is fully lined.

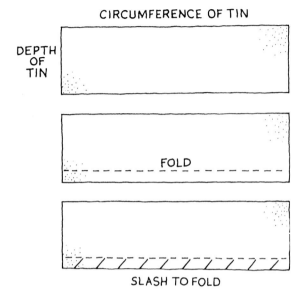

CIRCUMFERENCE OF TIN

DEPTH OF TIN

FOLD

SLASH TO FOLD

Another way of lining a square or rectangular tin, deep or shallow, is to stand the tin on a large piece of greaseproof paper, at least the size of the tin and its depth. See the diagram below. Mark with pencil around the base and then measure and rule in lines outside this which correspond to the *depth* of the tin. Cut at an angle from outer corner to inner corner at all four corners then fit the paper in the greased tin. The cut corners will overlap, and excess can be cut away. Grease again.

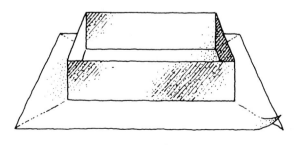

Baking cakes

The first necessity is to preheat the oven to the correct temperature. If you use gas or electricity, you must allow time for this. The correct oven temperature is vital for cake-making success, and if you're uncertain of your oven, buy or borrow an oven thermometer, and check it yourself.

Before turning on the oven, you may first have to adjust the position of the oven shelves, depending on the type of oven you have. If baking one cake, use the shelf in the centre position; if baking two cakes, one cake is usually on a shelf above centre, the other below. If you're baking several things at the same time, they will take longer to cook than a solitary cake. Keep an eye on them in the later stages.

Try not to open the oven door during the first stages of baking or move the cake tin, as both these actions will make the cake sink in the middle.

Telling when a cake is done

The principal signs of done-ness for most cakes are when the cake shrinks slightly from the sides of the tin and when the top of the cake springs back after being pressed lightly with the finger. The look and the smell can also be informative.

Fruit cakes need another test, which is to push a skewer into the centre. If the skewer comes out clean, the cake is ready; if there is some cake mixture adhering to the skewer, it needs a little longer – but check carefully. If a cake such as this looks as though it's browning too much on the top, cover with foil and cook for a bit longer at a lower temperature.

With biscuits and shortbread, test by eye, checking that the colour is right, not only on the top but on the underneath as well. Outside ones may do slightly more quickly than those in the middle. In this case, remove them to a wire rack to cool and return the rest to the oven for a few minutes extra cooking time.

Cooling cakes

Particular cooling instructions are attached to individual recipes. In general, though, leave cakes and biscuits in the tin or on the tray to contract, firm up and cool for a while before turning them out on to a wire rack to become completely cold. This prevents them sticking or perhaps breaking. Before turning out, run a knife quickly round the edges of the cake tin.

To turn a cake out of a loose-bottomed tin, stand the base on something like a large can so that the side can slip down, leaving the cake free, still standing on the tin base.

If the tin has been lined, peel off the paper very carefully. Special care is needed for thinner cakes such as roulades and Swiss rolls.

Certain cakes such as shortbreads and flapjacks are not cooled on a cooling tray as this would spoil their texture. Follow the instructions in the recipe.

Decoration

For family cakes keep decoration simple. A dusting of icing sugar or a sprinkling of demerara sugar is often enough. For a more special occasion, for example an Easter cake, you could decorate the finished cake with fresh flowers such as primroses, rose buds or pansies.

YEAST

There are many types of yeast other than fresh, which is difficult to come by these days. I now use fast-acting dried yeast with added Vitamin C, or ordinary dried yeast. The advantage of the former is you mix it in with the flour rather than mixing it with water and sugar and waiting for it to react. Some types of dried yeast require only one rising, which can save a lot of time. Always read the packet instructions carefully, and buy in small quantities.

Facing page 192: *Victoria Sandwich Cake (page 196) with slices of Coffee Cake and Chocolate Cake (pages 196–7)*

Left: *Carrot Cake (page 195)*

All-in-one Method

MADEIRA CAKE

This plain but delicious cake has good keeping qualities as it contains butter. The butter must be soft enough to mix easily with the other ingredients, but not oily.

INGREDIENTS

8 oz (225 g) self-raising flour
1 teaspoon baking powder
6 oz (175 g) butter, softened
7 oz (200 g) caster sugar
4 eggs
finely grated rind of 1 lemon
a strip of lemon citron peel, washed and dried (optional)

HOW TO MAKE

Heat the oven to 350°F/180°C/gas mark 4. Grease and line a 7 inch (18 cm) round cake tin with greased greaseproof paper.

Measure all the ingredients, except for the peel, into a bowl and beat well until smooth. Spread the mixture in the prepared tin and level the top.

Bake in the oven for 30 minutes until set, then carefully lift the peel on to the cake. Reduce the oven temperature to 325°F/160°C/gas mark 3, and cook for a further 1 hour. The cake should be shrinking away slightly from the sides of the tin and be pale golden in colour.

Cool in the tin for about 10 minutes, then turn out, peel off the paper, and finish cooling on a wire rack.

COOK'S TIP
When grating rind for a cake, whether orange or lemon, first wash and dry the fruit well. Grate the rind on the small holed side of the grater, making sure you scrape it all off the back of the grater, and add immediately to the sugar content of the recipe. The rind won't discolour this way, and the oils in the rind will be absorbed by the sugar.

CARROT CAKE

This really is gooey and delicious, and is my version of the carrot cake served après-ski in Switzerland. Have it, as the Swiss do, with a cup of hot chocolate, topped with whipped cream and a sprinkling of chocolate powder.

INGREDIENTS

8 oz (225 g) self-raising flour
2 teaspoons baking powder
5 oz (150 g) caster sugar
2 oz (50 g) walnuts, chopped
4 oz (100 g) carrots, peeled and grated
2 ripe bananas, mashed
2 eggs
¼ pint (150 ml) sunflower oil
a little vanilla essence (optional)

TOPPING
3 oz (75 g) soft margarine
3 oz (75 g) cream cheese
6 oz (175 g) icing sugar, sieved
a little vanilla essence (optional)

HOW TO MAKE

Heat the oven to 350°F/180°C/gas mark 4. Grease and line an 8 inch (20 cm) round cake tin with greased greaseproof paper.

Measure the flour and baking powder into a large bowl and stir in the sugar. Add the nuts, carrots and bananas and mix lightly. Make a well in the centre, add the eggs and oil, and beat well until blended, adding a little vanilla essence, if liked.

Turn into the prepared tin and bake in the oven for 1¼ hours until the cake is golden brown and shrinking away from the sides of the tin. A warm skewer pushed into the centre should come out clean. Turn out, remove the paper, and leave to cool on a wire rack.

For the topping, measure all the ingredients into a bowl and beat well until blended and smooth. Spread over the cake and rough up with a fork. Leave in a cool place to harden slightly before serving.

Serve cut into thin wedges.

VICTORIA SANDWICH CAKE

The most popular British cake. It can be flavoured in different ways (see the variations below). This amount of mixture makes a good deep sandwich cake. It is remarkably quick to make, just beat the ingredients together in one bowl. The cake can be filled and topped with white butter cream for an extra-special tea time or simply filled with jam and the top sprinkled with caster sugar. If you are making the sandwich to freeze, I prefer to freeze it unfilled, slipping a piece of silicone or greaseproof paper between the layers and then wrapping them in foil. To thaw, loosen the wrapping and leave at room temperature for 3 hours. Then fill and leave to thaw completely before serving.

INGREDIENTS

6 oz (175 g) soft margarine
6 oz (175 g) caster sugar
3 eggs, beaten
6 oz (175 g) self-raising flour
1½ teaspoons baking powder

FILLING AND TOPPING
about 4 tablespoons strawberry or raspberry jam
a little caster sugar

HOW TO MAKE

Heat the oven to 350°F/180°C/gas mark 4. Grease and line two 7 inch (18 cm) round sandwich tins with greased greaseproof paper.

Measure the margarine, sugar, eggs, flour and baking powder into a large bowl and beat well until thoroughly blended. Divide the mixture between the prepared tins and level the tops.

Bake in the oven for about 25 minutes, until well risen, and the tops of the cakes spring back when lightly pressed with a finger. Leave to cool in the tins for a few moments, then turn out, peel off the paper and finish cooling on a wire rack.

When completely cold, sandwich the two cakes together with the jam. Lift on to a serving plate and serve sprinkled with a little caster sugar.

Variations

Orange or Lemon   Add the finely grated rind of 1 orange or 1 lemon to the cake mixture. Serve sandwiched together with lemon curd.

Chocolate   Blend 2 tablespoons sieved cocoa with 3 tablespoons boiling water in the mixing bowl. Cool, then add the remaining ingredients and continue as above. (There is no need to decrease the amount of flour in the recipe.) Sandwich together with white butter cream (see below). If liked, spread extra butter cream on top and sprinkle with chocolate curls (see opposite).

Coffee Dissolve 2 heaped teaspoons instant coffee in the beaten eggs before adding to the bowl. Sandwich the cakes together with coffee butter cream (see below). Top with extra butter cream if liked.

WHITE BUTTER CREAM

A traditional filling and topping for cakes that can be flavoured or coloured to suit the cake.

INGREDIENTS

2 oz (50 g) soft margarine
6 oz (175 g) icing sugar, sieved
1 tablespoon milk

HOW TO MAKE

Blend the margarine, icing sugar and milk together until very light and fluffy.

Variations

Orange Add the grated rind of 1 orange to the butter cream.

Chocolate Leave out the milk, use only 4 oz (100 g) icing sugar and blend in the margarine with 2 oz (50 g) melted plain chocolate.

Coffee Add 1 tablespoon coffee essence to the butter cream.

COOK'S TIP
To make chocolate curls, also known as caraque, melt chocolate in a bowl over a pan of hot water, then spread very thinly on to a clean, scratchproof work surface. Leave until set, then, with a long sharp knife, shave it off the surface using a slight sawing action and holding the knife almost upright so the chocolate forms curls or flakes.

FAMILY FRUIT CAKE

Don't be tempted to be over-generous with the marmalade, otherwise the cake is likely to sink in the middle. Chop the peel in the marmalade if it is chunky.

INGREDIENTS

8 oz (225 g) soft margarine
8 oz (225 g) caster sugar
12 oz (350 g) self-raising flour
3 oz (75 g) glacé cherries, quartered
1 lb (450 g) mixed dried fruit
2 tablespoons marmalade
4 eggs

TOPPING
2 oz (50 g) flaked almonds

HOW TO MAKE

Heat the oven to 325°F/160°C/gas mark 3. Lightly grease and line a 9 inch (23 cm) deep round cake tin with greased greaseproof paper.

Measure all the ingredients into a bowl and mix until well blended. Turn into the prepared tin and level the top. Sprinkle with the flaked almonds.

Bake in the oven for about 2¼ hours until a fine skewer inserted into the centre comes out clean. Leave in the tin to cool for about 10 minutes, then turn out and finish cooling on a wire rack.

PINEAPPLE AND CHERRY CAKE

This is a really moist cake, and is best stored in the refrigerator and eaten within four weeks. The pineapple gives a very special flavour. Make sure you drain it thoroughly – use the juice in a fruit salad. (You could use canned apricots instead of the pineapple if liked.)

INGREDIENTS

2 oz (50 g) glacé cherries
8 oz (225 g) can pineapple pieces, thoroughly drained
5 oz (150 g) soft margarine
5 oz (150 g) light muscovado sugar
2 large eggs, beaten
7 oz (200 g) self-raising flour
2 tablespoons of the pineapple juice
12 oz (350 g) mixed dried fruit

HOW TO MAKE

Heat the oven to 325°F/160°C/gas mark 3. Grease and line an 8 inch (20 cm) deep round cake tin with greased greaseproof paper.

Cut the cherries in half, rinse under running cold water, then dry thoroughly. Chop the pineapple very finely.

Put the margarine, sugar, eggs, flour, pineapple juice, dried fruit, cherries and pineapple into a bowl and beat well until smooth. Turn the mixture into the prepared tin and level out the top.

Bake in the oven for about 1½ hours until golden brown and shrinking away from the sides of the tin. A fine skewer inserted into the centre should come out clean. Leave to cool in the tin, remove paper and store in a plastic container in the refrigerator.

Variation

Decorate the top, when cold, with rows of blanched almonds, walnuts and hazelnuts, alternating with glacé cherries. Top with an apricot glaze made by melting apricot jam in a pan and sieving it.

MINCEMEAT FRUIT LOAVES

MAKES 2 LOAVES

Make one to eat now and one for the freezer. Many moons ago I invented this mincemeat cake, and over the years I have varied the ingredients slightly. This version is made in 1 lb (450 g) loaf tins, as on more than one occasion Women's Institute members have told me how useful it is to sell on W.I. markets. You can, of course, double up this recipe and bake four at a time – much easier to fit in the oven than round tins! But do remember that the more you fill the oven, the longer the loaves will take to cook.

INGREDIENTS

2 eggs
5 oz (150 g) caster sugar
5 oz (150 g) soft margarine
8 oz (225 g) self-raising flour
12 oz (350 g) mincemeat
8 oz (225 g) currants
a few flaked almonds

HOW TO MAKE

Heat the oven to 325°F/160°C/gas mark 3. Grease and line the base of two 1 lb (450 g) loaf tins with greased greaseproof paper.

Crack the eggs into a large, roomy bowl and add all the other ingredients except the flaked almonds. Mix until well blended, then divide between the two prepared tins and level the tops. Sprinkle with flaked almonds.

Bake in the oven for about 1¼ hours, until risen, pale golden brown and shrinking away from the sides of the tin. A fine skewer inserted in the centre of the loaves should come out clean. Turn out of the tins and cool on a wire rack. Peel off the paper and store in an airtight tin.

BARA BRITH

A simple traditional Welsh tea bread that is deliciously moist and keeps well. Prepare it in the afternoon with the remains of the tea, leave to stand overnight and then make the tea bread the following morning.

INGREDIENTS

5 oz (150 g) currants
5 oz (150 g) raisins
5 oz (150 g) caster sugar
½ pint (300 ml) hot tea
10 oz (275 g) self-raising flour
1 egg

HOW TO MAKE

Put the fruit and sugar in a bowl and pour in the hot tea. Stir very well, cover with a plate to keep the heat in and then leave to stand overnight.

Next day, heat the oven to 300°F/150°C/gas mark 2. Grease and line a 2 lb (900 g) loaf tin with greased greaseproof paper.

Stir the flour and egg into the soaked fruit and mix very well. Turn the mixture into the tin and bake in the oven for about 1½ hours, or until the bread has shrunk from the sides of the tin and a fine skewer inserted in the centre comes out clean. Turn out, remove the paper and leave to cool on a wire rack.

Serve sliced, either spread with butter or just as it is.

VICTORIANA CHRISTMAS CAKE

An easy, different and special Christmas cake. The dried fruit is soaked for several days in sherry, which makes it very moist. This is not a really deep cake so do not expect it to rise to the top of the tin.

INGREDIENTS

1¼ lb (550 g) mixed dried fruit, including peel
4 oz (100 g) raisins, chopped
4 oz (100 g) currants
4 oz (100 g) glacé cherries, quartered
¼ pint (150 ml) medium or sweet sherry
6 oz (175 g) soft margarine
6 oz (175 g) dark soft brown sugar
grated rind 1 lemon
grated rind 1 orange
3 eggs
1 tablespoon black treacle
2 oz (50 g) blanched almonds, chopped
4 oz (100 g) plain flour
2 oz (50 g) self-raising flour
1 teaspoon mixed spice

HOW TO MAKE

Put the dried fruit and cherries in a container, pour over the sherry, cover with a lid and leave to soak for at least 3 days, stirring daily.

Heat the oven to 300°F/150°C/gas mark 2. Grease and line an 8 inch (20 cm) round cake tin with greased greaseproof paper.

Put the margarine, sugar, lemon and orange rind, eggs, treacle and almonds in a large bowl. Sift together the flours and mixed spice and add to the bowl. Mix together until evenly blended, then stir in the soaked fruit and sherry.

Spoon the mixture into the tin and smooth the top flat. Bake in the oven for 2 hours, then reduce the heat to 275°F/140°C/gas mark 1 and bake for a further 1¼ hours. (If the cake seems to be getting too brown on top, cover it very loosely with a sheet of foil.)

Test with a fine skewer to see if the cake is done. If the skewer comes out clean when inserted in the centre of the cake, it is cooked. If not, bake for a further 15 minutes. Leave to cool in the tin.

COOK'S TIP
Glacé cherries should always be washed and thoroughly dried before putting in a cake mixture. This prevents them sinking to the bottom of the cake as it cooks.

EASTER SIMNEL CAKE

This is now the traditional Easter cake, but originally it was given by servant girls to their mothers on Mothering Sunday. The cake is baked with a layer of marzipan in the middle, and then topped with more marzipan and glacé icing.

INGREDIENTS

6 oz (175 g) soft margarine
6 oz (175 g) light soft brown sugar
3 eggs
6 oz (175 g) self-raising flour
2 teaspoons mixed spice
10 oz (275 g) mixed dried fruit
2 oz (50 g) ground almonds
1½ lb (700 g) almond paste

DECORATION
a little pale yellow glacé icing made with 6 oz (175 g) icing sugar
sugar eggs and chickens

HOW TO MAKE

Heat the oven to 325°F/160°C/gas mark 3. Grease and line an 8 inch (20 cm) round cake tin with greased greaseproof paper.

Put all the cake ingredients, except for the almond paste, into a large mixing bowl and beat well with a wooden spoon until well blended. Place half the mixture in the bottom of the tin and level the top.

Take 12 oz (350 g) of the almond paste and roll it out to a circle the size of the tin and then place on top of the cake mixture. Cover with the remaining cake mixture and level the top.

Bake in the oven for about 1½ hours until evenly browned and shrinking away from the sides of the tin. Leave in the tin to cool for about 10 minutes, then turn out, peel off the paper and finish cooling on a wire rack.

With the remaining almond paste, make a long sausage, then lay this in a circle round the outside top of the cake. Flatten with your fingers and pinch the outside edge all round to decorate. Pour the icing into the centre and leave to set.

Decorate with sugar eggs and chickens.

COOK'S TIP

To make glacé icing, simply mix the sieved icing sugar in a bowl with enough warm water or lemon juice to make a pouring consistency. For 6 oz (175 g) icing sugar you will need about 1½ tablespoons of liquid. If you add too much liquid and the icing is too runny, just sift in more sugar.

BUTTER BISCUITS

MAKES ABOUT 30

These can be made by measuring all the ingredients straight into a blender or food processor and mixing until blended. Don't overlap biscuits while cooling or they will become misshapen as they cool and harden on the wire rack.

INGREDIENTS

4 oz (100 g) butter, softened
2 oz (50 g) caster sugar
grated rind of 1 lemon
5 oz (150 g) self-raising flour

HOW TO MAKE

Heat the oven to 350°F/180°C/gas mark 4. Lightly grease a baking tray.

Measure the butter and sugar into a bowl and beat until smooth. Stir in the lemon rind and gradually work in the flour. Form into balls about the size of walnuts and place on the prepared baking tray well spaced apart. Flatten each one with a fork dipped in water to prevent it sticking.

Bake for about 15–20 minutes, until pale golden brown. Cool on tray for a few minutes, then transfer to a wire rack to finish cooling.

Variations

Chocolate   Omit the lemon rind and replace 1 oz (25 g) flour with 1 oz (25 g) cocoa, sieved.

Orange   Use orange rind instead of lemon rind.

Vanilla   Omit lemon rind and add half teaspoon vanilla essence, or use 1 oz (25 g) vanilla sugar to replace 1 oz (25 g) of the caster sugar.

Almond   Omit lemon rind and 1 oz (25 g) self-raising flour and replace with ¼ teaspoon almond essence and 1 oz (25 g) ground almonds. Add 1 oz (25 g) chopped almonds for extra crunch.

Sultana   Add 3 oz (75 g) sultanas with the lemon rind. Flatten each biscuit with your hand rather than a fork before baking.

Walnut   Omit the lemon rind and add 2 oz (50 g) chopped walnuts. Press half a walnut on top of each biscuit before baking.

YUM YUMS

MAKES ABOUT
30

Otherwise known as melting moments. In warm weather, chill the mixture to make shaping easier.

INGREDIENTS

4 oz (100 g) soft margarine
3 oz (75 g) caster sugar
1 egg yolk
few drops vanilla essence (optional)
5 oz (150 g) self-raising flour
crushed cornflakes or porridge oats

HOW TO MAKE

Heat the oven to 375°F/190°C/gas mark 5. Grease two baking sheets.

Measure all the ingredients except the cornflakes or oats into a bowl and beat well. Take a teaspoonful of the mixture and roll it into a ball with wet hands to prevent sticking. Roll in cornflakes or oats and place on the prepared baking sheet, well spaced apart. Flatten slightly with your finger.

Bake in the oven for about 15 minutes, until very pale golden at the edges. Leave for a few moments to cool on the tray, then lift on to a wire rack to finish cooling.

Creaming Method

BUTTER ALMOND CAKE

A simple plain cake. It is essential to use butter as it adds to the flavour.

INGREDIENTS

6 oz (175 g) butter, softened
6 oz (175 g) caster sugar
4 eggs, beaten
4 oz (100 g) ground almonds
7 oz (200 g) self-raising flour
1 teaspoon almond essence

TOPPING
1 oz (25 g) flaked almonds

HOW TO MAKE

Heat the oven to 350°F/180°C/gas mark 4. Grease and line an 8 inch (20 cm) deep round cake tin with greased greaseproof paper.

Cream the butter and sugar together in a bowl until light and fluffy. Beat in the eggs, a little at a time. Gently fold in the almonds, flour and almond essence until thoroughly blended. Turn into the prepared tin and level the top. Scatter over the flaked almonds.

Bake in the oven for about 1¼ hours, until well risen and golden brown and a fine skewer inserted into the centre comes out clean. Leave to cool in the tin for a few minutes, then turn out, peel off the paper and finish cooling on a wire rack.

SPECIAL CHERRY CAKE

A classic cake. It is important to cut up the cherries and then wash and dry them thoroughly so that all moisture is removed, otherwise they will sink to the bottom of the cake.

INGREDIENTS

6 oz (175 g) glacé cherries
6 oz (175 g) butter, softened
6 oz (175 g) caster sugar
3 eggs, beaten
8 oz (225 g) self-raising flour
2 oz (50 g) ground almonds
finely grated rind of 1 lemon

HOW TO MAKE

Heat the oven to 350°F/180°C/gas mark 4. Grease and line a 7 inch (17.5 cm) round cake tin with greased greaseproof paper.

Cut each cherry into quarters, put in a sieve and rinse under running water. Drain well and dry very thoroughly on absorbent kitchen paper.

Cream the butter and sugar together in a bowl until light and fluffy, then add the eggs with 2 tablespoons of the flour, beating well. Lastly, fold in the remaining flour, the ground almonds, lemon rind and cherries. The mixture will be fairly stiff, which will help to keep the cherries evenly suspended in the cake while it is baking.

Turn into the prepared tin and bake in the oven for 1¼ hours, or until a fine skewer inserted in the centre comes out clean. Leave to cool in the tin for 10 minutes, then turn out and finish cooling on a wire rack. Store in an airtight tin.

SUNDAY TEA CHOCOLATE CAKE

MAKES 2 CAKES

A real Sunday best cake! Large, moist and luxurious.

INGREDIENTS

10 oz (275 g) caster sugar
6 tablespoons water
3 oz (75 g) cocoa
¼ pint (150 ml) milk
8 oz (225 g) soft margarine
4 eggs, separated
8 oz (225 g) self-raising flour
2 level teaspoons baking powder

ICING AND FILLING
3 oz (75 g) butter
2 oz (50 g) cocoa, sieved
6 tablespoons milk
8 oz (225 g) icing sugar, sieved
½ pint (300 ml) whipping cream, whipped

HOW TO MAKE

Heat the oven to 350°F/180°C/gas mark 4. Grease and line with greased greaseproof paper 2 × 8 inch (20 cm) sandwich tins.

Put 3 oz (75 g) of the caster sugar in a pan with the water and cocoa and mix to a thick paste. Cook gently until the mixture is thick and shiny. Stir in the milk and leave to cool.

Cream the margarine with the remaining sugar. Beat in the egg yolks with the cocoa mixture, then fold in the flour and baking powder. Whisk the egg whites until stiff then fold them into the mixture too. Divide between the tins and bake for about 40 minutes until the cakes spring back when lightly pressed with a finger. Turn them out, peel off paper and leave to cool on a wire rack.

To make the icing, melt the butter in a small pan, stir in the cocoa and cook gently for 1 minute. Remove from heat, and beat in milk and icing sugar. Leave to cool, stirring occasionally until icing has thickened. Split each cake in half, and sandwich cakes together with whipped cream. Spread chocolate icing over the tops.

AUSTRIAN BUTTER FINGERS

MAKES ABOUT
15–20

Always popular for tea time or coffee mornings. Keep an eye on the biscuits as they cook, and remove from the oven when they are just beginning to colour. If they turn dark they won't taste as nice.

INGREDIENTS

6 oz (175 g) butter, softened
2 oz (50 g) icing sugar
1/4 teaspoon vanilla essence
6 oz (175 g) plain flour
melted chocolate

HOW TO MAKE

Heat the oven to 350°F/180°C/gas mark 4. Cream the butter and icing sugar together in a bowl until light and fluffy. Add the vanilla essence and gradually work in the flour.

Put the mixture into a piping bag fitted with a large star nozzle and pipe fingers on to a baking sheet. Bake in the oven for about 10–15 minutes, until just beginning to colour.

Lift the biscuits on to a cooling tray and leave to cool, then dip each end in melted chocolate. Leave to set on baking parchment. Alternatively, sandwich pairs of fingers together with butter icing (see below), then dip in chocolate.

BUTTER ICING

INGREDIENTS

2 oz (50 g) butter, softened
4 oz (100 g) icing sugar, sieved
a little lemon juice

HOW TO MAKE

Beat the butter and sugar very well together until smooth and well blended. Add a little lemon juice to taste.

Rubbed-in Method

RATHER GOOD ROCK CAKES

MAKES 24

Rock cakes are made so quickly from store cupboard ingredients, and are full of fruit. I like mine to spread a bit, as it makes them lighter. If you like a more solid rock cake, then just add 1 tablespoon milk. Rock cakes are best eaten on the day they are made or at least the next day.

INGREDIENTS

8 oz (225 g) self-raising flour
2 teaspoons baking powder
4 oz (100 g) soft margarine
2 oz (50 g) golden granulated sugar
3 oz (75 g) sultanas
3 oz (75 g) currants
1 egg, beaten
2 tablespoons milk

TOPPING
a little demerara sugar

HOW TO MAKE

Heat the oven to 400°F/200°C/gas mark 6. Lightly grease two large baking trays.

Measure the flour and baking powder into a bowl, add the margarine, and rub in until the mixture resembles breadcrumbs. Add the remaining ingredients, except the topping, and mix together. Spoon out 12 rock cakes on each baking tray using two teaspoons. Sprinkle them with demerara sugar.

Put the two trays one above the other in the oven, swapping the trays over halfway through the cooking time. Bake for about 15 minutes, until just beginning to brown at the edges. Lift on to a wire rack to cool.

Variation

Spicy Rock Cakes   Add 1 level teaspoon of mixed spice to the flour and baking powder.

REALLY GOOD SHORTBREAD

MAKES 12
FINGERS

Butter makes the best shortbread, but for everyday you can mix butter and margarine half-and-half. A good shortbread is an even, pale, biscuity beige colour – lift it up gently to see if it's the same colour underneath. The recipe can be varied slightly in a number of ways. You can use cornflour, ground rice or semolina, each of which gives slightly different textures; cornflour gives the least crunchy texture, semolina the most crunchy. You can make it in a square tin for fingers, or roll out to a circle for wedge-shaped petticoat tails.

INGREDIENTS

4 oz (100 g) plain flour
2 oz (50 g) cornflour, ground rice or semolina
4 oz (100 g) butter, cut into pieces
2 oz (50 g) caster sugar
a little caster sugar, for dusting

HOW TO MAKE

Heat the oven to 325°F/160°C/gas mark 3. Grease a 7 inch (18 cm) shallow square tin.

Mix the flour with the cornflour, ground rice or semolina in a bowl. Add butter and sugar. Rub together with fingertips until the mixture is just beginning to bind together. Knead lightly, just until the dough forms a smooth ball.

Press the mixture into the prepared tin and bake in the oven for about 35 minutes, or until a very pale golden brown.

Remove from the oven and mark into 12 fingers. Leave the shortbread to cool in the tin, then sprinkle with caster sugar.

Variations

Wholewheat Shortbread   Use wholewheat flour instead of the 4 oz (100 g) plain flour.

MAKES
ABOUT 40

Butter and Almond Processor Shortbread   Put 3½ oz (90 g) self-raising flour, 2 oz (50 g) semolina, 4 oz (100 g) butter, 2 oz (50 g) caster sugar and a few drops of almond essence into a food processor and process until smooth. Scrape down sides and process briefly. Transfer the mixture to a piping bag fitted with a plain ½ inch (1.25 cm) piping nozzle. Pipe about 40 blobs on to a greased baking sheet. Press a split almond into the top of each biscuit. Bake in the oven at 350°F/180°C/gas mark 4 for about 15–20 minutes, until pale golden. Watch carefully as they quickly overbake.

OLD-FASHIONED RICH TEA SCONES

MAKES
ABOUT 15

Scones are lovely to serve at tea time or a coffee morning. For the lightest scones avoid handling the dough too much – it doesn't require kneading.

INGREDIENTS

8 oz (225 g) self-raising flour
2 oz (50 g) butter
1 oz (25 g) sugar
¼ pint (150 ml) milk and water, mixed
milk, for brushing

HOW TO MAKE

Heat the oven to 425°F/220°C/gas mark 7. Lightly grease a baking tray.
  Measure the flour into a bowl. Cut the butter into small pieces, then rub into the flour until the mixture resembles fine breadcrumbs. Stir in the sugar. Mix in enough of the milk and water to give a soft dough.
  Turn out on to a lightly floured surface and roll out thickly. With a plain cutter, cut into 1½ inch (4 cm) rounds.
  Arrange on the tray, brush the tops with a little milk and bake in the oven for about 10–15 minutes, until well risen and golden brown. Cool on a wire rack.
  Split open the scones and serve with butter.

Variations

Fruit Scones   Add 2–3 oz (50–75 g) dried fruit to the rubbed-in mixture in the bowl.

Very Special Cheese Scones   Add 3 oz (75 g) grated mature Cheddar cheese and salt and pepper to the breadcrumb mixture instead of the sugar.

Melting-fat Method

VERY MOIST GINGERBREAD

MAKES ABOUT
18 SQUARES

Gingerbread improves with keeping and is best made 2–3 days before you need it. When you come to cut it you will find it deliciously moist.

INGREDIENTS

4 oz (100 g) margarine
3 oz (75 g) dark muscovado sugar
¼ pint (150 ml) golden syrup
¼ pint (150 ml) black treacle
3 teaspoons ground ginger
½ teaspoon mixed spice
2 eggs
¼ pint (150 ml) milk
10 oz (275 g) flour
½ teaspoon bicarbonate of soda

HOW TO MAKE

Heat the oven to 325°F/160°C/gas mark 3. Line an 8 × 12 inch (20 × 30 cm) roasting tin with foil and lightly grease the foil.

Measure the margarine, sugar, syrup, treacle, ginger and spice into a pan and heat gently until melted and mixed. Beat the eggs into the milk. Sift the flour and bicarbonate of soda into a bowl, add all the other ingredients and beat well. Pour through a sieve, in case of lumps, into the prepared tin.

Bake in the oven for about 1¼ hours, until springy to the touch and just beginning to shrink away from the sides of the tin. Watch that it doesn't get too brown on top; if necessary, cover the top loosely with a piece of foil. Leave to cool completely in tin. Wrap in foil or clingfilm and store for 2–3 days before cutting.

FLAPJACKS

MAKES 12

These delicious flapjacks are quick and easy to make. Do mark into squares after cooling for 10 minutes; don't forget as the baked mixture hardens as it cools.

INGREDIENTS

4 oz (100 g) margarine
4 oz (100 g) demerara sugar
1 tablespoon golden syrup
5 oz (150 g) rolled oats

HOW TO MAKE

Heat the oven to 325°F/160°C/gas mark 3. Lightly grease a 7 inch (18 cm) shallow square tin.

Measure the margarine into a pan with the sugar and syrup and heat gently until the margarine has melted. Remove from the heat and stir in the oats. Mix well, then turn into the prepared tin and level the top.

Bake in the oven for about 35 minutes, until golden brown. Remove from the oven, leave to cool for 10 minutes, then mark into 12 squares. Leave in the tin to finish cooling.

CHOCOLATE KRISPIES

MAKES ABOUT
12–15

No need to use butter for this recipe. These are most children's all-time favourites. For the best results, they should be eaten on the day that they are made. This is usually no problem! Let the children make them themselves and try and persuade them that it is worth waiting for the krispies to set.

INGREDIENTS

2 oz (50 g) margarine
2 tablespoons drinking chocolate powder
1 rounded tablespoon golden syrup
2½ oz (62 g) rice krispies

HOW TO MAKE

Put the margarine in a saucepan and heat gently until it is melted. Stir in the drinking chocolate and golden syrup and mix well. Remove from the heat, tip in the krispies and stir very well so that they become evenly coated with the chocolate mixture. Using two spoons, pile the mixture into about 12–15 paper cases. Leave to harden in a cool room for about 30 minutes.

Store any krispies that are not eaten in an airtight tin.

CHOCOLATE JULIET

SERVES 6

A very rich uncooked chocolate cake, so serve thin slices – they can always come back for more. Serve straight out of the refrigerator.

INGREDIENTS

8 oz (225 g) milk chocolate
8 oz (225 g) margarine
2 eggs
1 oz caster sugar
8 oz (225 g) 'Nice' biscuits
2 oz (50 g) chopped raisins
2 oz (50 g) chopped nuts
1 oz (25 g) quartered glacé cherries

HOW TO MAKE

Line a small loaf tin, 7½ × 4 inches (19 × 10 cm) by 2½ inches (6 cm) deep, with foil.

Break the chocolate into small pieces and place in a pan with the margarine, then heat gently until melted. Beat the eggs and sugar together until blended, then gradually add the chocolate mixture a little at a time. Break biscuits into ½ inch (1.5 cm) pieces and stir into the chocolate mixture with raisins, nuts and cherries. Press the mixture into the prepared tin and smooth the top. Leave to set in the refrigerator for about 6 hours, or until firm, preferably overnight.

Turn out on to a serving dish and peel off the foil.

BRANDY SNAPS

MAKES 30

The quantities given in this recipe result in a lot of brandy snaps, but they keep very well in an airtight tin. If only a few are required, it is easy to make half the quantity. The mixture does not take long to make, but it does take a little time to lift the brandy snaps from the baking sheet and roll them up.

INGREDIENTS

4 oz (100 g) butter
4 oz (100 g) demerara sugar
4 oz (100 g) golden syrup
4 oz (100 g) flour
1 teaspoon ground ginger
1 teaspoon lemon juice

HOW TO MAKE

Heat the oven to 350°F/180°C/gas mark 4. Thoroughly grease several baking sheets and oil the handles of four wooden spoons.

Measure the butter, sugar and syrup into a saucepan and heat gently until the butter and sugar have dissolved. Allow the mixture to cool slightly and then sift in the flour and ginger. Stir well, adding the lemon juice.

Drop teaspoonfuls of the mixture on to the baking sheets at least 4 inches (10 cm) apart. It is best only to put four spoonfuls on the baking sheets at a time.

Bake in the oven for about 8 minutes, until the snaps are a golden brown. Remove from the oven and leave for a few minutes to firm, then lift from the tin with a sharp knife, using a sawing movement. At once, roll around the handle of the wooden spoons and leave to set on a wire rack. Slip out the spoons.

Store in an airtight tin as soon as they are cold.

They may be served just as they are with ice cream, mousses or soufflés but they are also good if you fill them with a little whipped cream and serve them with fruit.

COOK'S TIP

To measure syrup accurately, stand the empty mixing bowl or saucepan on the scales and spoon in the required amount of syrup. For less accurate weighing, one tablespoon holds approximately 1 oz (25 g) syrup. Syrup will slide easily off the measuring spoon if first dipped in hot water.

JAFFA CAKES

**MAKES ABOUT
12 SQUARES**

These very rich and sweet cakes are adored by Jaffa biscuit enthusiasts. If the weather or your kitchen are warm, store the Jaffa Cakes in the refrigerator otherwise they will be too soft to eat.

INGREDIENTS

3 oz (75 g) butter
3 oz (75 g) caster sugar
1 egg, beaten
3 oz (75 g) self-raising flour
8 oz (225 g) apricot jam
grated rind 1 small orange plus 1 tablespoon juice
6 oz (175 g) plain chocolate

HOW TO MAKE

Heat the oven to 325°F/160°C/gas mark 3. Brush an 11 × 7 inch (27.5 × 18 cm) Swiss roll tin with oil.

Measure the butter into a saucepan and very gently heat until it has just melted, but is not hot. Remove from heat, stir in the caster sugar, beaten egg and flour. Stir until smooth.

Spread the mixture over the prepared tin and bake in the oven for 25–30 minutes, until still soft but pale golden brown on top. Leave to cool.

Warm the apricot jam and sieve it if there are any big pieces of fruit. Stir in the orange rind and juice. Spread over the cold cake. Melt the chocolate in a bowl over pan of hot water and spread carefully over the cold apricot jam, making sure you go right up to the edges of the cake. Cut into squares when cold.

Whisked Sponges and Roulades

SWISS ROLL

Making a Swiss roll is quite simple if the ingredients are weighed accurately and the instructions closely followed. Make sure the eggs are at room temperature as they will give a greater volume when whisked.

INGREDIENTS

3 size 2 eggs, at room temperature
3 oz (75 g) caster sugar, warmed
3 oz (75 g) self-raising flour
caster sugar
raspberry jam

HOW TO MAKE

Heat the oven to 425°F/220°C/gas mark 7. Grease and line a 13 × 9 inch (33 × 23 cm) Swiss roll tin with greased greaseproof paper or silicone paper.

Whisk the eggs and sugar together in a large bowl until the mixture is light and creamy and the whisk leaves a trail when lifted out. Sieve the flour and carefully fold in using a metal spoon.

Turn the mixture into the prepared tin and give it a gentle shake so that the mixture finds its own level and spreads evenly into corners. Bake in the oven for about 10 minutes, until the sponge is golden brown and just beginning to shrink from the edges of the tin.

While the cake is cooking, cut a piece of greaseproof or silicone paper just a bit larger than the tin and sprinkle it with caster sugar. Heat about 4 tablespoons of jam in a small pan until it is soft enough to spread easily but not too hot or it will soak into the sponge.

Invert the cake on to the sugared paper. Loosen the lining paper and peel it off. To make rolling easier, trim the crisp edges (all four) from the sponge and make a score mark 1 inch (2.5 cm) in from one short edge, taking care not to cut right through. Spread the cake with jam, taking it almost to the edges. Fold the narrow strip created by the score mark down on the jam and begin rolling using the paper to keep a firm line.

Leave for a few minutes with the paper wrapped round it, to set. Lift Swiss roll on to a wire rack, remove paper and sprinkle with more sugar. Leave to cool completely.

CHOCOLATE BRANDY ROULADE

SERVES 6–8

A truly delicious pudding cake. Don't worry that the sponge cracks as you roll it, it is meant to!

INGREDIENTS

6 oz (175 g) plain chocolate, broken into small pieces
6 oz (175 g) caster sugar
6 eggs, separated

FILLING AND DECORATION
2 tablespoons brandy
½ pint (300 ml) double cream, whipped
icing sugar
fresh strawberries

HOW TO MAKE

Heat the oven to 350°F/180°C/gas mark 4. Grease and line a 13 × 9 inch (33 × 23 cm) Swiss roll tin with greased greaseproof paper or silicone paper.

Break the chocolate into a bowl and set the bowl over a pan of hot water to melt. Put the sugar and egg yolks in a bowl and whisk with an electric whisk on full speed until light and creamy. Carefully stir in the melted chocolate until blended.

Whisk the egg whites in a separate bowl until stiff, then fold gently into the chocolate mixture. Turn into the prepared tin and spread into the corners. Bake in the oven for about 20 minutes, until firm to the touch.

Remove from the oven, leave in the tin and cover with a piece of greaseproof paper or a clean folded tea towel and leave to stand for several hours or overnight.

Stir the brandy into the whipped cream. Dust a large sheet of greaseproof paper with icing sugar, turn out the roulade and peel off the paper. To make rolling easier, trim all four edges of the roulade and make a score mark 1 inch (2.5 cm) in from one of the shorter edges, being careful not to cut right through. Spread the roulade with the cream, fold the narrow strip created by the score mark over, and roll up like a Swiss roll, using the paper to help. Dust with icing sugar and place on a serving dish. Decorate with fresh strawberries.

Choux Pastry

CHOCOLATE ÉCLAIRS

MAKES 12
ÉCLAIRS

If you like the centres of the éclairs really dry, return them to the oven after splitting the side of each one to let the steam out. Lower the oven to 350°F/160°C/gas mark 3 and cook until the centre is dry – about a further 10 minutes, then leave to cool.

INGREDIENTS

CHOUX PASTRY
2 oz (50 g) butter
¼ pint (150 ml) water
2½ oz (65 g) flour, sieved
2 eggs, beaten

FILLING
½ pint (300 ml) whipping cream, whipped

ICING
2 oz (50 g) plain chocolate, broken into small pieces
2 tablespoons water
½ oz (15 g) butter
3 oz (75 g) icing sugar, sieved

HOW TO MAKE

Heat the oven to 425°F/220°C/gas mark 7. Lightly grease a large baking tray.

First make the choux pastry. Measure the butter and water into a small pan, bring slowly to the boil and allow the butter to melt. Remove from the heat, add the flour all at once, and beat until it forms a soft ball. Gradually beat in the eggs, a little at a time, to give a smooth shiny paste.

Turn the mixture into a piping bag fitted with a ½ inch (1 cm) plain nozzle and pipe 12 long éclair shapes, about 5–6 inches (13–15 cm) long on to the baking tray, leaving room for them to spread.

Bake in the oven for about 10 minutes, then reduce the heat to 375°F/190°C/gas mark 5. Cook for about a further 20 minutes until well risen and golden brown. Remove from the oven and split one side of each éclair to allow the steam to escape. Cool on a wire rack.

Fill each of the éclairs with a little cream. To make the icing, measure the chocolate, water and butter into a bowl. Heat over a pan of simmering water until the chocolate and butter have melted. Remove from the heat and beat in the icing sugar until smooth. Pour into a shallow dish, then dip each éclair into the icing to coat the top. Allow to set.

Bread and Yeast Doughs

SODA BREAD

MAKES ONE
LOAF

If you run out of bread, this is a quick and easy recipe to make. It is best eaten fresh as a tea bread or as a substitute for yeast-baked bread. If you do not have soured milk, fresh milk may be soured by adding 1 tablespoon lemon juice.

INGREDIENTS

1 lb (450 g) plain flour
1 level teaspoon salt
2 level teaspoons bicarbonate of soda
2 level teaspoons cream of tartar
1 oz (25 g) butter
about ½ pint (300 ml) soured milk

HOW TO MAKE

Heat the oven to 400°F/200°C/gas mark 6. Flour a baking sheet. Sift the flour, salt, bicarbonate of soda and cream of tartar into a bowl. Add the butter and rub in with your fingertips until the mixture is like breadcrumbs.

Make a well in the centre and stir in the milk. Mix to a scone-like dough with a round-bladed knife. Turn the dough on to a lightly floured surface and knead lightly. Shape into a 7 inch (17.5 cm) round, flatten slightly and then place on the baking sheet.

Mark the round into four with the back of a knife and bake in the oven for about 35 minutes, until it is well risen and golden brown. Leave to cool on a wire rack. Serve sliced, spread with butter.

DROP SCONES

MAKES
ABOUT 20

Quick and easy to make from ingredients likely to be in the larder. They're delicious warm, spread with butter and strawberry jam. Very good made with self-raising wholewheat flour too. The cooked drop scones are wrapped immediately in a tea towel to trap the steam and keep the scones soft and springy.

INGREDIENTS

4 oz (100 g) self-raising flour
1 oz (25 g) caster sugar
1 egg
¼ pint (150 ml) milk

HOW TO MAKE Grease a non-stick frying pan or griddle. Stand it on the hob on medium heat until hot.

Measure the flour and sugar into a bowl and make a well in the centre. Add the egg and half the milk and beat to a thick batter. Stir in the remaining milk.

Spoon the mixture on to the hot pan in tablespoonfuls, spacing them well apart. When bubbles rise to the surface, turn the pancakes over with a palette knife and cook on the other side for a further 30 seconds or so, until golden brown.

Lift off and keep wrapped in a clean tea towel to keep them soft. Continue cooking until all the batter has been used. Serve them warm.

CRUMPETS

MAKES
ABOUT 20

These freeze well and are fun to make as they are cooked on the top of the oven and the characteristic holes appear before your very eyes.

INGREDIENTS

1 1/2 teaspoons dried yeast
1/2 teaspoon sugar
1/2 pint (300 ml) tepid water
12 oz (350 g) strong white flour
1/2 teaspoon salt
8 fl oz (250 ml) milk
oil for greasing

HOW TO MAKE Put the yeast and sugar into the warm water, stir well to mix and leave in a warm place until it froths.

Measure the flour and salt into a large bowl, pour in the yeast mixture and the milk and mix well to make a thick batter. Beat well, cover and leave in a warm place for about 1 hour, until the surface is bubbly. Beat well again to mix. Pour into a jug.

Grease some crumpet rings and a heavy-based frying pan. Place the greased rings on the frying pan and leave to become heated through. Pour some batter into each ring to about half the depth. Cook for about 5–7 minutes until the tops are dry and full of holes.

At this point, the crumpets will shrink away from the sides of the rings which now can be removed and set aside. To finish cooking, turn the crumpets over and cook for another minute until pale golden. Continue with the rest of the batter, ensuring the rings are well greased each time.

To serve, toast the crumpets on each side and spread with butter. Serve hot.

WHITE, BROWN OR GRANARY BREAD

MAKES TWO 1 lb
(450 g) LOAVES
OR ONE 2 lb
(900 g) LOAF

To make a lighter wholemeal or granary loaf, substitute half the quantity of flour with strong white flour – this also makes the dough easier to handle. Brown flour absorbs more liquid than white so increase the water accordingly.

INGREDIENTS

1½ lb (675 g) strong white, granary or wholemeal flour
2 teaspoons salt
¾ oz (20 g) butter, cut into pieces
¾ oz (20 g) fresh yeast (or dried yeast according to makers'
*   equivalent)*
about ¾ pint (450 ml) tepid water

HOW TO MAKE

Grease two 1 lb (450 g) loaf tins or one 2 lb (900 g) tin. Measure the flour into a large bowl, add the salt and rub in the butter until the mixture resembles fine breadcrumbs. Make a well in the centre, crumble in the yeast and then pour in the water. Mix by hand and knead into a ball in the bowl.

Turn out on to a clean dry surface and knead for about 4 minutes (brown bread will not require as long). Return the dough to the bowl, cover with clingfilm and leave to rise in a warm place fo 1–1½ hours until double in size.

Knock back the dough and knead again for 2–3 minutes, then divide in half if making two loaves. Slightly flatten the ball of dough with the heel of your hand and fold in the two opposite sides, slightly overlapping, then roll up like a Swiss roll. Place the dough in the tin or tins with the folded part underneath. Cover with oiled clingfilm and leave to prove for about 30 minutes (with brown bread as soon as a few 'pin' holes begin to appear the loaf is ready to bake).

Meanwhile, heat the oven to 425°F/220°C/gas mark 7. Remove the clingfilm and bake in the oven for about 20–30 minutes for two tins, 35–40 minutes for a 2 lb (900 g) loaf, until evenly browned and when the loaf is turned out a hollow noise is made when the loaf is knocked on the base.

Variations

Crown Loaf   Use half the quantity of dough to make 12 equal sized balls. Place in a greased 8 inch (20 cm) shallow cake tin and bake for 25 minutes.

Rolls   After the second kneading divide the dough into 16 equal pieces. Shape into balls (or other shapes, see opposite) and place on a greased baking sheet. Bake for about 20 minutes until golden brown and the rolls sound hollow, when tapped on the bottom. White rolls can be sprinkled with sesame seeds before proving, and brown and granary rolls can be sprinkled with cracked wheat.

Shaping rolls

Knots   Roll out each piece of dough to a 6 inch (15 cm) length. Tie each one into a simple knot.

Plaits   Divide each piece of dough into three. Shape into three equal lengths. Place side by side and pinch one set of ends together. Plait the three lengths, then pinch the other ends together and tuck underneath.

BRIOCHES

MAKES 12

Best served warm and if there happen to be any left, then they make an excellent breakfast with butter and marmalade. Use easy-blend dried yeast – you simply mix it in to the flour – there's no mixing with water and sugar and waiting for it to go frothy.

INGREDIENTS

9 oz (250 g) strong plain white flour
1 oz (25 g) caster sugar
2 oz (50 g) butter, cut into pieces
½ oz (15 g) easy-blend dried yeast
3 tablespoons tepid milk
2 eggs, beaten
a little beaten egg, to glaze

HOW TO MAKE

Measure the flour and sugar into a large mixing bowl and rub in the butter until the mixture resembles fine breadcrumbs. Stir in the yeast until thoroughly blended, then add the milk and eggs and work together to form a soft dough.

Knead until smooth in the bowl, then turn out on to a lightly floured surface and knead for at least 5 minutes. This kneading can be done in a food processor and will take 60 seconds. Return the dough to the bowl, cover with clingfilm and leave in a warm place for about 1 hour, until the dough has doubled in size. Lightly grease 12 fluted brioche moulds or deep fluted patty tins.

Knead the dough again on a floured surface, then divide into 12 equal pieces. Cut off a quarter from each piece, then form the larger part into a ball and place in the greased tins. Firmly press a hole in the centre of each ball and place the remaining small piece of dough on top of this. Cover all the brioches with clingfilm and leave to prove for another 45 minutes, until light and puffy.

Heat the oven to 450°F/230°C/gas mark 8. To bake the brioches, glaze with a little beaten egg and bake in the oven for 10–12 minutes, until golden brown. Gently lift out of the moulds and allow to cool on a wire rack. Serve warm with butter balls for a special occasion.

DANISH PASTRIES

MAKES 16

These are easy and quick to make using easy-blend dried yeast. They also freeze well!

INGREDIENTS

PASTRY
8 oz (225 g) strong plain flour
¼ teaspoon salt
6 oz (175 g) butter
1 sachet of easy-blend dried yeast
5 tablespoons tepid water
1 egg
1 oz (25 g) caster sugar
a little beaten egg, to glaze

FILLING AND TOPPING
4 oz (100 g) white almond paste
a little glacé icing made with 4 oz (100 g) icing sugar
1 oz (25 g) flaked almonds, toasted
1 oz (25 g) glacé cherries, washed, dried and chopped

HOW TO MAKE

Measure the flour and salt into a bowl and rub in 1 oz (25 g) of the butter. Add the yeast and blend in. Make a well in the centre, add the water and the egg blended with the sugar. Draw in the flour from the sides and mix to a soft dough. Turn out on to a floured surface and knead. Put the dough into a polythene bag and chill for 10 minutes.

Mash the remaining butter until it is spreadable. Take the chilled dough from the refrigerator and roll out to an oblong about 12 × 10 inches (30 × 25 cm). Spread the butter down the centre of the dough. Fold the two long sides of the pastry inwards so that they are just overlapping to encase the butter. With the folds at the sides, fold the bottom third up and the top third down. Return it to the polythene bag and chill for a further 10 minutes. Roll out again to an oblong, then fold into three. Repeat this process and chill again for 10 minutes. The dough is then ready for shaping (see opposite).

After shaping, arrange the pastries on baking trays, cover with polythene, and leave to prove for about 20 minutes in a warm place, until beginning to look puffy. Meanwhile, heat the oven to 425°F/220°C/gas mark 7. Brush each pastry with beaten egg again, and bake in the oven for about 15 minutes, until golden brown. Lift on to a wire rack to cool.

Spoon a little of the icing over each pastry whilst they are still warm. Sprinkle some of them with flaked almonds and some with small pieces of glacé cherry.

Shaping Danish pastries

Crescents Take half the pastry and roll out to a 9 inch (23 cm) circle. Divide the circle into eight wedges. Place a small amount of almond paste at the wide end of each wedge, and brush with beaten egg. Roll them up from this end towards the point, and bend them round to form a crescent.

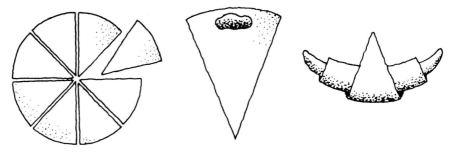

Star Shapes Roll out half the remaining dough to form a 6 inch (15 cm) square. Cut the square into four. Place a small amount of almond paste in the centre of one square. Make cuts from each corner almost to the centre, brush with beaten egg, then lift the left-hand corner of the bottom triangle into the centre to cover part of the paste. Repeat with the other 3 triangles to form a star. Shape the remaining squares in the same way.

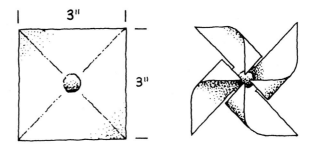

Kite Shapes Roll out the remaining dough very thinly to form an 8 inch (20 cm) square. Cut the square into four. Place a small amount of almond paste in the centre of one square. Cut ½ inch (1.5 cm) inside the square as shown below, A to B and C to D, then brush with beaten egg. Lift both cut corner strips and cross them over the almond paste in the centre. Repeat this with the remaining squares.

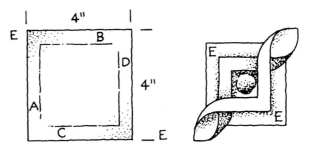

Sauces and Accompaniments

All the sauces are simple to make, and many can be made in advance and stored until needed. Probably the sauce requiring most care is Hollandaise, but if you follow the instructions carefully, whether making by hand or in a food processor, you will achieve a perfect result. Hollandaise is served warm, and should be made just before it is needed as it can't successfully be kept warm or be reheated. A white sauce, on the other hand, can be kept warm by standing the pan in a larger pan of simmering water, with the top of the sauce covered closely with a piece of wet greaseproof paper to stop a skin forming.

Should you by mistake make a lumpy sauce or custard, rather than put it through a sieve just process it in the food processor until smooth again. It will be corrected in a flash.

Leftover fresh gravies and sauces (except those with added cream or of the Hollandaise kind) freeze well for up to a month. Thaw then reheat and stir briskly.

I also give recipes for flavoured butters – garlic being the most popular – and accompaniments such as Garlic Bread, Croûtons and various savoury stuffings. Serving suggestions are included in each recipe.

GARLIC BUTTER

Use for garlic bread, tossing cooked vegetables in, cooking mushrooms or topping grilled steaks.

INGREDIENTS

8 oz (225 g) butter
4 cloves garlic, crushed
salt and freshly ground black pepper

HOW TO MAKE

Cut the butter into chunks and put in a blender or food processor with the garlic and seasoning. Process for a few moments until smooth. Turn into a glass container, cover well and store in the refrigerator until required. It can be stored for up to 1 month.

Variation

Garlic Herb Butter Put a good bunch of leavy herbs, such as basil, marjoram, dill, tarragon and parsley into the blender or processor and process for a few moments until roughly chopped, then add the butter, garlic and seasoning and continue as above.

CUCUMBER SAUCE

Serve with cold salmon and trout. If preferred, use Greek-style yoghurt instead of cream.

INGREDIENTS

½ cucumber, diced
2 teaspoons salt
¼ pint (150 ml) mayonnaise (see page 126)
¼ pint (150 ml) whipping cream, whipped
juice of ½ lemon
salt and freshly ground black pepper
2 tablespoons snipped dill

HOW TO MAKE

Place diced cucumber on a plate and sprinkle with salt. Leave to stand for 30 minutes, then rinse and thoroughly dry on absorbent kitchen paper. Blend together the mayonnaise and cream, then stir in the lemon juice, seasoning, cucumber and dill. Turn into a serving bowl and chill well.

MINT SAUCE

Serve with roast lamb or grilled lamb chops.

INGREDIENTS

a bunch of mint (about 8 good large sprigs)
2 teaspoons caster sugar
1 tablespoon boiling water
about 2 tablespoons vinegar

HOW TO MAKE

Wash the mint and shake off the excess water, then remove the leaves from the stems. Chop the leaves finely either by hand or in a blender or food processor. Place the sugar in a sauceboat with the boiling water and stir until dissolved. Add the chopped mint and vinegar to taste. Add a little more sugar, if liked.

MINT SAUCE CONCENTRATE

The best time to make this is in June when mint is at its best.

INGREDIENTS

½ pint (300 ml) distilled vinegar
8 oz (225 g) sugar
6 oz (175 g) mint leaves, finely chopped

HOW TO MAKE

Measure the vinegar and sugar into a pan and heat slowly, stirring, until all the sugar has dissolved. Increase the heat and bring to the boil, then add the mint and remove from the heat. Pour into screw-top jars. Dilute with extra vinegar to make it into a mint sauce to accompany roast lamb.

INSTANT YOGHURT SAUCE

Leafy herbs are best in this light sauce. Serve it with cold fish such as trout and salmon. For a richer sauce use Greek yoghurt.

INGREDIENTS

small bunch of fresh herbs, such as basil, tarragon, parsley, dill
juice of ½ lemon
½ pint (300 ml) natural yoghurt
salt and freshly ground black pepper

HOW TO MAKE

Put the herbs in a blender or food processor and process for a few seconds until roughly chopped. Add the lemon juice, yoghurt and seasoning. Process for a few seconds. Check the seasoning and serve well chilled.

SAUCE ROUILLE

A spicy hot sauce to compliment the richness of Bouillabaise (page 24).

INGREDIENTS

1 small can pimentoes, drained
1 clove garlic
1–2 fresh chillies, seeded
salt
1 tablespoon olive oil

HOW TO MAKE

Measure all the ingredients into a blender or food processor and process until smooth. Check for seasoning – it should be spicy hot.

HORSERADISH SAUCE

Serve with roast beef and steaks. Grated horseradish root is available in jars from good delicatessen shops.

INGREDIENTS

¼ pint (150 ml) double cream
2 tablespoons grated horseradish
1 teaspoon cider or white wine vinegar
salt and freshly ground black pepper
a little caster sugar

HOW TO MAKE

Lightly whip the cream and add the horseradish. Stir in the vinegar and seasoning. Add a little sugar to taste and blend thoroughly. Turn into a small serving dish, cover with clingfilm and chill before serving.

PESTO

MAKES ABOUT ½ PINT (300 ML)

A delicious sauce to toss hot spaghetti in or to add to cooked vegetables. Quickly made in a blender or food processor, it can be stored in the refrigerator for up to 3 weeks in a screw-top jar. Fresh parsley can be added with the basil, if liked.

INGREDIENTS

2 oz (50 g) fresh basil leaves
2 cloves garlic
2 tablespoons pine nuts
4 fl oz (120 ml) good quality olive oil
2 oz (50 g) Parmesan cheese, grated
salt and freshly ground black pepper

HOW TO MAKE

Measure the basil, garlic and pine nuts into the blender or food processor and process until the herbs are finely chopped. With the machine running, add the oil in a fine stream until the paste is creamy. Transfer to a bowl, add the Parmesan and seasoning to taste. Mix well together, then pack into a screw-top jar for storing.

MUSTARD DILL SAUCE

Serve with Gravadlax (see page 64) or cured herrings. Goes well with cold ham.

INGREDIENTS

3 tablespoons Dijon mustard
2 tablespoons caster sugar
1 tablespoon white wine vinegar
1 egg yolk
1/4 pint (150 ml) sunflower oil
salt and freshly ground black pepper
2 tablespoons chopped fresh dill or 1 tablespoon dried dill weed

HOW TO MAKE

Whisk the mustard, sugar, vinegar and egg yolk together in a bowl using a small balloon whisk, then add the oil, whisking well until it is the consistency of mayonnaise. Season with salt and pepper and stir in the dill.

BASIC WHITE SAUCE

This is the basis for many sauces and can be altered to give either a pouring sauce or a thick coating sauce. The recipe below is for a pouring sauce. For a coating sauce, increase the amounts of butter and flour to 2 oz (50 g) each and use the same amount of liquid.

INGREDIENTS

1 1/2 oz (40 g) butter
1 1/2 oz (40 g) flour
1 pint (600 ml) milk
salt and freshly ground black pepper

HOW TO MAKE

Melt the butter in a saucepan, add the flour and cook for 1 minute stirring. Gradually blend in the milk and bring to the boil, stirring until thickened. Cook for 1–2 minutes. Season to taste.

Variations

Cheese Sauce   Add 4 oz (100 g) well-flavoured Cheddar cheese, grated, and 1 teaspoon Dijon mustard to the thickened sauce.

Parsley Sauce   Add 2 tablespoons chopped parsley to the sauce.

Mustard Sauce   Add 1 tablespoon any mustard, 1 good teaspoon sugar and 1 tablespoon vinegar to the thickened sauce.

Onion Sauce   Finely chop 1 large onion and fry until soft in 1 oz (25 g) butter. Add it to the thickened sauce. Purée in a blender or food processor if a smooth sauce is preferred, then reheat.

CAPER SAUCE

Serve with boiled mutton or lamb.

INGREDIENTS

1½ oz (40 g) butter
1½ oz (40 g) flour
1 pint (600 ml) stock from the cooked mutton or lamb
2 tablespoons capers
1–2 teaspoons vinegar from capers
1 teaspoon prepared mustard
salt and freshly ground black pepper
a little sugar
2 tablespoons single cream or top of the milk

HOW TO MAKE

Melt the butter in a pan, stir in the flour and cook for 1 minute. Gradually blend in the stock from the mutton and bring to the boil, stirring until thickened. Stir in the capers, caper vinegar mustard, seasoning to taste and a little sugar. Add the cream and pour into a warm sauceboat.

BREAD SAUCE

Serve with roast chicken, turkey and game.

INGREDIENTS

2 whole cloves
1 onion
1 pint (600 ml) milk
about 4 oz (100 g) white breadcrumbs
salt and freshly ground black pepper
knob of butter

HOW TO MAKE

Stick the cloves into the onion and place in a pan with milk. Bring gently to the boil, remove pan from the heat and leave to infuse for 30 minutes.

Remove the onion from the milk, then stir in the breadcrumbs, seasoning and butter. Reheat the sauce almost to boiling point. Remove from heat, cover with a piece of damp greaseproof paper and keep warm until ready to serve.

FRESH HERB CREAM SAUCE

Wonderful fresh tasting sauce, ideal to serve with fish and it takes only seconds to make in a blender or food processor. Experiment with other fresh herbs to vary the flavour.

INGREDIENTS

3 oz (75 g) butter, melted
juice 1 lemon
1 rounded teaspoon flour
½ pint (300 ml) single cream
1 egg yolk
salt and pepper
1 tablespoon snipped dill or chives

HOW TO MAKE

Measure all the ingredients except the seasoning and herbs into a blender or food processor and process until smooth. Transfer to a small bowl and stand it over a pan of simmering water for about 10 minutes, stirring from time to time until thickened and will coat the back of a spoon. Season to taste and stir in the herbs. Transfer to a bowl or sauceboat to serve.

Variation

Crab Sauce   Drain 1 small can crabmeat, mash with a fork and combine with the sauce when thickened. Heat through.

HOLLANDAISE SAUCE

Serve with asparagus, artichokes, salmon or other fish.

INGREDIENTS

2 teaspoons lemon juice
2 teaspoons wine vinegar
3 egg yolks, at room temperature
4 oz (100 g) unsalted butter, softened
salt and freshly ground black pepper

HOW TO MAKE

Measure the lemon juice and vinegar into a bowl, add the egg yolks and whisk well with a balloon whisk. Place the bowl over a pan of hot water and continue whisking. Gradually add the softened butter, whisking until the sauce thickens and all the butter has been added. Season and serve.

Variation

To make in a food processor, place blade in position, heat the bowl by pouring in about 1 pint (600 ml) boiling water, switch on briefly then throw water away. Add the lemon juice and vinegar, switch on then add the egg yolks. With the machine running, pour piping hot butter through the funnel. Process until thick, season to taste and serve at once.

APPLE SAUCE

Serve with pork, duck or goose.

INGREDIENTS

1 lb (450 g) cooking apples
5 tablespoons water
juice of ½ lemon
1 oz (25 g) butter
sugar to taste

HOW TO MAKE

Peel, core and slice the apples. Place in a pan with water and lemon juice, cover and cook gently until soft. Beat well with a wooden spoon or purée in a blender or food processor until smooth. Add the butter and sugar to taste.

CRANBERRY SAUCE

Serve with roast turkey, pheasant, goose or roast pork.

INGREDIENTS

6 oz (175 g) caster sugar
¼ pint (150 ml) water
8 oz (225 g) fresh cranberries

HOW TO MAKE

Measure the sugar and water into a small pan and stir over a low heat until the sugar has completely dissolved. Wash the cranberries and remove any stalks. Add to the pan and bring to the boil, then simmer gently for about 10 minutes, until the berries are tender, stirring from time to time. Remove from the heat. Turn into a small serving dish and serve warm.

CUMBERLAND SAUCE

Serve with cold ham or gammon.

INGREDIENTS

2 oranges
2 lemons
2 shallots, finely chopped
1 lb (450 g) redcurrant jelly
2 heaped teaspoons Dijon mustard
¼ pint (150 ml) port
2 teaspoons cornflour
1 tablespoon water

HOW TO MAKE

Peel the oranges and lemons with a potato peeler. Cut the peel into very fine strips. Place the shallots in a small pan, cover with water and boil for 2 minutes. Add the strips of peel and boil for a further 2 minutes, then drain and set aside.

Cut the oranges and lemons in half, squeeze juice from the fruit and place in a small pan. Add the redcurrant jelly, heat until the jelly has melted and combined with the fruit juice, then add the mustard and port.

Mix the cornflour with the water. Pour a little of the sauce on to the cornflour, mix together, then pour the cornflour into the saucepan, stir well and gently bring to the boil, stirring until thickened. Simmer for 1 minute, then leave to cool. Keeps in the refrigerator for up to 3 weeks.

TOMATO SAUCE

Serve with simple meat dishes and spaghetti.

INGREDIENTS

1 rasher streaky bacon, snipped
1 onion, chopped
1 oz (25 g) flour
14 oz (400 g) can chopped tomatoes
¼ pint (150 ml) chicken or vegetable stock (see page 14)
salt and freshly ground black pepper
1 tablespoon Worcestershire sauce
1 teaspoon sugar
1 bay leaf
1 fat clove garlic, crushed

HOW TO MAKE

Heat the bacon gently in a small non-stick pan over a low heat until the fat runs out. Add the onion and cook gently for about 5 minutes. Stir in the flour and cook for 1 minute. Add the tomatoes and stock and bring to the boil, stirring until thickened.

Stir in the remaining ingredients, cover and simmer for about 20 minutes. Remove the bay leaf and reduce the mixture to a purée in a blender or food processor. Return it to the pan, reheat, then taste and check the seasoning before serving.

BARBECUE SAUCE

Serve with grilled meat or beefburgers. You can vary the flavour by adding half a jar of mango chutney, chopped.

INGREDIENTS

1 oz (25 g) butter
1 tablespoon oil
1 onion, finely chopped
14 oz (400 g) can chopped tomatoes
3 tablespoons water
2 tablespoons lemon juice
1 tablespoon brown sugar
2 teaspoons made mustard
½ teaspoon paprika
½ teaspoon chilli powder
salt and freshly ground black pepper

HOW TO MAKE

Heat the butter and oil in a pan and gently fry the onion until soft. Add all remaining ingredients, bring to the boil and simmer for about 20 minutes. If you like a smooth sauce, process in a blender or a food processor until smooth. Taste and adjust the seasoning.

BUTTERSCOTCH SAUCE

Wonderful with vanilla ice cream.

INGREDIENTS

2 oz (50 g) butter
4 tablespoons soft brown sugar
2 tablespoons golden syrup
squeeze of lemon juice

HOW TO MAKE

Measure butter, sugar and syrup into a pan and heat gently, stirring until the sugar has dissolved. Bring to the boil and cook for 1 minute. Stir in the lemon juice and serve at once.

CHOCOLATE SAUCE

Serve with ice cream or pour over profiteroles. Cocoa burns easily, so add it to the butter away from heat. This sauce reheats well and keeps well in the refrigerator for up to 2 weeks.

INGREDIENTS

1 oz (25 g) butter
1½ oz (40 g) cocoa, sieved
4 fl oz (120 ml) boiling water
5 oz (150 g) granulated sugar
few drops vanilla essence

HOW TO MAKE

Melt the butter in a small pan, then remove from the heat and stir in the cocoa. Mix well and gradually add the boiling water. Stir in the sugar, bring to the boil and simmer for about 5 minutes, without stirring. Take great care as it can boil over. Remove from the heat and stir in the vanilla essence.

MELBA SAUCE

Wonderful sauce to go with fresh peaches and home-made ice cream. The same sauce can be made with strawberries, and then there is no need to sieve as the seeds are so small.

INGREDIENTS

8 oz (225 g) fresh raspberries
4 oz (100 g) icing sugar

HOW TO MAKE

Put the raspberries and sugar into a blender or food processor. Process for a few seconds until smooth, then sieve into a bowl to remove the pips.

PROPER CUSTARD SAUCE

Serve hot with traditional puddings or cold as part of an old English trifle. For a richer custard, use single cream instead of milk. The teaspoon of cornflour prevents the custard curdling.

INGREDIENTS

½ pint (300 ml) milk
3 egg yolks or 2 whole eggs
1 tablespoon vanilla caster sugar
1 teaspoon cornflour

HOW TO MAKE

Heat the milk in a small pan until almost boiling. Beat the egg yolks, or whole eggs, sugar and cornflour together in a small bowl. Pour on the hot milk, stirring well the whole time. Return the sauce to the pan and heat until it thinly coats the back of the spoon. Strain through a sieve if using whole eggs. Serve hot or cold.

COOK'S TIP
Do not boil a sauce which contains cream or egg yolk. If the sauce becomes too hot it will curdle.

BRANDY BUTTER

Good with mince pies and Christmas pudding. Any that is left will keep for up to 3 months in the freezer.

INGREDIENTS

8 oz (225 g) unsalted butter
1 lb (450 g) icing sugar
8 tablespoons brandy

HOW TO MAKE

Cream the butter with a wooden spoon to soften. Gradually beat in the icing sugar until the mixture is light and fluffy. It can be done in a food processor, if wished. Beat in the brandy.

Turn into a pretty serving dish and chill before serving. If made a long time in advance leave at room temperature for about 30 minutes before serving.

GARLIC BREAD

If you are using a large French stick, you will need additional butter.

INGREDIENTS

1 French stick
2 fat cloves garlic, crushed
salt and freshly ground black pepper
3 oz (75 g) butter

HOW TO MAKE

Heat the oven to 400°F/200°C/gas mark 6. Make wide diagonal cuts through the bread, then lay it on a large piece of foil. Beat the garlic and seasoning into the butter. Butter both sides of the bread and ease it back into its original shape. Spread any remaining butter over the crust. Wrap in the foil and bake in the oven for about 15 minutes, opening the foil for the last 5 minutes to crisp the top.

Variation

Herb Bread   Herb bread is a nice alternative to garlic bread or for those who wish to avoid the pungent smell of garlic. Use fresh green herbs, such as parsley, chives or spring onion tops, plus if you like a little of some of the following: dill, chervil, lemon thyme, mint, marjoram or basil. Use about 2 tablespoons of finely chopped herbs and beat into the butter with the seasoning.

MELBA TOAST

These wafer thin slices of toast are perfect for serving with soup or dips and they keep crisp in a biscuit tin for a month or so.

INGREDIENTS

8 thin slices of white bread, crusts removed

HOW TO MAKE

Toast bread in a toaster or under the grill until pale golden. At once, hold the toast flat and carefully cut each slice of bread through the doughy middle between the toasted edges, using a sharp knife. Cut in half diagonally, if liked. Arrange on the grid in a grill pan uncooked side uppermost. Grill until very pale golden, watching carefully to make sure it doesn't burn. The corners will curl up and look attractive.

OVEN BAKED CROÛTONS

Serve warm with soup, or sprinkled on leafy salads. The conventional way of making croûtons is to fry the tiny cubes of bread in deep fat until pale golden brown. If you have a pan of deep fat, make them in this way. However, I prefer to do a half loaf at a time before winter sets in and keep the made croûtons in the freezer. It saves having to set to and make small quantities. The other half of the loaf I make into white breadcrumbs, and the crusts also into breadcrumbs for stuffings. Both these go in the freezer in separate bags.

INGREDIENTS

½ loaf white sliced bread
3 oz (75 g) butter
6 tablespoons oil

HOW TO MAKE

Heat the oven to 425°F/220°C/gas mark 7. Cut the bread slices into finger strips, then into cubes. Measure butter and oil into a roasting tin then put in the oven on a high shelf to melt the butter. Add cubes of bread and toss in the fat. Bake in the oven, tossing frequently until pale golden, for about 10 minutes. Take great care not to let them get too brown. They should be pale golden – the colour of perfect fried bread. If necessary, add a little more oil if they look a bit dry during cooking. Drain on absorbent kitchen paper.

Variation

Garlic Croûtons   Add 2 crushed garlic cloves to the butter and oil when it is melted.

FRIED BREADCRUMBS

Serve hot with roast game birds or mix with cheese for a crunchy topping on cauliflower cheese or pasta dishes with cheese sauces.

INGREDIENTS

2 oz (50 g) butter
4 oz (100 g) fresh breadcrumbs

HOW TO MAKE

Melt the butter in a frying pan and stir in the crumbs as the butter foams. Stir from time to time over a low heat until all the crumbs are golden brown.

GAME CHIPS

Serve with roast game birds such as pheasant and quail.

INGREDIENTS

potatoes, peeled
deep fat for frying

HOW TO MAKE

Thinly slice the potatoes and immerse in cold water to prevent discoloration. Drain and dry well on absorbent kitchen paper. Deep fry until pale golden, then drain on absorbent kitchen paper.

CHIPOLATA SAUSAGES

Serve with roast turkey.

INGREDIENTS

chipolata sausages

HOW TO MAKE

Grill the sausages under a medium grill for about 10–15 minutes turning to brown evenly. If you prefer small sausages, twist each one in the middle to make it half the size, then cut in two.

BACON ROLLS

Serve with roast turkey.

INGREDIENTS

streaky bacon rashers

HOW TO MAKE

Cut the rind from streaky bacon rashers and stretcher them on a wooden board, using the back of a knife, so they are twice their original size. Cut each rasher in half and roll up. Place rolls on skewers and grill for about 6 minutes under a moderate grill, turning so they brown nicely all round.

YORKSHIRE PUDDING

This is the traditional accompaniment to serve with roast beef. It is essential to preheat the Yorkshire pudding tin or patty tins before pouring in the batter. If you are expecting a crowd for Sunday lunch cook the pudding first thing in the morning. Leave in the tin and reheat for 8–10 minutes just before lunch to recrisp.

INGREDIENTS

4 oz (100 g) flour
¼ level teaspoon salt
2 eggs, beaten
½ pint (300 ml) milk and water mixed, less 2 tablespoons
a little fat or dripping

HOW TO MAKE

Heat the oven to 425°F/220°C/gas mark 7. Sift the flour and salt into a bowl, make a well in the centre and blend in the egg and a little milk and water. Using a wire whisk blend to a smooth paste, then blend in the remaining liquid to make a batter. Beat really well until smooth and the consistency of pouring cream.

Melt a little fat in the bottom of a shallow Yorkshire pudding tin or in the base of a 12 hole deep patty tin and heat until very hot. Remove from the oven and pour in the batter. Cook a large Yorkshire pudding for about 30 minutes, until well risen, golden brown and crisp, and small ones for about 15 minutes.

SAGE AND ONION STUFFING

Serve with roast pork and roast goose.

INGREDIENTS

1 lb (450 g) onions, chopped
½ pint (300 ml) water
3 oz (75 g) butter
1 level teaspoon dried sage
8 oz (225 g) fresh breadcrumbs
salt and freshly ground black pepper

HOW TO MAKE

Place the onions and water in a pan and bring to the boil. Simmer for about 15 minutes, then drain well. Stir in the remaining ingredients and mix well.

If preferred, turn into a well buttered dish, dot the top with a little more butter and cook in the oven with the joint or bird for about the last 30 minutes of cooking time.

LEMON AND THYME STUFFING

Use to stuff a 14–16 lb (6.5–7.25 kg) turkey.

INGREDIENTS

1 oz (25 g) butter
1 onion, chopped
1 lb (450 g) pork sausage meat
4 oz (100 g) fresh breadcrumbs
grated rind and juice of 1 lemon
salt and freshly ground black pepper
1 teaspoon chopped fresh thyme or ½ teaspoon dried thyme

HOW TO MAKE

Melt the butter in a pan, add the onion and fry gently for about 10 minutes, until soft. Transfer to a bowl and add the remaining ingredients. Mix well together.

CHESTNUT STUFFING

Use to stuff a 14–16 lb (6.5–7.25 kg) turkey. If you cannot get frozen chestnuts, use a 1 lb 15 oz (880 g) can of whole chestnuts in water, or 8 oz (225 g) dried chestnuts soaked overnight in cold water, then drained.

INGREDIENTS

1 lb (450 g) frozen chestnuts, thawed
8 oz (225 g) streaky bacon, chopped
2 oz (50 g) butter
4 oz (100 g) fresh breadcrumbs
1 egg, beaten
1 bunch watercress, finely chopped
salt and freshly ground black pepper

HOW TO MAKE

Chop the chestnuts coarsely. Fry the bacon slowly to allow the fat to run out, then add the chestnuts, increase the heat and fry until the bacon is crisp and the nuts begin to brown. Lift from pan with a slotted spoon and transfer to a bowl.

Add the butter to the pan with the residual fat. When melted, add the breadcrumbs and fry until brown. Turn into the bowl with the bacon and chestnuts. Add the remaining ingredients and mix well.

Preserves

Jams and jellies are a good way of using up a glut of summer fruit, and making your own preserves means that they are free from artifical colourings and preservatives. This chapter includes jams, jellies, marmalade, lemon curd and chutneys.

MAKING JAM AND MARMALADE

Equipment

A preserving pan or really large saucepan is essential to allow plenty of headroom for fast boiling. A good one to choose is stainless steel or aluminium. If you haven't a pan with a capacity of more than 8 pints (4.5 litres), make small quantities of preserve using 12 oz (350 g) fruit.

Save used screw-top jars for your own jam and marmalade making, it's much less trouble than fiddling with wax discs and cellophane tops. Stick on attractive labels with the name and date.

Sugar

Granulated sugar is the most economical, but you must make sure it is completely dissolved before boiling. Preserving sugar is more expensive, but less likely to stick to the bottom of the pan. It is a good sugar to use for jellies or special jam and marmalade because it produces little scum. Jam sugar has added acid and pectin, making it excellent for use with fruit that has a poor setting quality. The jam sets quickly which gives a better fresher flavour, especially to soft fruit jams such as strawberry and cherry.

Fruit

Choose under-ripe rather than over-ripe fruit for a good set. Over-ripe fruit will produce a poor quality jam or marmalade which may not set well.

The fruit should be dry when picked. When making marmalade, take care that the orange peel is really tender before the sugar is added. It will not soften further after the sugar is added – it will just become tough and dark.

Testing for a set

The simplest way to test for a set is to spoon a little jam or marmalade on to a cold saucer, leave for a minute, then push the jam with a finger. If the surface wrinkles, then setting point has been reached. If not set, boil for a few minutes more. While testing take the pan off the heat so the jam or marmalade does not overcook.

When setting point has been reached, leave the jam or marmalade in the pan off the heat to cool slightly. This will help to prevent the fruit or peel floating to the top of the jar when it is potted.

Pour into clean glass jars with screw tops. Label clearly when cold.

MAKING JELLIES

Equipment

The equipment needed is much the same as for jam only with the addition of a jelly bag. If you are not sure it is worth investing in a jelly bag, use a clean strong pillowcase for straining through. Jelly bags have loops or rings at the top and they can be hung from a stand, upturned stool or just simply from a hook on a high shelf.

Fruit

Choose fruit in peak condition. There is no need to remove stalks of currants, peel apples or hull berries as all that stays in the jelly bag. Apples should be cut up into small pieces.

Fruits which contain less pectin, such as cherries and brambles, need lemon juice added to the extracted juice, otherwise the jelly will not set. If you are not sure if you are using a high pectin fruit, test for pectin content (see below).

Testing for pectin content

After the juice has simmered and the skins are soft take 1 teaspoon of the juice with as little seeds and skin as possible, leave it to cool in a cup or glass. When cool, add 1 tablespoon methylated spirit and shake them together. Leave to stand for 1 minute. If a jellylike lump forms, then there is plenty of pectin in the fruit. If the clot is not too firm, the pectin content is moderate; if it breaks into piece: the pectin quantity is low.

Adding pectin

To boost the quantity of pectin in a fruit with a low amount, you can make another fruit jelly from apples, redcurrants or gooseberries, all of which have a high content, and mix it with one lacking pectin. Fruits low in pectin are strawberries, cherries and blackberries. Added lemon juice helps too.

Another way is to buy commercial pectin and carefully follow the manufacturer's instructions. Too much pectin spoils the jelly flavour.

A third method is to use a jam sugar which has added pectin. Sometimes this will cause the jelly to be slightly cloudy.

Dissolving the sugar

Make sure the sugar has dissolved before beginning the full rolling boil for a set. If you add the sugar before heating the juice, the colour of the jelly at the end will be deeper – which you might like with a pale fruit such as apple or gooseberry. Normally, the sugar is added after the juice is heated.

Testing for a set

Test for a set in the same way as for jam and marmalade.

MAKING CHUTNEYS
Equipment

A varied number of wonderful chutneys can be produced inexpensively at home without specialist equipment. You need a large stainless steel, aluminium or enamel pan with a thick base to prevent the chutney burning. Brass, copper or tin give a metallic taste to the chutney. Chutney does not boil up and over like jam, so the pans can be three-quarters full at the start of cooking.

Keeps jars with screw-on lids like coffee or pickle jars. The lids must have a plastic coating or be made of plastic, otherwise they will corrode when in contact with the vinegar. Cellophane tops are not suitable as the chutney dries out and shrinks, and you may be storing it for quite a time in the store cupboard.

Choosing ingredients

Fresh, frozen or dried fruit can all be used. The best fresh and frozen being apples, pears and rhubarb and all stoned fruits such as plums, apricot, peaches and mangoes. Oranges and lemons add extra flavour, and dates, raisins and sultanas are useful additions too.

Green and red tomatoes are popular bases for chutneys as are onions, celery, marrows, courgettes, beans and so on.

Spices, peppers, garlic and chillies can be

added to make endless delicious combinations. An economical addition is whole mixed pickling spice, which is available in most supermarkets. It can be ground up in a blender or coffee mill, or left whole and tied in a piece of muslin. It is dropped in the pan during cooking and removed at the end. Half an ounce (15 g) is enough to flavour a 7–10 lb (3.15–4.5 kg) batch of moderately spiced chutney. If you prefer a more mellow taste, halve the amount in recipes and add more at the end when tasting.

Keeping chutneys improves their flavour as they take time to mellow. Store for a couple of months before eating.

Sugar

White or brown may be used, light muscovado in particular improves the flavour and colour of the chutney. White or pale sugars are better for delicately flavoured chutneys such as tomato or apricot.

STRAWBERRY JAM

MAKES ABOUT
3½ lb (1.6 kg)

Strawberries are low in pectin and acid, so specially-formulated jam sugar gives a trouble-free set without loss of flavour due to long boiling.

INGREDIENTS

1 lb 12 oz (800 g) strawberries, about 2 lb (900 g) before
*   preparation*
2¼ lb (1 kg) jam sugar
knob of butter

HOW TO MAKE

Remove any over-ripe or bad strawberries. Place the rest of the strawberries in a large pan and crush with a potato masher. Add the sugar and stir over a low heat until completely dissolved. Increase the heat and bring to a fast rolling boil for 4 minutes. Remove from the heat, test for a set (see page 241) and, when setting point is reached, stir in the knob of butter to reduce the scum. Pot, seal and label.

COOK'S TIP
If an opened jar of jam or honey has gone hard and sugary, stand the jar in a pan of water and heat gently until sugariness disappears.

RHUBARB AND GINGER JAM

MAKES ABOUT
5 lb (2.25 kg)

A fresh tasting jam to make when there is a glut of rhubarb in the garden. For a more special jam, add about 4 oz (100 g) chopped crystallised or stem ginger at the end of cooking for a more gingery flavour.

INGREDIENTS

3 lb (1.4 kg) rhubarb (prepared weight)
3 lb (1.4 kg) sugar
juice of 3 lemons
1 oz (25 g) fresh root ginger

HOW TO MAKE

Cut the rhubarb into chunks, layer it in a large bowl with the sugar, pour over the lemon juice, cover and leave to stand overnight.

Next day, bruise the ginger by placing it in a small polythene bag and hitting it with a wooden rolling pin or mallet. Remove from the bag and tie up in a piece of muslin. Place in a large saucepan or preserving pan. Add the rhubarb and all the juice. Heat gently, stirring occasionally, until all the sugar has dissolved. Increase the heat, bring to the boil and continue to boil until setting point is reached. Test for a set (see page 241) after about 15 minutes and stir to prevent the bottom of the pan burning. Remove from the heat, discard the bag of ginger and stir in the chopped crystallised or stem ginger, if using. Pot and seal and label.

GOOSEBERRY AND ELDERFLOWER JAM

MAKES ABOUT
12 lb (5.4 kg)

Gooseberries and elderflowers are in season at the same time.

INGREDIENTS

6 lb (2.7 kg) gooseberries, topped and tailed
1½ pints (900 ml) water
12 large heads of elderflowers
8 lb (3.6 kg) granulated sugar

HOW TO MAKE

Put the gooseberries into a large pan with the water. Tie the elderflower heads in a piece of muslin and add to the pan. Bring to the boil, cover and simmer until the fruit is soft. Mash with a potato masher to break down any fruit still whole. Remove the elderflower bag, squeezing out all the liquid. Add the sugar and stir over a low heat until completely dissolved. Increase the heat and bring to the boil for about 10 minutes. Test for a set (see page 241), then when setting point is reached, pot, seal and label.

LEMON CURD

MAKES 3 SMALL
JARS

Once made store in the refrigerator and use within 3 months.

INGREDIENTS

4 oz (100 g) butter
8 oz (225 g) caster sugar
finely grated rind and juice of 3 lemons
5 egg yolks or 3 whole eggs, beaten

HOW TO MAKE

Measure the butter and sugar into a double saucepan or bowl and stand over a pan of simmering water, stirring occasionally until the butter has melted. Add the lemon rind and juice, then add the egg yolks or whole eggs. Mix well together and cook for about 25–30 minutes until the curd thickens, stirring from time to time. Remove from the heat, strain if whole eggs were used, then pot, seal and label.

SEVILLE ORANGE MARMALADE

MAKES ABOUT
5 lb (2.25 kg)

Sound family marmalade made from whole fruit. If you haven't time to make marmalade in January and February when Sevilles are available, freeze them, then make marmalade when you feel like it! Don't thaw the fruit first as this spoils the colour of the marmalade.

INGREDIENTS

1½ lb (675 g) Seville oranges
1 lemon
2½ pints (1.5 litres) water
3 lb (1.4 kg) granulated sugar

HOW TO MAKE

Put the oranges, lemon and water in a large pan and weight down the fruit with a plate if they bob up to the surface. Bring to the boil, cover and simmer for about 1 hour, until the skins are tender. Remove the fruit from the pan and leave until cool enough to handle.

Cut fruit in half, scoop out the flesh and pips and add to the water in the pan. Bring to the boil and cook for 6 minutes without a lid. This extracts the pectin for a good set. Strain through a sieve, pressing well with a spoon to extract all the liquid. Save the liquid and discard the pips.

Cut each orange half into half again and then into strips of the desired chunkiness. Return the sliced skins to the liquid in the pan, add the sugar and stir over a low heat until the sugar has completely dissolved. Turn up the heat and boil rapidly for about 10–15 minutes until setting point is reached (see page 241). Remove from the heat, allow to cool a little, then pot, seal and label.

THREE FRUIT MARMALADE

MAKES ABOUT
5 lb (2.25 kg)

Sweet oranges and sharp grapefruit and lemons combine to make a good marmalade when Seville oranges are not in the shops.

INGREDIENTS

1½ lb (675 g) mixed fruit, including 2 lemons, 1 grapefruit and
*   oranges*
2 pint (1.1 litre) water
3 lb (1.4 kg) granulated sugar

HOW TO MAKE

Cut the fruit in half and squeeze the juice into a large pan, saving all the pips and pith – scrape out the halves with a spoon to remove any stubborn pith. Put all the pips and pith into a piece of muslin and tie into a bag. Add the bag to the pan. Cut fruit shells in half again, then slice to the desired chunkiness and put in the pan. Pour on the water and bring to the boil, then cover with a lid and simmer until the peel is tender when squeezed between thumb and finger.

Remove the bag of pips, squeezing out all the liquid. Add the sugar and stir over a low heat until completely dissolved. Increase the heat and bring to a full rolling boil, cook for about 10 minutes, then test for a set (see page 241). Remove from the heat, allow to cool a little, then pot, seal and label.

Variation to the method

Slice the peel in a food processor, if preferred. First cut the fruit shells in half for the second time. Fit a slicing disc in the processor and pack the feed tube with as much peel as possible as this helps to keep the slices straight. Turn on the machine and press the peel down with the feed tube plunger. Some pieces may have to be put through a second time if not fine enough. Alternatively, fit the metal blade in the processor bowl and chop the peel very finely.

Marmalade variations

It's always nice to have more than one variety of marmalade and any of the following can be added to the marmalade recipes:

Dark Marmalade   Add 1 level tablespoon black treacle with the sugar.

Whisky Marmalade   Add 3 tablespoons whisky before potting.

Ginger Marmalade   Add chopped stem ginger at the end, before potting. If you like really gingery marmalade, add 1 teaspoon ground ginger when adding the sugar, in addition to the stem ginger.

APRICOT AND ORANGE MARMALADE

MAKES ABOUT
8 lb (3.6 kg)

Dried apricot pieces are cheaper than whole dried apricots and are perfect for this marmalade.

INGREDIENTS

4 oz (100 g) dried apricot pieces
1¼ pints (750 ml) boiling water
1 lb 14 oz (850 g) can prepared Seville oranges
5 lb (2.25 kg) granulated sugar

HOW TO MAKE

If the apricot pieces are large chop them up a little. Put them in a bowl and cover with the boiling water, then leave to soak for at least 1 hour.

Pour the contents of the can of oranges and the sugar into a preserving pan or two smaller pans if you don't have one big enough to hold 10 pints (6 litres). Add the apricots and their soaking water and heat gently, stirring until the sugar has completely dissolved.

Increase the heat, bring to the boil and boil briskly for 10 minutes. If using two pans, boil for 8 minutes. Remove from the heat, test for a set (see page 241) and, if necessary, boil for a further 2 minutes. Allow to cool, then pot, seal and label.

REDCURRANT JELLY

It is difficult to give a precise weight for the redcurrants and sugar as jelly is made by allowing 1 pint (600 ml) of fruit juice to each 1 lb (450 g) sugar.

INGREDIENTS

about 6 lb (2.7 kg) redcurrants
granulated sugar

HOW TO MAKE

Put the redcurrants in a pan and cook over a gentle heat until the currants are soft. Mash with a potato masher to make sure all the currants are broken.

Spoon the fruit pulp into a jelly bag and leave to strain overnight – warn everyone not to squeeze the bag or it will make the jelly cloudy! Next day, measure the juice into a pan, adding 1 lb (450 g) sugar to each 1 pint (600 ml) of juice. Stir over a low heat until all the sugar has dissolved. Bring to the boil for about 1 minute, then test for a set (see page 241). Pot, seal and label.

SAGE JELLY

Mint can be used instead if you enjoy the more traditional flavour. Crab apples could also be used.

INGREDIENTS

3 lb (1.4 kg) cooking apples
juice of 2 lemons
good bunch fresh sage
water
granulated sugar

HOW TO MAKE

Cut up the apples and put in a large pan with the lemon juice. Add a few sprigs of sage and enough water to cover apples. Bring to the boil, then simmer until the fruit is reduced to pulp.

Spoon the fruit pulp into a jelly bag and leave to strain overnight. Next day, measure the juice in a pan, adding 1 lb (450 g) sugar for each 1 pint (600 ml) of juice. Stir over a low heat until the sugar has dissolved. Tie some sage in a bunch and add to the pan. Increase the heat and boil for about 5 minutes, then test for a set (see page 241). Remove the bunch of sage and add some finely chopped sage, if liked. Allow to cool a little, then pot, seal and label.

RED TOMATO CHUTNEY

MAKES ABOUT
4 lb (1.8 kg)
INGREDIENTS

Good to make when homegrown tomatoes are plentiful.

6 lb (2.75 kg) tomatoes
8 oz (225 g) onions, chopped
1/2 pint (300 ml) distilled vinegar
1/2 oz (15 g) whole mixed pickling spice
3/4 lb (350 g) sugar
1 teaspoon paprika
pinch of cayenne
3/4 oz (20 g) salt

HOW TO MAKE

Peel the tomatoes, about 1 lb (450 g) at a time, by placing them in a bowl and pouring over boiling water; leave for about 1 minute, then drain and peel. Cut into quarters, put into a pan with the onions and cook until thick and pulpy.

Add the vinegar and the whole spice tied in a piece of muslin, then cook again until thick and pulpy. Add the sugar, remaining spices and the salt and stir until the sugar has dissolved. Cook until thick and pulpy. Remove the muslin spice bag, then pot, seal and label.

APRICOT AND ONION CHUTNEY

MAKES ABOUT
3 lb (1.4 kg)

A mild-flavoured chutney made with dried apricot pieces.

INGREDIENTS

8 oz (225 g) dried apricot pieces
¾ pint (450 ml) water
4 oz (100 g) seedless raisins
1 lb (450 g) onions
1 lb (450 g) sugar
½ pint (300 ml) distilled vinegar
freshly ground black pepper
1 teaspoon ground cumin
2 teaspoons salt

HOW TO MAKE

Soak the apricots in the water overnight. Next day, drain the apricots, reserving the soaking water. Chop the apricots, raisins and onions and put in a preserving pan or large saucepan with the sugar, reserved soaking water and the vinegar. Cook over a gentle heat, stirring until the sugar has dissolved. Bring to the boil, then simmer until the chutney is thick and pulpy, stirring occasionally to prevent sticking. Add pepper to taste and the cumin and salt. Pot, seal and label.

APPLE, PEPPER AND DATE CHUTNEY

MAKES ABOUT
8 lb (3.6 kg)

This is the ideal way of using up windfall apples.

INGREDIENTS

4 lb (1.8 kg) cooking apples (prepared weight)
4 red peppers
8 oz (225 g) stoned dates
1 oz (25 g) fresh root ginger, peeled
½ oz (15 g) whole mixed pickling spice
2 tablespoons salt
2 teaspoons mixed spice
1½ pints (900 ml) distilled vinegar
2 lb (900 g) light muscovado sugar

HOW TO MAKE

Peel, quarter and core apples, then chop coarsely either by hand or in a food processor. Halve and seed the peppers, then cut into dice. Chop the dates. Grate or finely chop the ginger. Tie the whole spices in muslin.

Put all the ingredients in a large pan and heat slowly until the sugar has dissolved. Increase the heat and bring to a fast boil. Reduce the heat and simmer for about 30–40 minutes, until reduced to a thick consistency, stirring occasionally to prevent it burning. Pot, seal and label.

Herbs and Spices

A–Z OF FRESH HERBS

Store fresh herbs separately, standing in a mug of water covered with a polythene bag in the refrigerator. Most will keep for up to 10 days. When fresh aren't available, use frozen or dried. If replacing fresh herbs in a recipe with dried, halve the quantity needed.

Basil
Wonderful herb with salads and tomatoes. Used a great deal in Italian cookery.

Bay
The leaves of the evergreen bay tree, these are usually used in cooking when dried. One or two bay leaves is the average number for a recipe. Use for stocks, casseroles and stews. Remove before serving. It is also used to flavour milk for use in white sauces.

Borage
An easy herb to grow. It is mainly used in drinks such as Pimms and in fruit salad. The pretty blue flowers can also be crystallised.

Bouquet Garni
A term often used in savoury recipes. It is literally the French for 'faggot' or bundle. The traditional ingredients are parsley, bay leaf and thyme tied up in a bundle with string and used together in recipes with pepper-corns. Sometimes marjoram is added to the bunch. The whole bouquet garni is lifted out just before serving.

Chives
Bright green shoots with a delicate onion flavour. Add, snipped with scissors, to scram-bled eggs, omelettes, pâtés and salads. Use, also, to garnish salads tossed in mayonnaise.

Keep in a polythene bag in the refrigerator for up to 3 days.

Dill
The feathery leaves (dill weed) are used as a herb and the dried seeds as a spice. The leaves are especially good with fish and new potatoes. It has a much milder flavour than fennel.

Fennel
Has a mild aniseed flavour. It is a classic flavouring to use with oily fish as it counteracts the oiliness.

Garlic
A white or whitish-red bulb made up of many individual cloves. It is not strictly a herb but is used like one. Peel each clove, then crush with a garlic press or with the flat side of a knife with a little salt on a board. Use sparingly, about 1 or 2 cloves for a recipe.

Marjoram
Good with pizzas, meat and stuffings. Oregano is wild marjoram, popular in Italy.

Mint
The second most popular herb after parsley. Mainly used for mint sauce, new potatoes and lamb. Goes well in salads. There are many varieties with different flavours – apple mint has the most delicate flavour.

Parsley
The most popular herb in Britain today. Par-sley can either be chopped on a board or the heads quickly snipped with scissors in a cup or mug. Use the stalks as flavouring in soups and casseroles; lift out before serving. Use snipped or chopped for flavour and colour in

creamy white soups and sauces. Scatter chopped parsley over savoury dishes to add colour contrast. Keep chopped parsley in a container in the refrigerator for a few days – very handy for sprinkling over new potatoes or adding to a dish of boiled onions at the last moment.

Rosemary
Both fresh and dried forms are popular. Add fresh sprigs to the lamb or chicken roast, or use rosemary in soups and casseroles of these meats. Just a few chopped spikes are good blended with other herbs in savoury recipes.

Sage
Sage is usually used dried and crumbled, though fresh leaves are useful for threading on skewers with meats for kebabs. Sage goes especially well with pork and veal. Delicious in stuffing with onions. Using sparingly.

Tarragon
A tender herb which goes well with chicken, lamb and fish. The French variety has a much better flavour than the prolific Russian tarragon.

Thyme
Fresh common thyme has a distinctive, strong, aromatic flavour: lemon thyme also has a lemon tang. Thyme is an important constituent in mixed herbs. Use for meat, game and poultry dishes. Take leaves from the stem and roughly chop; use about $\frac{1}{2}$ teaspoon for each recipe. In some recipes use a couple of sprigs and lift them out before serving.

Note: As a general rule, use half the quantity of dried herbs to fresh herbs. Drying them accentuates the flavour.

A–Z OF SPICES

There are many different spices used in cooking but here are a few of my favourites.

Buy in small quantities and store in a dark, dry place – preferably not glass jars or on an open shelf as exposure to light affects the flavour. With all types of spice the flavour is best when freshly ground.

Allspice
Looks like peppercorns but tastes like a combination of cinnamon, cloves, ginger and nutmeg. Ground allspice is an important ingredient in mixed spice. Good with savoury and sweet foods and often used in mincemeat.

Caraway
A pale brown seed used to flavour breads and cheeses, cabbage dishes and soups. Can be used whole or ground.

Cardamom
Slightly pungent, highly aromatic pods containing seeds. Green and white are the most common, while brown or black cardamoms are much larger and more pungent. Use whole or ground in savoury and sweet dishes.

Chilli Powder
Very very hot ground chilli peppers. Use with caution. Superb for chill con carne. Chilli seasoning is milder.

Cinnamon
The bark of the cinnamon tree. Bought in sticks or ready-ground. Used in punches and goes well with apples and dried fruits.

Cloves
The dried flower bud of a tropical shrub. Use whole or ground in apple and ham dishes and in hot punches. Remove whole cloves from dish before serving.

Coriander
One of the most important spices in Indian cookery. The leaves can be used fresh (as a herb) and the seeds whole or ground.

Cumin
Thin yellowish brown seeds with a fragrant aroma. An ingredient of chutneys, chilli and curry powders.

Ginger
The root of the ginger plant, used fresh, dried or ground. The stem is also crystallised. Fresh root ginger freezes well and can be grated from frozen. Dried ground ginger is used in baking, and fresh in Chinese stir fry dishes.

Green Peppercorns
Fresh green peppercorns are piquant and peppery without being overpowering. Take off the stem, lightly crush the berries with the flat side of a knife. Usually about ½ teaspoon is required. Store, covered in a container in the refrigerator for up to 3 weeks. Use for peppered steaks, in casseroles and in piquant sauces for meat and fish.

Juniper
Fragrant spicy berries used in marinades for rich meats, in pâtés, meat stews and with cabbage. The berries are also used to flavour gin.

Mixed Spice
A blended mixture of ground spices including cinnamon, allspice, cloves and nutmeg. Used in rich fruit cakes, biscuits and fruit breads.

Nutmeg
A hard seed used ground or finely grated to flavour milk puddings, egg custards, baked goods and punches. Whole nutmegs keep for years.

Paprika Pepper
Ground mild Hungarian red peppers. Adds a touch of colour to savoury dishes and is the traditional flavouring for Hungarian goulash.

Pepper
White peppercorns are the inside of the black peppercorn. Both can be used ground. Use white pepper for white and pale sauces when the speckling of black pepper would spoil the appearance. Like all spices, the flavour is best when freshly ground.

Pickling Spice
A mixture of whole spices used to flavour pickling vinegar for preserves.

Saffron
The stamens of the saffron crocus. It takes 75,000 flowers to yield 1 lb (450 g) saffron and is the most expensive spice. Soak a good pinch in 2 tablespoons warm water to extract the colour and flavour and to soften the stamens before using.

Tumeric
A cheaper alternative to saffron, when you want to colour a dish yellow. Used in curries, piccalilli, rice and egg dishes.

Vanilla
Vanilla pods are the dried unripe pods of a tropical climbing orchid. Don't throw away after using, instead rinse and store in a jar topped up with sugar. The sugar will be flavoured and scented with the vanilla, and can be used in biscuits, cakes and custards when a vanilla flavour is required. The more usual way of using vanilla is in essence form.

Index